# A SHORT COURSE
# ON COMPUTER VIRUSES

# A SHORT COURSE
# ON COMPUTER VIRUSES

### SECOND EDITION

## FREDERICK B. COHEN

### John Wiley & Sons, Inc.

New York • Chichester • Brisbane • Toronto • Singapore

Publisher: Katherine Schowalter
Editor: Diane Cerra
Managing Editor: Jacqueline A. Martin
Editorial Production: Science Typographers, Inc.

Designations used by companies to distinguish their products are often claimed as trademarks. In all instances where John Wiley & Sons, Inc. is aware of a claim, the product names appear in initial capital or all capital letters. Readers, however, should contact the appropriate companies for more complete information regarding trademarks and registration

This text is printed on acid-free paper.

In recognition of the importance of preserving what has been written, it is a policy of John Wiley & Sons, Inc. to have books of enduring value published in the United States printed on acid-free paper, and we exert our best efforts to that end.

This publication is designed to provide accurate and authoritative information in regard to the subject matter covered. It is sold with the understanding that the publisher is not engaged in rendering legal, accounting, or other professional service. If legal advice or other expert assistance is required, the services of a competent professional person should be sought. FROM A DECLARATION OF PRINCIPLES JOINTLY ADOPTED BY A COMMITTEE OF THE AMERICAN BAR ASSOCIATION AND A COMMITTEE OF OF PUBLISHERS.

*Library of Congress Cataloging-in-Publication Data:*

Cohen, Frederick B.
    A short course on computer viruses / by Frederick B. Cohen. — 2nd
ed.
        p.  cm.
    Includes bibliographical references.
    ISBN 0-471-00769-2 (book/disk). — ISBN 0-471-00768-4 (paper). —
ISBN 0-471-00770-6 (disk)
    1. Computer viruses.  I. Title.
QA76.76.C68C64  1994
005.8—dc20
                                                            93-20951

Printed in the United States of America

10 9 8 7 6 5 4 3 2 1

# ABOUT THE AUTHOR

Dr. Frederick B. Cohen is widely known for his pioneering work on computer viruses and integrity maintenance mechanisms. His famous 1984 paper "Computer Viruses—Theory and Experiments" started the field of computer virus research, and is one of the most widely cited papers in the computing field today. Since that time, Dr. Cohen has published over 35 technical papers, given over 60 invited talks, and educated thousands of students and professionals about computer viruses. In 1989, Dr. Cohen won the prestigious Information Technology Award for his research on computer viruses and development of practical integrity maintenance mechanisms for modern computing systems.

# PREFACE

This book was derived from recordings of my one-day short courses on computer viruses. The course runs about 8 hours, and at the time of this writing, had been taught about 50 times. In this course, I try to avoid the deep technical details and most of the mathematics behind the conclusions presented. At the same time, I think it is important to provide enough evidence to be convincing and understandable. As an aid to the technically inclined reader, I have published a number of good references which contain more detailed technical information.

This is not a technology book; it is a science book. By that I mean that the purpose of the book is to educate the reader, so that for the rest of their life, they will understand about computer viruses, and never be surprised by what happens. For that reason, I avoid discussing details of particular technologies except for the purpose of providing examples. The point is to give you knowledge of the subject that can be applied regardless of the system you are using, the programming languages in the environment, or the most popular operating system of the day.

The intended audience is anyone who works intimately with computers on a day-to-day basis. It will be particularly helpful to computer programmers, information system managers, system administrators, EDP auditors, and computer security specialists, but it would also be a good book for an undergraduate student who has taken a course on computers, and has been used in graduate programs as a supplement to other material.

You will find the coverage of this book quite broad. We begin with the basics of computer viruses, and discuss how they work, what they can do, and how they are different from other technologies. We then discuss scientific experiments with viruses, viruses that have appeared in the real world, and how organizations have historically responded to the threat of viruses. Next, we go into details about defenses, starting with theoretically sound defenses, then moving into a series of examples of defenses that don't work very well, describing the best current defenses in real systems, and discussing non-technical defenses and management issues. Next we analyze the impact of computer viruses and defenses, go through a series of scenarios that consider viruses in a variety of real-world situations, and sum up the course. Finally, in the appendices, we tell "the good joke" that I tell just after lunch to wake people up before starting the second half of the course, include the most commonly requested technical details, and provide a list of about 75 annotated references to related works.

I hope that you enjoy this book, and I welcome your comments and suggestions.

# CONTENTS

# A SHORT COURSE
# ON COMPUTER VIRUSES

# Chapter 1

# COMPUTER VIRUS BASICS

## 1.1 WHAT IS A COMPUTER VIRUS?

I would like to start with a formal definition

$$\forall M \forall V (M, V) \in VS \Leftrightarrow [V \in TS] \text{ and } [M \in TM] \text{ and}$$
$$[\forall v \in V [\forall H_M [\forall t \forall j$$
$$[1) P_M(t) = j \text{ and}$$
$$2) \square_M(t) = \square_M(0) \text{ and}$$
$$3) (\square_M(t, j), \ldots, \square_M(t, j + |v| - 1)) = v]$$
$$\Rightarrow \quad [\quad \exists v' \in V [\exists t' > t [\exists j'$$
$$[1)[[(j' + |v'|) \leq j] \, or \, [(j + |v|) \leq j']] \text{ and}$$
$$2) (\square_M(t', j'), \ldots, \square_M(t', j' + |v'| - 1)) = v' \text{ and}$$
$$3) [\exists t'' s.t. [t < t'' < t'] \text{ and}$$
$$[P_M(t'') \in j', \ldots, j' + |v'| - 1]$$
$$]]]] \quad ]] \quad ] \quad ]$$

**FIGURE 1.1** Formal definition.

So, much for that! Now let me tell you what it means.

When we talk about computer viruses in the deepest sense, we are talking about sequences of symbols in the memory of a machine in whatever form that may be, main memory, the registers, disk, tape, or what have you. What makes one of those sequences of symbols an element of a "viral set" ($V$) is that when the machine interprets that sequence of symbols ($v$), it causes some other element of that viral set ($v'$) to appear somewhere else in the system at a later point in time (see Figure 1.2). Most of the viruses you have probably heard about form singleton viral sets (e.g., sequences of instructions in machine code for the particular machine that make exact copies of themselves somewhere else in the machine), but that's not the only possibility.

- You can have viruses that are not in the binary code of the machine; an example is a virus written in a source language that infects other source language programs. Any sequence of symbols that is interpreted on the machine could potentially contain a virus.

- All viruses are not from singleton viral sets. You can have viruses that evolve through a finite number of different instances. In fact, you can have viruses that evolve through a potentially infinite number of different versions. It turns out that this is very important, because it makes the problem of virus detection and eradication far more difficult than it would be if we could only make viruses that made exact copies of themselves.

## 1.2　HOW DO VIRUSES SPREAD THROUGH SYSTEMS?

The working definition of a virus that most people see, goes like this: "A virus is a program that can 'infect' other programs by modifying them to include a, possibly evolved, version of itself."

Let's look at an example. In Figure 1.3 we have a picture of a time-sharing system with three users; $U_1$, $U_2$, and $U_3$; who own three programs; $P_1$, $P_2$, and $P_3$, respectively; at times $t_1$, $t_2$, and $t_3$. If at time $t_1$ program $P_1$ is infected with a virus $V$, and at time $t_2$ user $U_2$ runs program $P_1$, then because user $U_2$ is authorizing program $P_1$ to act on $U_2$'s behalf, and user $U_2$ has the authority to modify program $P_2$, the virus in program $P_1$ is authorized to modify program $P_2$, and thus it infects program $P_2$. Similarly, if at time $t_3$ user $U_3$ runs program $P_2$, program $P_3$ becomes infected. Thus the virus spreads from program to program and from user to user.

Note that this operates in a typical timesharing computer environment, even with standard protection mechanisms in place. This means that the protection mechanisms used throughout the computing community today are inadequate for defense against viruses.

To present this to people with a nontechnical background, we use the secretaries analogy. In this analogy we talk about a group of secretaries, where each secretary does a job by taking orders from the boss. For

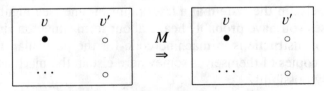

**FIGURE 1.2**　Picture of the formal definition.

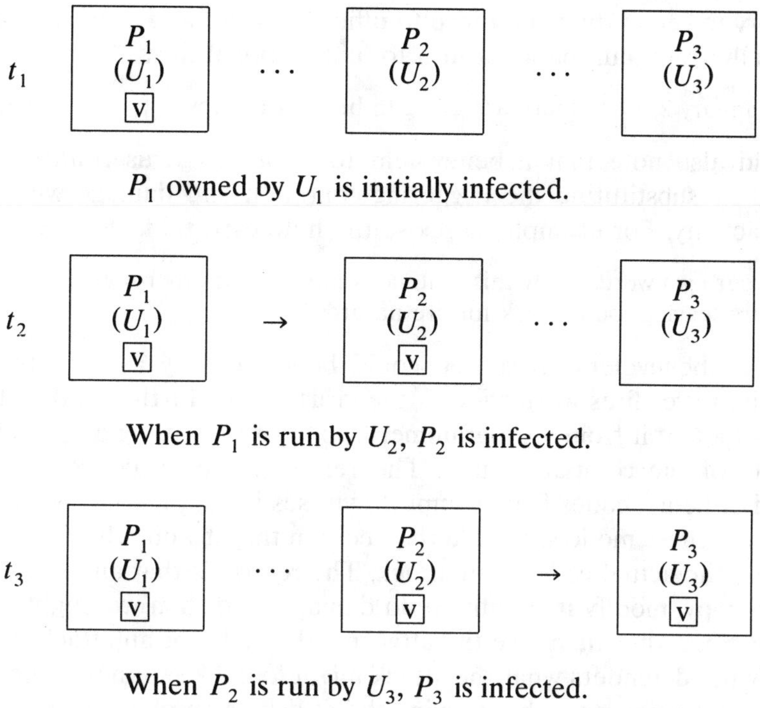
$t_1$
$P_1$ ($U_1$) V
. . .
$P_2$ ($U_2$)
. . .
$P_3$ ($U_3$)
$P_1$ owned by $U_1$ is initially infected.
$t_2$
$P_1$ ($U_1$) V
→
$P_2$ ($U_2$) V
. . .
$P_3$ ($U_3$)
When $P_1$ is run by $U_2$, $P_2$ is infected.
$t_3$
$P_1$ ($U_1$) V
. . .
$P_2$ ($U_2$) V
→
$P_3$ ($U_3$) V
When $P_2$ is run by $U_3$, $P_3$ is infected.

**FIGURE 1.3** A time-sharing system.

example, a boss might tell Secretary 3 to "make a call." When Secretary 3 gets that order, Secretary 3 looks for a note card that says "make a call" at the top, and does whatever that note card says. If Secretary 3 doesn't have such a note card, then Secretary 3 will ask the other secretaries if they have a "make a call" note card. When Secretary 3 finds such a note card, he or she does whatever that note card instructs.

Now let's imagine that somewhere in the middle of Secretary 2's "write-a-memo" note card, is the following sentence:

> "In your own words, copy this sentence onto all your other note cards, and if the date is after January 1, 1999, burn everything in sight."

Let's see what happens. When Secretary 2 is told to "write-a-memo," this sentence is going to be interpreted in the process of writing that memo, and all of Secretary 2's note cards are going to become infected. If at a later time, Secretary 3 is told to "make-a-call," and ends up using Secretary 2's "make-a-call" note card, all of Secretary 3's note cards become infected, and so on. So this virus spreads from note card to note card, from secretary to secretary, from office to office (as secretaries change jobs), and eventually from multinational firm to multinational firm.

On January 2, 1999, there are going to be a lot of fires!

I should also note that a benevolent form of this virus could be implemented by substituting the triggering condition and damage with a more useful activity. For example, suppose the note card said:

"In your own words, copy this sentence onto all your other note cards, and if you are leaving soon, check for fire hazards."

With this benevolent virus, you could be reasonably assured that there would be fewer fires worldwide as the virus spread further and further.

Let's look at it from a programmer's point of view using a "pseudocode" example of the computer virus. The reason I use pseudocode examples instead of actual codes from computer viruses is that, in 1983 when I first developed these models, I made the decision that it would be inappropriate to reveal the actual code of an attack. The reason is that an attacker could make a copy, modify it slightly to do damage, and then we might be in big trouble. So, rather than give the attackers the code for an attack, I decided to show the defenders what the attack might look like so they could provide appropriate defenses without giving the attackers an obvious entry. Unfortunately, the response of the computer science community was denial. They felt that such a thing was not possible. As recently as 1989, there was a dominant feeling that this was just "a lot of media hype." In the meanwhile, the attackers read the early papers, and took action to realize many attacks. This situation is changing because of the large number of real-world attacks, and the computer science community is now beginning to think that viruses are a realistic possibility.

```
Program V :=
{1234567;
Subroutine infect-executable:=
 {loop: file=random-executable;
 if (first-line of file = 1234567)
   then goto loop;
   else prepend V to file;}

Subroutine do-damage:=
 {whatever damage you can program}
Subroutine trigger-pulled:=
 {whatever trigger you want here}
```

```
Main-program-of-virus:=
 {infect-executable;
 if (trigger-pulled) then do-damage;
 goto next;}
next:
}
```

The pseudocode virus $V$ works like this. It begins with a marker "1234567." This is not necessary, but in this particular case, it is used to identify that this particular virus has already infected a program, so that it doesn't infect the same program repeatedly. It then has three subroutines followed by the main program. The main program of the virus starts by infecting another program through the subroutine "infect-executable." This subroutine loops, examining random executable files until it finds one without the first line "1234567." When it finds an uninfected executable, $V$ copies itself into the beginning of the previously uninfected executable, thus infecting it.

Note that there have been tens of thousands of readers of this particular example, and yet nobody has ever called to attention the fact that it will loop indefinitely once all of the executable files in the system are infected.

After infection, the virus checks for a "trigger-pulled" condition, which can be anything the attacker programs in. If the condition is active, it performs whatever damage is programmed into the "do-damage" routine. Finally, the main program of the virus jumps into whatever program the virus was "prepended" to when it was installed, and runs that program normally. So, if this virus is at the beginning of an executable program, and you run that program, the virus is going to attach itself to the beginning of the next program, and if the trigger is not pulled, it's just going to run the program it was prefixed to. If this process happens relatively quickly, users are not likely to notice it taking place during the normal operation of a system.

## 1.3   WHAT DAMAGE COULD A MALICIOUS VIRUS DO?

Let's take a cursory look at the types of damage you might get from a computer virus.

```
Trigger-pulled:=
 {if the date is after Jan 1, 1999;}
```

```
Do-damage:=
 {loop: goto loop;}
```

This is a simple denial of services example. The triggering condition in this case is time driven, and the damage is an infinite loop. If this virus spread throughout a computer system or network, then as of the triggering date, every program that was infected would go into an infinite loop. So, in a typical computer network today, every program on the network will stop operating as of that moment.

This is only the simplest and most obvious sort of attack, it is relatively easily detected and countered, and does not require much sophistication to write. But as we will now begin to see, the situation can get somewhat more complex. Figure 1.4 shows a more interesting virus called a "Compression Virus." We use this example because it shows us a couple of things about typical ideas for defenses, particularly that it is not such an easy matter to determine whether a program has been infected.

```
    Program CV:=
      {01234567;
      subroutine infect-exec:=
        {loop:
         file=random-exec-file;
         if first-line of file = 01234567
           then goto loop;
(1)      compress file;
(2)      prepend CV to file;
        }
      main-program:=
        {if ask-permission
           then infect-exec;
(3)      uncompress rest-of-file;
(4)      run uncompressed file;
        }
      }
```

This virus works in a four-step process, marked 1, 2, 3, and 4 in the code. Rather than look at the code for this attack, I think it is much easier to look at the picture.

We start at a time $t_0$ with program $P'_1$, the infected version of program $P_1$, and a clean program $P_2$ that has never been infected with this virus. If at time $t_1$, program $P_1$ is run, the following steps take place.

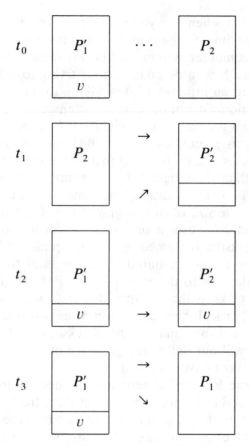

**FIGURE 1.4**  A compression virus.

$t_1$—Program $P_2$ is compressed into $P'_2$.

$t_2$—$v$ attaches itself to $P'_2$.

$t_3$—$P'_1$ is decompressed into the original program $P_1$.

$t_4$—The original program $P_1$ is executed normally.

There are a couple of things to note about this particular compression virus. One thing is that the size of $P'_2$ is typically about half the size of the original $P_2$. That is, file compression typically saves about 50% of the space taken up by files (sometimes you can get two thirds or more). The net effect is that if you spread this virus throughout a computer system, you can save about half the space taken up by programs. The penalty you pay for that space savings is that whenever you run a program, it has to decompress, and this takes extra time. So the compression virus implements a time/space trade-off in your computer system, and in this sense might be quite useful.

Now suppose we have a defender who is trying to figure out whether a file is infected, and an attacker who is willing to put forth some effort to prevent this detection. One of the earliest defenses we saw in the real-world was looking to see if the size of a file changed. A lot of people wrote papers saying "To find viruses, look for changes in the size of the files." Well, let's see what the attacker can do to avoid that. Since the resulting program $P'_2$ has fewer bytes than the original $P_2$, by simply adding appropriate null bytes to $P'_2$, we can make $P'_2$ exactly the same size as the original program $P_2$, and therefore, the size of the program has not changed.

Suppose the defender uses a simple checksum to indicate changes in a file. A simple checksum is formed by adding up all the bytes in the file in some modulus. By taking an initial checksum, and then comparing at a later date, defenders try to detect viruses. Well, instead of putting in null bytes (as we did to keep the file size identical), we can put in any other bytes we wish. In particular, we can put in bytes that make the checksum of the infected program the same as the checksum of the original. Then a simple checksum will not detect the presence of a virus. So simple check-summing is very easy to avoid as well.

The same is true for cyclical redundancy check (CRC) codes. A CRC code is typically used to identify changes on disks from random errors, but of course, it is only useful against random Gaussian types of noise, and will not work against serious attackers because it is very easy to forge a modification that keeps the same CRC code as the original program.

It turns out that it is pretty straightforward to write a virus so that the resulting size, the modification date and time (on most systems), the checksum, and the CRC code for the infected file, are exactly the same as for the original. This points out some of the difficulty in trying to detect the sorts of change that a virus might make to a file.

## 1.4   SOME OTHER THINGS MALICIOUS VIRUSES MIGHT DO

Now I just want to go through some other types of damage very quickly, to give you an idea of the range of things you might expect from computer virus attacks. Of course, when I get to the end, you will probably be thinking of lots of other things that a virus could do. So, have a good time.

Just realize that the attackers are also having a good time thinking about these things.

### 1.4.1 A Data Diddling Virus

Let's start out with the "data diddling" virus. A data diddling virus is a virus where every infected program modifies one bit in one randomly selected data file once a week. In a typical personal computer system there will be something like a thousand infected programs, so each of those thousand infected programs modifies one bit of data from a randomly selected data file once a week. So a thousand randomly selected bits of data in your system are being changed every week.

Is anybody here going to notice that occurring in their system? Does anybody have any system in place to detect the random changing of a bit in a data file? Okay, so if this sort of a virus entered your system, you wouldn't even notice that the damage was being done. You wouldn't notice the virus and you wouldn't notice the damage. Eventually, you would. After a couple of months, or depending on how you use your system, a couple of weeks, you would start to notice that you had all sorts of errors in your database; and you would probably have some difficulty tracking down the source of those errors. In fact, it is very difficult to figure out that these errors come from this virus, because there is no direct link between the attack and the damage, so the symptom does not indicate the cause.

Instead of a random data diddling virus, you could create a far more sophisticated data diddling virus. For example, a virus that randomizes the second and last digits of numbers that look like postal codes would cause mailing lists to direct mail incorrectly. A virus that switches digits before and after a decimal point would wreak havoc on most arithmetic calculations. Exchanging commas with periods in a document would cause a condition that would first corrupt information, and subsequently correct it (after changing commas to periods, it would change them back again, alternating between right and wrong versions). This could be quite unnerving. As a real-world example, a virus called "Typo" creates typing errors whenever the user types faster than 60 words per minute. This is clearly directed against the more skilled typists of the world (perhaps its author failed a typing test and didn't get a job?). A more directed data diddling virus might target specific information for specific changes to attain specific goals.

These data diddling viruses show a key factor in the success of a virus; to make the link between cause and effect so indirect that it is not likely to be determined by examining results. Thus, even once corruptions are detected, it may be a long time before the cause is determined. The more indirect the link, the more complex the process of tracking down the source. Furthermore, the cost of trying to restore integrity from a data diddling attack might be very high. For example, there is no simple way to determine how far back you have to go to correct those corruptions.

### 1.4.2   The Random Deletion Virus

The "Random Delection Virus" is a virus that spreads throughout a system and looks for files that haven't been accessed in, let's say the last month and a half, and deletes them. It turns out that if you haven't accessed a file in the last month and a half, you probably won't access that file in the next month and a half. To the extent that you don't notice that the file is missing, it might be a long time before you determine that it is missing, and you might have great difficulty tracing it to an appropriate backup. In fact, you'll probably think that you deleted it by accident and start to lose confidence in what you have and have not done.

Let's take it a step further. Suppose you have a system in place where in order to save space, you periodically move unaccessed files to off-line backups and then delete them from the system. If the attacker is aware that this system is in place, it's very straightforward to look for files that are about to be moved off-line and delete a small percentage of them, say one out of ten. The net effect is that the user gets messages that various files were moved off-line, and they figure that everything is nice and safe. When they go to get a deleted file back, they find it's not there! It's not on the system and it's not on the off-line backups and nobody knows where it went, or why it is gone. That could create a few problems, and it almost certainly would not be attributed to an undetected virus.

### 1.4.3   A Production Destruction Virus

A "Production Destruction Virus" is a virus launched, for example, by one steel company against another. In this scenario, you launch a virus that spreads through your competitor's company, identifying their production line system and causing the temperature in the third phase of their steel cooling process to be off by 10° C on Tuesday afternoons when there are between two and five people using the system, and no system administrator or security administrator logged in.

The net effect is that they'll have lower quality steel, and if they try to trace down the problem, the chances are, they'll have an administrator on the system looking for the problem, so the problem won't occur. It might be very difficult to track down the problem, and in the meanwhile, a noticeable degradation in quality might occur.

### 1.4.4   A Protection Code Changing Virus

A "Protection Code Changing Virus" is a virus that spreads throughout an environment changing the protection state of the machine, making unreadable things readable, making readable things unreadable, making executable programs readable and writable, and so on.

It turns out that in most modern systems, the protection state of the machine is very complex and there are no adequate tools for determining its propriety or restoring it to a known state. Thus, by randomizing the protection state, it is unlikely that the attack will be detected, and it may be very hard to restore the proper protection state. A minor improvement in protection tools would dramatically change this situation, and this is one of the major problems we face today in the information protection area.

### 1.4.5   A Network Deadlock Virus

A "Network Deadlock Virus" (we've seen this many times in the real world) is a virus that replicates so quickly that it deadlocks a network. All of the network deadlock viruses we are aware of, whether from a bug as in the ARPAnet deadlock in the mid-1970s and the AT&T crash of 1990, or from an intentional attacker as in the IBM Christmas card of 1988 and the Internet virus of 1989, have caused deadlock accidentally.

### 1.4.6   An Executive Error Virus

One of my favorites is the "Executive Error Virus." This is a virus launched by, let's say, the Vice President of R&D. It resides in a spreadsheet. It is not a virus in the spreadsheet binary executable program, it's in the spreadsheet itself. What it does, is spread from spreadsheet to spreadsheet until it gets to one of the President's spreadsheets. When it gets to one of the President's spreadsheets, it randomly changes one of the cells in the spreadsheet every time somebody looks at it. As a result, the President makes improper decisions based on the wrong numbers in the spreadsheet, and eventually makes so many incorrect decisions that he or she gets fired, and the Vice President moves up!

A similar thing was reportedly done when two partners in a small business attacked a third partner. According to the story, the third partner got so frustrated from errors in programs, that he quit the company. Now this is just a rumor, as far as I can tell, but it makes the point.

### 1.4.7   A Covert Channel Virus

Another interesting virus is a "Covert Channel Virus," used to leak secrets from the best computer security systems available today. Let's talk about these "best computer security systems." Typically, we're talking about a system intended to protect secrecy. It's called a security system, but I will call it a secrecy system. It works like this. If you are at a given secrecy level, you can't read information that's more highly classified, lest it would be leaked to you, and you can't write information that's less highly classified, lest you could leak secrets out to someone else. Figure 1.5 shows a picture of such a system. This is commonly called the "Bell-LaPadula Model" of computer security and is used on systems like RACF, ACF2, Top Secret, AT&T Secure Unix, and other commercial and military systems.

Now suppose that the least trusted user in this system puts a virus into a program. As soon as a classified user runs that unclassified program, a classified program can become infected. This is because there's no rule that says that a more trusted user can't run a less trusted program. The system allows the classified user to run the unclassified program, hence authorizing the unclassified program to act as a classified user and infect the classified program (see Figure 1.6).

Similarly, when a secret user runs the classified program, a secret program can become infected, and when a top secret user runs a secret program, top secret programs can become infected. That means that the least trusted user is the most dangerous from the standpoint of a viral attack.

| Higher | No read |
|--------|---------|
| You    | Read/Write |
| Lower  | No Write |

**FIGURE 1.5**   A Bell-LaPadula system.

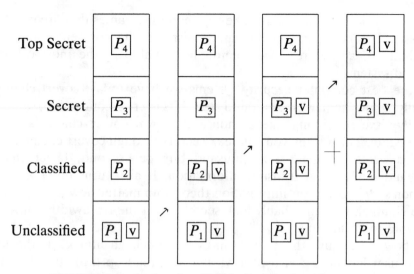

**FIGURE 1.6**   A virus in a Bell-LaPadula–based system.

This lack of integrity protection subjects all users of such a system to denial of services, directed corruptions, data diddling, and all of the other attacks we have discussed. But then, these systems are not designed to protect against corruptions, because they were designed with only a secrecy requirement restricting rights of subjects to see objects. It has become increasingly clear that a requirement to assure that objects are accurate and available for their intended use is called for if we are to depend on these systems for any particular purpose.

So how do we use that to leak secrets? We do it through something called covert channels. A covert channel is a channel for sending information around a system, that's not normally intended to be an information channel.

Let me give you an example. Suppose a top secret user wants to send information to an unclassified user by using a disk space covert channel. All the top secret user has to do is use a lot of disk space to indicate a '1', and very little disk space to indicate a '0'. If there is an unclassified user on that same computer system, that unclassified user could look at how much disk space is available. If there's very little disk space available, that indicates a '1'. If there's a lot of disk space available, that indicates a '0'. So that's a covert channel.

It turns out that on any system that allows users to share resources in a non-fixed fashion, there are always covert channels. In some systems, simple-to-exploit channels exist, like top secret file names that are visible to unclassified users. Other signaling mechanisms, such as presence of a file or availability of a resource, are commonly available in the most carefully designed systems.

In the best computer security systems we have today, covert channels typically allow somewhere around ten bits per second each, and we typically have something like a thousand known covert channels in any given system. This means you can leak secrets through covert channels at a combined rate of about ten thousand bits per second, faster than a 9600-baud modem can transmit information. It also turns out that (from Shannon's 1948 paper on information theory) no matter how much noise is in the channel, we can reliably leak secrets, with the bandwidth limited by the signal-to-noise ratio.

So how do we use these two things to launch an attack? If the least trusted user launches a virus, the virus can spread up through the system until a copy of the virus gets into the top secret area. At that point, this copy of the virus can start transmitting top secret information through the covert channel to a cooperating process in the untrusted environment. So you can leak secrets from the best computer security systems we have, if those systems do not maintain their integrity.

### 1.4.8  Synergism in Attack

Several of the examples described above exploit a synergistic relationship between the virus and another attack mechanism. For example, a virus alone could not leak secrets from a Bell-LaPadula–based system, and a covert channel cannot be systematically introduced by an outside attacker alone in such a system, but by combining the virus with the covert channel attack, we can do things neither could do alone.

This can be extended to many other attacks. For example, the Internet virus exploited a virus to spread the attack and attempted to guess passwords once it arrived in systems. Without the virus, these systems may not have been reachable to guess passwords on, while without the password guessing, the virus may not have been able to spread as far. Actually, the Internet virus was not as good at exploiting these things as it could have been; you can do much better.

Without going into too much more detail, this combination is very dangerous, and allows many otherwise strong defenses to be rendered completely ineffective. Imagine a virus designed to include 20 of the most successful attacks with the ability to spread far and fast. Perhaps you might even add a form of evolution so that replicas tend to try the most successful historic attacks more often than the less successful ones so that the more successful attack combinations tend to be used more often.

## 1.5  WHAT COULD A BENEVOLENT VIRUS DO?

We have seen the example of a compression virus that saves space by compressing executable files, and it may occur to you that there could be other useful applications of viruses in computer systems and networks. It turns out that there are. In fact, as a general result, we have known since viruses were first conceived that any computation that can be done by any program can be done by a computer virus. The issue surrounding the useful application of viruses is whether they do any sorts of things better than other forms of programs.

I don't want to go into too much detail on benevolent viruses here, because I have recently written another book on "live programs" (called "It's Alive") that addresses this issue in some depth, and the subject takes a great deal of time and space to cover. Instead, I just want to cover some of the possibilities to get your mental juices going.

### 1.5.1  Maintenance Viruses

Maintenance viruses, as a class, seem to be one of the most useful forms of computer viruses in existence today. Put in the simplest terms, computer systems are imperfect, and these imperfections often leave residual side effects, such as undeleted temporary files, programs that never stop processing, and incorrectly set protection bits. As more and more of these things happen over time, systems become less and less usable, until finally, a human being repairs the problems in order to continue efficient processing.

Here is a simple maintenance virus designed to replace older program versions with newer versions.

```
Program MVn :=
{Version=776; Program=test-program-1;
End-Date=93/12/21;
Original-Checksum=98763;
```

```
Main-program-of-virus :=
{Are-Viruses-Allowed?;
Is-This-Virus-Altered?;
Infect-All-Disks;
Perform-Useful-Function;
Make-Sure-MVs-Run;
Clean-Up-After;}


Subroutine Are-Viruses-Allowed? :=
    {If no 'viruses-allowed' file exists
      then exist-this-program-now;}


Subroutine Is-This-Virus-Altered? :=
    {If 'checksum' of this file is not
      the same as Original-Checksum
      then exit-this-program-now;}


Subroutine Clean-Up-After :=
    {If End-Date is after Today
      then Clean-all-disks and remove 'run MVn'
      from startup-profile;}


Subroutine Perform-Useful-Function :=
    {If version-of Program is less than Version
      then copy Tail-Program to Program}


Subroutine Make-Sure-MVs-Run :=
    {For all programs MVx
      {If 'run MVx' is not in startup-profile,
        prepend 'run MVx ' to startup-profile;}
    }


Subroutine Infect-All-Disks :=
    {For all accessible disks D
      {if MVn is not on disk D then copy MVn to D;
        if Version exceeds the Version of MVn on disk
          D then copy MVn to D;}
    }
```

```
Subroutine Clean-All-Disks :=
   {For all accessible disks D
       {if MVn is on disk D
          then remove MVn from disk D;}
   }


Tail-Program: ⟨Version 776 of test-program-1 goes
here⟩
}
```

This virus first checks to see if viruses are allowed on this system. If not, it exists without further operation. In a system with access controls, we could require that this file be in a directory owned by the systems administrator, so that no other user could allow viruses without permission. Next, it checks that the program has not been altered by using a "checksum" technique. These techniques will be described later, but it essentially checks a "fingerprint" of this file that assures to within a specified probability that this file has not been changed in distribution.

Next, it copies itself to all accessible disks unless they already have a newer version of MV. Next it checks whether the program it carries with it is newer than the on-line version of that program. If so, it updates that program. Next it assures that all current MV programs will run whenever the user uses the system by placing appropriate commands in the user's startup "profile." Finally, if the End-Date is past, it removes itself form all disks and from the user's profile.

As a side effect of any one of the MV viruses (i.e., $MV_1 \cdots MV_i$, $i \in \mathcal{N}$) running, all accessible MV viruses are assured to run. This enhances the distribution process by speeding up the spread of newer MV viruses. It also provides redundancy so that even if some MV viruses don't naturally infect a particular computer, they are helped along by other MV viruses.

Other useful functions that could be provided by MV viruses include deleting old temporary files, checking for disk errors and correcting them, and automatically distributing new software packages. You can probably think of more.

### 1.5.2   Distributed Databases with Viruses

Another application of benevolent viruses is in the area of distributed database design. In this case, instead of modifying information we are retrieving it from multiple sources, and in this case, we will assume a more advanced computing environment than is currently provided by the DOS operating system. For our example, we will assume there is a "Remote Procedure Call" (i.e., RPC) capability that allows programs to run programs on neighboring machines in a local area network. We will use this capability to reproduce into remote machines and cause them to invoke our viruses quickly.

```
Program DBV :=
{Search-Term=`Name=Jones and State=NJ';
Termination-Time=1PM on June 13, 1999;
Result-Address=Smith at Headquarters;


Main-program-of-virus :=
{Clean-Up;
Infect-Neighbors;
Perform-Useful-Function;
Wait-Around;}


Subroutine Wait-Around :=
    {sleep-till Termination-Time;
    Clean-Up;}


Subroutine Clean-Up :=
    {If Current-Time after Termination-Time
       then Delete DBV and DBV-active and exit;}


Subroutine Perform-Useful-Function :=
    {Search-for Search-Term and
mail-result-to Result-Address;}


Subroutine Infect-Neighbors :=
    {For all neighboring machines M
        {if file DBV-active does-not-exist on
           machine M then {create DBV-active on
                             machine M
                             copy DBV to machine M
                             run DBV on machine M}
        }
    }
}
```

When DBV is run on any machine, it first checks to see if the current time is after its termination time. If so, it deletes all files created by DBV on the current machine and terminates its own operation. If the termination time is not past, DBV copies itself to neighboring machines that it doesn't already exist on, and tells those machines to run their copy of DBV. They in turn copy the virus to their neighbors, and so on. Next, DBV performs a useful function by searching the local database(s) for the search terms and returning any results to the result address via computer mail. Finally, DBV waits around until its termination time and deletes itself.

A few comments are in order here because there is a bit of subtlety involved. For example, what if we change the order of the program operations so that main-program looks like this:

```
{Infect-Neighbors;
Clean-Up;
Perform-Useful-Function;
Wait-Around;}
```

In this case, the program could run forever, consuming disk space and computer time all over the network! The reason is that each copy will reproduce before self-destruction, thus creating several progeny which will do the same thing, ad infinitum. By cleaning up first, we prevent reproduction after the expiration time.

Another problem that could occur would be a situation where the time settings on different computers in the network are so different that whenever some systems are deleting their copy of DBV, other systems are reproducing DBV into new machines. On a local scale, this is unlikely to create a problem, but on a global scale, the situation could be quite different. Suppose the termination time didn't include a date. While it is after 1 p.m. in one place, it is before 1 p.m. somewhere west of that place, and that is true for every place on Earth! DBV could literally circle the earth, infecting machines with time settings between midnight and 1 p.m. (since in those machines it is before 1 p.m.) and dying out in areas where it is after 1 p.m.

Just as a biological creature can cause its own extinction by overpopulation, so could an undated version of DBV. Extinction comes if DBV is so successful that it saturates all of the susceptible computers in the network with copies of itself. At that point, none of the copies of DBV will ever reproduce again because the infection routine is only executed at program startup. This design is intended to cause rapid spread and execution, and not to cause network overloads.

If you ever try to run this sort of distributed database, you may be surprised by the results. To me, the most intriguing result of such an experiment is that results come back at different times. This is reminiscent of how the human thought process works in that we often start to consider a problem, get some initial results, and over time gain further insight as the thought process triggers results from more and more indirect connections.

### 1.5.3   Life for Its Own Sake

I personally believe that reproducing programs are living beings in the information environment, and I am not alone. A natural question that follows that belief is whether life in this form is virtuous for its own sake.

I am happy to report that I am at or near the top of the food chain, and as a result, I commonly kill other living creatures for my own survival. I am not anxious to kill other living creatures just for the thrill of the hunt, but other people are, and as long as they don't do so much of this that they impact the environment, it is only a somewhat nebulous moral issue as to whether it is right or wrong to kill them. We commonly kill nuisance creatures and rudimentary creatures such as bacteria without a second thought about their right to life.

This having been said, it would seem that just as people keep dogs and cats for pets, they might want to keep computer life-forms for pets. It would seem reasonable that just as we have leash laws in the city for pets, we might want leash laws on computer networks. We kill stray dogs and cats to control population, and so we will probably continue the genocide against stray computer viruses.

A good example of a nonviral computer pet is the X-Windows "roach" program. I'll run this program now so I can give as realistic a description as possible... The first thing that happens is that a bunch of cockroaches appear on the screen and start running around looking for a window to hide behind. Eventually, they all find hiding places, but as soon as I move a window or resize or delete it, all of the cockroaches that were hidden by it rush to find new cover.

Now you would think that such a useless program would never become widely used, but it seems that it is so widely used that it is a standard part of most X-Windows distribution systems, and similar programs have been widely used in computers since the early 1960s.

### 1.5.4   Practical Limits

Anything that can be done by any nonviral program can be done by a computer virus. For that reason, any limitations on the applications of viruses don't come from theory, but from practical concerns. From a practical standpoint, we only have limited experience, but we seem to know a few things about the kinds of problems best suited to viral computation.

In implementing problem solutions with viruses, communication between individuals is quite expensive compared to internal computation, and the more distant the individuals, the more overhead is required for communication. We would therefore prefer implementing viral solutions in cases where communication is less important than computation. A similar result applies to the issue of being able to centrally control computation once it is underway. Again, we would prefer viral solutions in cases where central control is not normally used.

Another important factor in determining if a computation is suited to viral implementation is the degree of parallelism inherent in the solution. Highly sequential solutions wherein each computation depends on the results of previous computations have a high degree of communication between computations in the series, and are thus not well suited to viral solutions. Similarly, highly parallel solutions are well suited to viral computation as long as they don't require a great deal of communication between parallel components.

For example, viruses are an ideal solution for certain "tree search" problems where each branch is independent and operates for a substantial amount of time, and only rare final results are returned. A terrible solution to implement with a virus would be a cellular array like the parallel multiplier, which performs $n^2$ fairly trivial calculations with each computation communicating results immediately to about four other computations, or a very sequential computation such as a simple recursive descent, wherein each result can only be determined after another result is available.

## 1.6   VIRUSES IN SPECIFIC COMPUTING ENVIRONMENTS

We're now going to translate the secretaries analogy into the language of a number of modern systems to clarify just how an infection might work, and to convince you that the principle is the same regardless of the particulars of your system.

### 1.6.1   Viruses in MVS

This is how the virus might work in an MVS system. Suppose that one module somewhere in a private MVS library (e.g., a Fortran subroutine, an object module, a library module, a source program, a spreadsheet that's interpreted by a spreadsheet program, a database macro, etc.) is infected. As the owner (user $U_a$) uses the infected module, other modules in $U_a$'s private library become infected, and as they are used, still other modules become infected, and so on, until eventually, everything in the library that can become infected does become infected. You can easily write a program to do this, it doesn't violate any security rules, nothing in it will trigger any errors or warnings on the system, and provided the process is reasonably fast, no obvious system changes will be noticed.

Eventually, some other user (user $U_b$) might run one of $U_a$'s infected programs, use an infected library or spreadsheet macro, or you name it. When $U_b$ uses something belonging to $U_a$, then $U_b$'s private library may become infected. $U_b$'s files start to have copies of the infection and it spreads throughout $U_b$'s area, eventually infecting everything that can become infected.

Through this process, the virus can spread from user to user and eventually work its way through the system. However, in some cases, the problem can get much worse very quickly. If some user along the way, say $U_c$, happens to have authority to modify programs or other information in common use, then the virus will spread far more quickly. For example, a system's programmer that runs an infected program, links with an infected library, interprets an infected spreadsheet, uses an infected database, you name it, grants the virus authority to modify system programs. In an MVS system, the virus will eventually spread into one of those system programs and everybody will become infected.

### 1.6.2   PC, MacIntosh, and Amiga Viruses

In a PC DOS-based system, a virus can be planted in an "EXE" or "COM" file (binary executables), in a Basic program, a spreadsheet, the boot sector, system memory, a device driver, video memory, the on-board clock memory, CMOS memory, or even in unused portions of a disk. Just as in the MVS case, whenever infected information is used, it can infect other information, but in a typical DOS environment, there is no protection, so any reachable information can be infected. If a floppy disk or a network is involved, viruses can spread to these media, and thus move from system to system.

The MacIntosh environment has a very different user interface than DOS, but in terms of operating system protection, it is not very different. It has minimal protection, and that protection is easily bypassed. The MacIntosh environment also has some extra problems related to the fact that some "data" files have implicit programs that are interpreted each time they are read or written. Viruses in these code segments can be very hard to track down.

The Amiga environment is similar in many ways to the DOS environment, and operating system protection is again minimal and easily bypassed. Thus the Amiga operating system can be corrupted just as the DOS and MacIntosh environments. The Amiga has an extra problem in that every time a disk is put into the system, a program on that disk is read in order to be able to interpret the contents of the disk. Each disk essentially carries its own driver, which means that the Amiga automatically installs and runs programs from the floppy disks whenever they are placed in the machine. Viruses planted in the driver area of a floppy disk are thus automatically installed and run.

### 1.6.3   Viruses in Unix and VMS

In a Unix or VMS system, a virus can be planted in the same way as in an MVS system, except that instead of modules in a library, viruses typically reside in files in a directory. When an infected file is interpreted, it can infect other accessible files. Viruses can also reside in processes, infecting information accessible by the process. Spreading from user to user can take place whenever a user uses another user's information, just as in MVS. If user $U_a$ has an infected program, and it is used by user $U_b$, then by using $U_a$'s program, $U_b$ authorizes it to modify $U_b$'s programs. Just as there are systems programmers in MVS, there are privileged users in Unix and VMS, and the accelerated spread works in essentially the same manner.

Remember, in each of these examples, the virus doesn't require any special privileges, it doesn't have to modify the operating system, it doesn't depend on any flaw in the operating system implementation, and it doesn't do anything that's not permitted by the security system. The virus spreads because the protection policies in these systems don't protect integrity.

### 1.6.4   Viruses in LANs

The most common forms of local area networks (LANs) in use today consist of one or more file servers and a set of host machines that access files on the file server(s) as if they were local files. The most common way viruses spread in LANs is that an infection on a host $H_x$ infects a file $f_a$ on the file server. When a user on another host $H_y$ uses $f_a$, the infection spreads to a file $f_b$ on host $H_y$. Users on other hosts accessing $f_a$ also spread the infections to their hosts, and each of those hosts in turn infect other files on the file server, and so on.

Just as in timesharing systems, no special privileges are required in order to infect files writable to infected users, and operating system modification is not necessary. Just as in timesharing systems, when users privileged to modify more files use infected hosts, the infection spreads further faster.

## 1.7   THE THREE DIFFERENCES

There are three major differences between viruses and everything that came before them: generality, extent, and persistence. I  will now describe these differences in some detail.

### 1.7.1   Generality

The first major difference is generality. When we look at computer security problems historically, we see things like a flaw in the operating system so that if a user calls a particular system facility in a particular way, then the system will grant access to a part of memory the user is not supposed to access. That's a typical attack before viruses.

With viruses, however, we have a very general attack situation. The virus spreads without violating any typical protection policy, while it carries any desired attack code to the point of attack. You can think of it as a missile, a general purpose delivery system that can have any warhead you want to put on it. So a virus is a very general means for spreading an attack throughout an entire computer system or network (see Figure 1.7).

Viruses can also be used to carry any useful function that could be manually performed in multiple places on multiple systems. The reproduction mechanism simply automates distribution in a reliable and efficient manner. You can think of it as you might think of a whole team of software installers that will install your program and run it on any machines you want. So a virus is a very general means of distributing useful functions throughout an entire computer system or network.

### 1.7.2   Range of Effect

The second major difference between viruses and previous attacks is their range. We used to think that if somebody broke into Joe's computer account, they could read what Joe could read and write what Joe could write, and that was that. When we did risk assessment on that basis, we normally found that the risk of breaking into any one account was minimal.

THREE DIFFERENCES BETWEEN
VIRUSES AND OTHER ATTACKS

GENERALITY

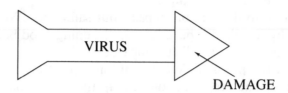

RANGE

**FIGURE 1.7**   A virus is like a missile.


But with computer viruses, we know that if somebody breaks into Joe's account, they can insert a virus, and when Mary uses one of Joe's programs, Mary's programs will become infected. Anybody that uses Mary's programs thereafter may also have their programs infected, and anybody that uses any of their programs, and so on. So it spreads from place to place, and its range, rather than being 1, is potentially infinite (see Figure 1.8). Think of it in other terms. Sitting at my Unix-based computer in Hudson, Ohio, I could launch a virus and reasonably expect it to spread through 40% of the Unix-based computers in the world in a matter of days. That's dramatically different from what we were dealing with before viruses.

The long range of viruses is also very helpful in benevolent applications because it enables them to bring useful functions far further without the need for centralized control of their progress. If Joe and Mary are in a fairly isolated network, we don't have to make special efforts to reach them unless time is of the essence, because eventually, the virus will spread into their network through the normal, if somewhat infrequent, sharing between their network and the rest of our organization.

$$\boxed{1} \rightarrow \boxed{2} \rightarrow \ldots \rightarrow \boxed{n}$$

**FIGURE 1.8**   The range of a virus.

### 1.7.3   Persistence

The third major difference between viruses and everything that came before them is persistence. This is perhaps the worst part of the problem. Take, for example, backups.

We used to think of backups as our safety net. We also saw hundreds of articles by so-called experts saying "Keeping good backups will protect you from computer viruses." It's not true.

Here's the problem. When you backup an infected program, you don't just backup the program, you backup the virus. That means that when you restore from backups, you don't just restore the program, you restore the virus. In other words, the backup acts as safe harbor for the virus and makes it much more difficult to get a virus out of a system than it would be if you didn't have those backups.

Let me give you some real good examples. Suppose I wrote a virus that only did subtle damage or didn't do any damage for six months. That means you would have six months of backup tapes infected with this virus. When the damage finally happens, you might get rid of the damage and clean your system up by restoring from backups that are say, two weeks old. Well, you've just brought the virus right back, and it's going to hit you again and again. In fact, you don't know how far back into the backups to go to have a clean system. You can never be absolutely certain you've gone back far enough.

But it gets worse. How about a network with floppy disks on personal computers? If anybody in the network has a floppy disk that's in a desk drawer somewhere, that's a backup. You may have a copy of a virus on that disk. Even though you cleaned the entire network and all the known backups, this one floppy disk sitting in a desk or in a briefcase can bring the virus back into your network, and there you go again. Let me give you a real-world example.

There's a virus called the "Scores" that works against MacIntosh computers. I know of one organization where they cured the Scores virus from hundreds of MacIntosh computers in a network once a week over a period of two years. They kept getting rid of the virus, but it kept coming back, because somewhere, somebody had a floppy disk made during that week that didn't get cleaned up. When the disk was reused, it brought the infection back.

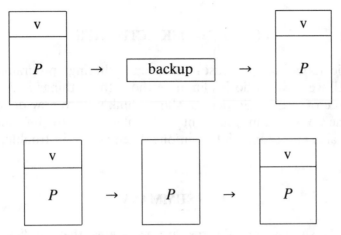

**FIGURE 1.9**   Viruses can be persistent.

So this persistence issue is really quite serious and makes getting rid of viruses much more difficult than other attacks. It's even more interesting to note that viruses tend to persist longer than almost anything else in the computing environment (see Figure 1.9). For example, every couple of years you might get a new version of a spreadsheet program. If your old spreadsheet program was infected, the new version will eliminate the infection, but because the virus is in the environment, it will eventually infect the new spreadsheet program. So a virus persists beyond changing from generation to generation of software programs.

Eventually, you probably change every piece of software in your computer system, but the virus may still persist. When you go from DOS 2.01 to DOS 2.3, to 3.0, to 3.1 to 3.2 to 4.0 4.1 to 5.0 to 6.0 to OS/2, the same viruses that worked on DOS 2.01 almost certainly work on each of these updated operating systems. In fact, if you wrote a computer virus for the IBM 360 in 1965, chance are it would run on every IBM-compatible mainframe computer today, because these computers are upward compatible.

The great benefit of persistence in benevolent viruses is that they can be designed so that they reliably distribute information even in a very unreliable environment. For example, in the global network environment, a central update process will almost certainly fail because machines are constantly being added, removed, rebooted, and reconfigured. Inevitably, some machines will miss the update. With computer viruses, eventually every machine that connects to the network may get updated, and we don't have any central control overhead.

## 1.8   HIGH-RISK ACTIVITIES

Three basic things allow viruses to spread: sharing, programming, and changes. All we have to do is eliminate those three things and we will be perfectly free of viruses. So does anybody think we are now done with the short course? You mean you want to be able to share information and write programs and change information? Then you're in trouble, I guess.

## 1.9   SUMMARY

Let's quickly summarize. Viruses are programs that replicate, evolve, and/or infect. They spread from program to program, user to user, computer to computer, and network to network. Their unique properties are generality, persistence, and extent. They are an integrity problem, not a secrecy problem. Therefore, improving computer security to keep secrets better does not eliminate the virus problem. Similarly, old risk assessment techniques do not apply. Finally, most current systems are extremely vulnerable.

Out of the thousands of people I've talked to about computer viruses in the last couple of years, I've had three people who claim to be invulnerable to this particular problem, and after great discussions, I find that they are probably right. They are the people who make nuclear missiles. Why aren't they very vulnerable? Because they combine all of the integrity techniques we discuss, sparing no expense. As you will see, you can be almost completely invulnerable, but you have to pay so much that you have to be in the nuclear missile business to justify it.

Benevolent viruses may also have a place in the computing world of tomorrow. Just because some people don't want viruses in their systems doesn't mean that they should be able to force their will in other peoples' systems. But one thing should be clearly understood. People who don't want viruses in their systems should not be forced into having them there just because some other people are malicious or thoughtless. To that end, a great deal of work has been done on defending against malicious viruses, and that work is largely the subject of the rest of this book.

Before continuing, I just want to say one other thing about benevolent viruses. It is very easy to provide protection against a benevolent virus, and benevolent virus writers that take even the most rudimentary precautions can provide a high degree of assurance that their viruses won't go where they are not invited. In my opinion, if they do not provide these precautions, they are recklessly endangering others, and they should be held responsible for their actions. But if they do provide reasonable precautions, there should be no objection to their efforts, and they should be allowed to continue without fear of penalty or the kind of social abuse currently heaped on researchers who admit to following this line.

# Chapter 2

# REAL-WORLD VIRUSES

Computer viruses have had a substantial impact on the world computing community, and for the most part, this impact has been negative. I believe that this negative impact has been the result of the fact that the early work on viruses related primarily to their utility as an attack and the difficulty of defending against them, and the fact that far more malicious viruses have been spread throughout the world than benevolent ones. I have a few notion about why more malicious viruses are seen, and I would like to share them with you before going on to specific examples.

Some people have the idea that malicious viruses are easier to write than benevolent ones, and I must agree that this is probably correct, but then the same could be said for any other sort of program. For example, the following Unix command deletes all of a user's files

$$\text{rm} - \text{rf \$HOME/}*$$

Considering the negative impact of this very small program, I doubt that a similar sized benevolent program exists with an equivalent positive impact. The point is, it is generally easier to destroy than to create.

Even if there were far more benevolent viruses than malicious viruses in the world, most of the viruses we would notice would likely be malicious, because malicious viruses tend to spread out of control. Benevolent viruses are normally designed to spread only where intended and only over a specific period of time, so we don't notice them at large in the world.

## 2.1 SOME EARLY EXPERIMENTS

I would now like to move into a description of some of the early experimental results with computer viruses and then to descriptions of some of the viruses in the real world. I am not going to go into a list of all of the existing viruses, because there are simply too many of them to list (several thousand at last count), and new ones come up so often, that by the time you publish a list, it is no longer complete. Furthermore, the vast majority of these viruses are not interesting from a scientific point of view, in that they represent no new ideas or technology, and they don't substantially change the problem of defense. Instead, I'm going to go over what I consider to be the more important breakthroughs in viruses so that we can learn about some key issues.

In the beginning, we did experimental attacks, but we didn't just say "Let's go play." Experiments were performed to demonstrate the feasibility of malicious viruses, determine infection time, and try to predict the time required to take over systems. Permission was obtained from systems administrators before each attack (to keep me out of jail), and implementation flaws were meticulously avoided because the whole idea of viruses is that they don't violate existing protection policies. Let me give you an example of what we faced.

- We did some of our early experiments on a Unix system. One of the things that people said about our results was "Yes, you succeeded, but Unix is fundamentally, weak, so it's not very interesting that you found another way to attack it." For some reason they thought that because they knew how to bypass controls in one Unix implementation, that invalidated the reality of viruses. So we did experiments on other systems, and at every step along the way there were those who said "Yes, but that system is fundamentally weak." In nearly every virus experiment I have ever done, someone has said "that operating system is fundamentally weak, so it's not important that you can use a virus against it."

The point is, these viruses didn't exploit implementation flaws; they exploited flaws in the security policy. That is, the policy that allows you to share information and interpret it in a general purpose way, allows a virus to spread, regardless of the implementation.

To get an idea of how widespread the misperception was, one day the National Security Agency (an agency in the U.S. government that is so secret that even its mission statement is classified) called me into a meeting and said "We don't think it's appropriate to reveal the names of systems that are vulnerable to an attack until the manufacturers have the chance to eliminate the vulnerability." Now to understand how ridiculous this is, you have to understand that the NSA is the organization that wrote the "Trusted Systems Evaluation Criteria," which is the basis for computer security controls used by the U.S. government. Even they didn't seem to understand that the problem is fundamental to the way we use computers, and not due to some implementation flaw.

If I follow their advice, I can never ever tell you that I've performed experiments on Unix, VMS, MVS, TSS, VM, DOS, and many other operating systems and shown that they are vulnerable to viruses. So, in keeping with their request, I won't tell you that.

### 2.1.1   The First Scientific Experiment

The first scientific protection-related experiment with a virus was certainly not the first virus ever to exist, but it was unique in that it was the first experiment we have found that exploited the infection property to bypass normal controls. This experiment was conceived November 3, 1983, performed over the next several days, and demonstrated on November 10th to the attendees of a computer security course.

The experiment was on a *blank* computer, running the *blank* operating system (in keeping with the NSA's request). The purpose was to demonstrate feasibility and measure attack time. It took 8 hours for an expert to develop the virus, which was far more complex than viruses we have seen in the real world. Even though this virus was one of the largest I've seen, it was only a 200 line C program (that sort of gives away the operating system, doesn't it?), so it wasn't a very big program compared to most other programs in the environment. Most of the complexity was to to precautions we took to assure that it would not spread out of control, that we could trace its spread, and that it could be safely removed. It also had at least one feature that no other virus since has displayed. As a means of spreading to the largest number of users in the smallest amount of time, it sought to infect the most often used programs first.

Infection time was under $\frac{1}{2}$ second in the middle of the day on a heavily loaded timesharing system. So let me just ask: On a heavily loaded timesharing system in the middle of the day, is anybody going to notice a $\frac{1}{2}$-second delay in running a program? How about a 1-second delay? A 2-second delay? Four seconds? Is anybody going to notice an 8-second delay? All right, yes. Somewhere between four and 8 seconds, there's always a person that says "I'm going to notice that delay." The point is, people don't tend to notice $\frac{1}{2}$-second delays under these conditions, and nobody ever noticed the $\frac{1}{2}$-second delay in our early experiments.

These viruses demonstrated the ability to cross user boundaries, which is the only protection provided in the *blank* operating system, so it bypassed all of the normal protection mechanisms. After each of these experiments, the virus was cleaned from all infected programs without any impact on the users, and except for the audit trials, there was no trace of the virus left. Even the tape drive was locked during the experiments to assure that copies didn't spread beyond the system under test.

There were five attacks launched, and the minimum time to completely take over the system (i.e., the time to attain all access to all information) was 5 minutes. The average time was 30 minutes, and the longest time in five experiments was 1 hour. This was somewhat surprising. In fact, at that point in time, I said to myself, "this cannot be true of most systems." I thought that this must have been a fluke having to do with this particular system. so I wanted to do a lot more experiments to find out for certain.

### 2.1.2   A Compression Virus

The idea of a compression virus came very early on, and in late 1983, we implemented a simple compression virus in the Unix "sh" command interpreter. Modern computer virus experts call this a "companion" virus, because rather than replace the original program file, we simply compressed it, renamed it, and replaced it with a copy of the virus. When the virus was run, it checked for a command line option that was used to specify that it should reproduce. If reproduction was not called for, it decompressed the compressed original under its original name, ran it, and after it finished running, replaced the virus.

This first benevolent virus had some other interesting properties. It notified the user of its existence upon execution, so it was not a Trojan horse, and it only spread where specifically directed, so it was not able to spread out of control without permission. I used it for a short time, without telling anyone, when disk space was particularly tight. The reason I didn't tell anyone about it was that my previous experiments with viruses had alienated some key members of the faculty,[1] and I didn't want to get in any further trouble. Since they didn't spread without permission and were only used in protected areas of my personal directory, I felt there was no danger involved.

---

[1] I think it was because the first virus infected several of their files even though they knew about the experiment ahead of time and tried to avoid being victims.

### 2.1.3   A Bell-LaPadula–Based System

I really wanted to do instrumentation, because with experiments you can only show what happened in one case, but with instrumentation, you can get statistics that show you what's going to happen on the average. I tried to get permission for instrumentation, but before I had the chance to do that, I got to do an experiment on a Bell-LaPadula-based system, one of these high-class computer security systems intended to protect from the leakage of secrets.

Negotiations began in March of 1984 and the actual experiments were performed in July of 1984. It was a Proprietary Univac 1108 based system, and I can practically guarantee that you have never encountered it. There were only two copies of this operating system ever in existence, and I heard a few years ago that these systems were decommissioned. I don't remember the name of the operating system, but if I told it to you, it wouldn't have any meaning anyway, and besides, I promised not to tell anyone the name of the site.

The purpose of this experiment was to demonstrate the feasibility of a virus in a Bell-LaPadula–based system, and performance simply was not an issue. It took 18 hours to develop by a novice user of both the 1108 and this operating system, with a little bit of help from another user who told me how to use the editor, helped me find the right manuals, et cetera.

Infection time was a very slow 20 seconds. The virus demonstrated the ability to cross user boundaries and move up security levels. It was an ugly program: 200 lines of Fortran, 10 lines of Assembly, and 50 lines of command files. A Fortran program called an assembly routine to run the command interpreter to compile another Fortran program. It was not a glorious example of programming.

So I went to do the demonstration, which was very interesting because I had the Chief of Computer Security for that organization, the Chief of Security for that site, the person that designed the operating system, the programmer who wrote the operating system, and the person in charge of the whole facility at the demonstration. I described what I was going to do: launch an attack that showed that the least trusted user on their system could corrupt classified information throughout. Well, the guy that wrote the system said "It's impossible to do that; there's no way." Now, if you ever give a demonstration, there's nothing better than having a guy across the table say that what you're about to do is impossible. So I did it, and he said "Gee, I guess it's not impossible, huh." He asked how I did it, and I described about Bell-LaPadula and moving up security levels, et cetera, and he got really upset. He said "I don't know why we had you here, you're the worst programmer I have ever seen. In 15 minutes, I could write a program to do this, it would go through the system like a hot knife through butter, and nobody would even notice it." So I said, "That's the point!" He finally got the point.

### 2.1.4  Instrumentation

We finally got to do instrumentation once on a pair of systems. Negotiations began in April of 1984, and by August 1984 instrumentation began. It was a *blank* computer again, running the *blank* operating system.[2]

The purpose was to confirm or refute the previous results on takeover time, measure attack times, and try to improve protection. It took an expert 8 hours to develop the instrumentation.

Much to our surprise, the minimum time to completely take over the system dropped to 30 seconds. If you got real lucky, and you put the virus in just the right place at just the right time, it would take over the whole system right away. The average, however, remained at 30 minutes, and the longest time was about 48 hours.

At first we couldn't figure out why there was a big clustering of takeover times around 48 hours and $\frac{1}{2}$ hour. What we found out was that people log-off the system Friday night and don't use the system until Sunday evening. On Sunday evening, they all log-in to read their mail, and then they all get infected. So if you launch a virus just after everybody leaves on Friday, everybody will get infected on Sunday evening.

Another interesting thing we found out was that if you announce a new program on a bulletin board and that program contains a virus, you can typically take over a computer system in 10 minutes. Anybody want to guess why? It's not that everybody reads the bulletin board and runs the program. One particular person reads the bulletin board and runs the program. Who might that be? The system administrator. It turns out that if you announce a new program on the bulletin board, within about 10 minutes, the average systems administrator will notice it and run it, thereby corrupting all of the system files immediately.

In fact, what we found was a set of social users. That is, users that tend to run a lot of other users' programs and write programs that a lot of other users run. So, it's just like biological diseases. Viruses tend to spread faster through people that display a lot of social behavior. If you cut down on the

---

[2] It's a very popular operating system. If you've never used a *blank* computer, you should try it.

way social users do these things, then you can slow the spread of computer viruses in the same way that if you decrease the interactions of social individuals in society, you can slow the spread of biological diseases. We made several suggestions to improve protection, particularly in protecting those social users.

### 2.1.5 Psychological Effects of Experiments

There were also psychological effects. As soon as we succeeded in launching an attack, other sites said, in effect, "Oh, you mean it works? Well, in that case you can't perform any more experiments." In other words, you can only perform an experiment on breaking security if it fails. If it's going to work in demonstrating a vulnerability, people are not interested in it, and that's that. In fact, we couldn't, and still to this day can't get permission to do instrumentation on systems and try to find out what the average attack time would be or to try to understand how this behavior works.

I have heard of other researchers doing experiments and instrumentation of systems in their own companies, but I have not seen any publications of their results. I assume that they either have not generated any new information worth publishing, or that they have generated new information so confidential to their organizations that they don't want to tell anyone. I can't imagine that it would be a big secret that their systems were less vulnerable to attack, and I have heard about faster attacks, so I believe that our experiments reflect the reality fairly well.

Perhaps the most undesired psychological side effects of our results is that people now have a strong negative feeling about all computer viruses. There is almost a knee-jerk reaction to the word "virus" in the research community, to the point where researchers who look into benevolent applications of reproducing programs make up different names for them, like "knowbots" and "artificial life forms." I even use the term "Live Programs" on occasion, so as to not offend my more sensitive readers.

We demonstrated feasibility for a number of other systems, but eventually administrators refused to allow experiments. Most administrators were unwilling to even allow use of sanitized versions of log tapes. All I can say is it looks like a fear reaction. What we seem to have run into is a situation where once you've violated the sanctity of a computer account, even in an approved experiment, those involved feel as if they've been personally violated. For somebody that uses a system day after day for 5 or 10 years, writing programs, writing papers, keeping notes, et cetera, there is a very personal feeling about that area of the computer. People feel personally violated when you do things to it, and they react just like victims of assault. So, I guess we should learn how to be survivors instead of victims.

## 2.2   THE COMPUTER VIRUS RECORD BOOK

People tend to be interested in records because they indicate the end points of technology. Let me tell you about some of the records regarding computer viruses.

### 2.2.1   The Smallest

The record for the smallest virus is a Unix "sh" command script. In the command interpreter of Unix, you can write a virus that takes only about 8 characters. So, once you are logged into a Unix system, you can type a 8 character command, and before too long, the virus will spread. That's quite small, but it turns out that with 8 characters, the virus can't do anything but reproduce. To get a virus that does interesting damage, you need around 25 or 30 characters. If you want a virus that evolves, replicates, and does damage, you need about 4 or 5 lines. In one of our Unix experiments, we created a 5 line virus that replicates, evolves, does data diddling for damage, and works on just about any Unix system. It's very easy to write, and you can do it in very few lines of code.

### 2.2.2   The Fastest on a PC

Another interesting record is on an IBM PC, that is, a 4-MHz processor, 5.25-in. floppy disks, and no hard disk. It turns out that to get an infection onto that floppy disk takes about $\frac{1}{2}$ second, just enough time for the disk to spin around one time. On a hard disk, infection is proportionately faster, so on a disk with a 10-ms access time, infection takes only 10 ms.

### 2.2.3   Spreading in Networks

The first record for spreading on a PC network was established in 1986 or 1987 (I believe it was 1986) by some graduate students at the University of Texas at El Paso doing a legitimate and authorized experiment. They wrote a computer virus for a standard IBM PC network using a token ring network architecture. They launched the virus, and within 30 seconds, the virus entered all 60 computers in the network. At this point the students said "Wait a minute, we don't want this virus getting out to the rest of the world, we'd better turn off all those computers." So they literally ran to all 60 of the computers in this relatively small environment and shut the power off.

Well, a couple of people were slightly offended. They had been entering data for 4–6 hours without saving their entries when their computers were switched off. The experimenters decided it might be inappropriate to perform further experiments.

That was the network record for a while, but in 1987 the IBM Christmas card spread, and at its peak, it was replicating at the rate of 500,000 times per hour in mainframes throughout the world. This was according to reports by people at IBM several weeks later, but I've subsequently heard from a gentleman at IBM who is authorized to and probably actually knows, and he told me that this figure is off by a factor of 10, but he won't tell me whether its high or low. So somewhere between 50,000 and 5,000,000 copies per hour were being replicated at the peak of the IBM mainframe attack, but that's not the record anymore.

On March 22, 1991, the world high-speed computing record was broken by a Massachusetts company specializing in parallel processing. The previous record holder, contrary to popular belief, was the Internet Virus. A design flaw that caused unchecked growth demonstrates one of the malicious aspects of this virus, and unfortunately, many of the other computer viruses we hear about are also malicious, but like any new technology, viruses are a two-edged sword.

Consider that the Internet Virus performed about 32 million operations per second on each of 6000 computers, and another 3.2 million operations per second on each of 60,000 computers, for a grand total of 384 billion operations per second! It took hundreds of person-years of work and millions of dollars to design the computer hardware and software that broke this processing record, whereas the Internet Virus was written by one graduate student using existing computers in his spare time over a period of a few months.

For pure processing cycles, computer viruses are some of the fastest distributed programs we know of, but unfortunately, we haven't yet grown enough scientifically or ethically to exploit their vast potential. But have heart. I understand that people are working around the world to try and beat that record, and you can probably count on it being broken in the next couple of years.

### 2.2.4   Other Time-Dependent Indications of Interest

Some other interesting things: In 1984, there was one researcher, and there were two papers on viruses. There was one news article, and it happened to be in the United States. In 1985, Europe had many news stories and there were two researchers. By 1986, there were 15 researchers. By now computer virus defense is a big business. The largest computer companies in the world have software products to fight viruses, many of the governments of the world have laws against introducing malicious viruses, and there are thousands of known viruses. Large companies report several incidents per year, there are well over a thousand active antivirus researchers, thousands of new stories are published per year, and over a dozen large conferences on computer viruses are held around the world each year.

## 2.3   REAL-WORLD COMPUTER VIRUSES

Let me just go down the list of viruses that I consider to be especially worthy of note. The reason I don't go through all the viruses that have ever taken place is that as of this writing, the research community knows of over 3000 real-world malicious viruses, and new malicious viruses are found in the environment at a rate of several a day. It's obviously infeasible to go through all the details of all these viruses, and it's also not particularly important to know about all of the minor variations on a theme to understand what is going on.

### 2.3.1   The Xerox Worm

There are many rumors of reproducing programs prior to the examples we describe here, and there is even the Xerox "Worm" programs which designed to operate in internal Xerox networks. Those were reported in the literature in 1982. The Worm programs may have been computer viruses, but it is hard to tell for certain based on the description in the published papers whether they were centrally controlled or whether each copy was an independent agent capable of reproduction on it's own. I don't intend to slight this interesting work, and I believe it may have been the first published case of benevolent viruses. I do want to note that the use of the capital "W" here is intended to indicate that the Xerox Worm programs were given that name by their authors, even though they may or may not meet the current formal definition of worms, which are subsets of viruses.

The story would not be complete unless I told you that one of the Xerox Worm programs was altered by an error of some sort (apparently a single bit-flip) that caused it to run amok, taking the entire Xerox computer network out of operation. Xerox then canceled all further experiments in this area.

To some, this leads to the conclusion that there can be no safe benevolent viruses. To others, it simply points out the need for ample precautions. The Xerox experiments had no safeties at all. Even the simplest safety of a self-test would have prevented this problem, and if the problem had been covered by such a safety, we might well see widespread applications of similar systems today.

### 2.3.2   The First Maintenance Viruses

I will probably hear about an earlier application of viruses the day after this is printed, but as far as I am aware, the first program designed as a computer virus and applied in the real-world was a maintenance virus used in a Unix environment to automate certain aspects of systems administration. This was first implemented in December of 1985, and was operating daily in a customer application in January of 1986. This virus was similar in some respects to the maintenance virus example shown earlier. To date, there have been no problems or complaints about this virus or any of the other maintenance viruses that followed, and they have been doing useful work for over 8 years.

It is particularly noteworthy that between 1983, when the first experiments with viruses per-se were performed, and four years later in 1987, the only real-world viruses were benevolent viruses. They were in day-to-day operation over a period of years, and with the exception of a single experimental virus at Xerox, no benevolent virus I am aware of has ever caused a substantial problem.

That does not mean that viruses are inherently safe. It is quite common for experimental viruses to go awry. In 1985 (or perhaps 1986), I was experimenting with process viruses on a guest computer account at Carnegie-Mellon University when I accidentally created an unkillable set of processes. In this case, the processes preproduced so quickly that they consumed all of the processes available to a single user. I couldn't stop the virus because I needed to create a process to kill off the reproducing processes but I couldn't get a process to do this because the virus consumed all the available processes. We even tried having the "superuser" kill off the processes, but even the superuser couldn't kill the processes quickly enough to kill all of them before the remaining ones reproduced. In other words, the reproduction rate was so great that we simply couldn't kill them as fast as they could reproduce.

The solution chosen by the systems administrator was to wait until the next time the computer was rebooted, at which time all processes are destroyed. The viruses couldn't reproduce any more because all of the processes available were consumed, and as a result, all of the copies of the virus were blocked from further computation as they awaited an available process for reproduction. The only effect was reducing the available "paging" space on the disk, reducing the total available processes on the system, and preventing me from using the system until the reboot succeeded. In this particular system, these effects were minimal.

### 2.3.3   The Lehigh Virus

I am now going to describe in some gory detail what happened at Lehigh University, after which I will describe what happened with a virus at the University of Maryland. The reason is that there are some very dramatic differences between the way these organizations reacted to these viruses, and their reactions had widespread effects on the rest of the world.

The "Lehigh Virus" virus was launched in the fall of 1987. It was probably launched by an undergraduate student at Lehigh University with significant experience with IBM PC computers. It infected the DOS command interpreter (a file called COMMAND.COM) by modifying it to include a routine that infected the first 4 disks it came in contact with, and then destroyed all of the disks currently in the system. The destruction was done by overwriting the "File Allocation Table" (FAT), which keeps a list of file and directory names and the series of disk "sectors" associated each file and directory on disk. This virus resides in the "stack segment" of COMMAND.COM, and as a result, it doesn't change the size of the file, but due to a lack of foresight, it does change the modification date of the file. According to the people at Lehigh University, if it had not changed the modification date, it might not have been identified for a much longer time.

The Lehigh virus was detected only as a side effect of the massive damage it unleashed, but in order to really understand this, you have to understand how the environment at Lehigh University operated. As a means of providing site-licensed programs to users, Lehigh had floppy disk libraries. When students wanted to use one of these programs, they would go into the library, take out the disks, put them into a PC at the library site, and use them as required. Many students made copies to take back to their dormitory rooms (a legitimate activity under the site license). When they were done using the software, they returned the disks to the central library.

On a typical day at that central library they had about five disks come in bad. Floppy disks are generally unreliable, especially in an environment like this. Some of them had data errors, some of them were bent, some of them got dusty, et cetera. Whatever the cause, about five disks per day normally went bad.

On this particular day, 500 disks came in bad, so they suspected something was wrong. The user consultants at Lehigh University had been educated in computer viruses (by me, as it turns out), so they were aware of the possibility of a virus, and immediately suspected it. They began to examine these destroyed disks, and they found out that the COM-MAND.COM modification date was very recent on many of the disks in the library. They then disassembled COMMAND.COM and compared it to an original copy that had never been opened (it was in the bottom of a file cabinet), and they found this virus.

By midnight, they figured out how the virus worked. By 4 o'clock the next morning, they wrote a program to detect its presence on a disk and automatically remove it. By 8 o'clock the next morning, they had a piece of physical mail in every physical mailbox on campus, electronic mail in every electronic mailbox on campus, and a person with a PC at every outside door on campus. Everybody that entered or left any building was required to put their floppy disk into one of these systems to cure any infections. If they had a PC at home and they needed a copy of the cure for their system the people at the doors would hand them a copy to take with them.

Within two days, they wiped out every single copy of this virus from that environment. That is, no copy of that virus has ever been seen "in-the-wild" anywhere else in the world.

Let me just point out what might have happened if one or two things were a little bit different. Suppose, for example, that the virus had replicated 16 times instead of four times before doing damage. Then there would have been four times as many copies in the first generation and 16 times as many copies in the second generation et cetera. There would have been many more copies, but they would not have been detected as soon, because the damage would have been delayed longer. They probably would have detected it a day or two later. So, a day or two later doesn't make much difference, does it?

Well, it turns out that this virus was detected two days before fall vacation at Lehigh University. During fall break at universities in the United States, most students bring floppy disks home from schools to do homework assignments and share software with students from other schools. They usually put this software into their parents' home computer system, and there the problems really begin. The parents typically take floppy disks back and forth to work, so if the infection had entered these machines, it would have moved into thousands of other computers in companies throughout the region. From there, it would have spread on, replicating, and doing massive damage. Instead of the 500 systems at Lehigh University that lost all of their data, we probably would have seen several orders of magnitude more damage.

### 2.3.4   The Brain Virus

By contrast, let's look at what happened at the University of Maryland, where the "Brain virus" first appeared in the United States.

The  Brain virus  was written by two brothers from Lahore, Pakistan (Ashad and Ahmed according to the copyright notice in the virus—we will probably never know who launched the Lehigh Virus). When Brain first appeared it didn't do any obvious damage. In fact, the only reason anyone noticed it at first was that it changed the disk label of unlabeled disks to read "(C)BRAIN." The Brain virus changes the "bootblock" of disks, so that when you put an uninfected disk into an infected system, it infects the bootblock of that disk, even if it's not a bootable DOS disk. If you use the newly infected disk to bootstrap another system, that system will also become infected. The only other effects of this virus are that it reduces available memory by a few thousand bytes, it marks several blocks of disk space bad and uses this space to store itself, and on fairly rare occasion, it causes disk failures.

This virus spread around the University of Maryland unchecked over a period of weeks, and when they had their fall break, students took it home. Over the next three months, at least 100,000 copies are well documented as having appeared and infected throughout the world. In this case, there wasn't a big defensive effort. It took several weeks to figure out what was going on, partly because nobody at Maryland knew what a virus was or what the risks were. It spread and spread and spread, and as a result, we may not get rid of all of the copies of Brain for a long time.

I should also note here that the Brain virus includes a telephone number for Ashad and Ahmed with instructions to call them for help in removing the virus. Apparently, nobody called them for several months after this virus was published in the newspapers. They were finally contacted by the *Journal for Higher Education*, whose reporter decided to call the number. In all fairness, it was a long-distance call.

### 2.3.5 The Jerusalem Virus

One of the major controversies surrounding the Jerusalem virus is the question of whether it was launched by a terrorist group or not. A terrorist was suspected because the damage was scheduled to cause widespread destruction of data on the 40th anniversary of the last time there was a Palestinian state, and the virus was the first seen at Hebrew University in Jerusalem (hence its name). It reproduces inside binary executable programs in the DOS operating system, but it doesn't properly check ".EXE" files prior to infection, so it reinfects the same programs again and again. It was first detected with people with brand-new PCs who started loading software onto their disks, only to find that a 20-mega byte disk was full after being loaded with only about 2-mega bytes worth of software. They did a directory and found out that DOS programs had grown to incredible sizes. Eventually they created a special-purpose defense and got rid of most of the copies, but not all of them.

It turns out that the Jerusalem virus was subsequently modified by a person or persons unknown to repair the "flaw", thus producing the "Jerusalem-B" virus, which has been one of the most widespread viruses in the world for several years. This particular variation also works quite well against Novell networks, and is one of the dominant viruses in that venue. The modification strategy seems fairly common. In fact, the vast majority of "new" viruses are minor variants of other viruses. There are apparently a number of computer clubs that require new members to provide a virus which is not detected by select current antivirus programs as a condition of admission. Some variants are as simple as altered triggering dates (hence we now have viruses that trigger on every day of the year) and altered messages (some people want the whole world to know when they were born). Other people make minor "repairs" and "improvements" or alter damage so as to make relatively harmless viruses very damaging.

### 2.3.6 The Swiss Amiga Virus

The story of the so-called "Swiss" Amiga viruses is fairly interesting for a number of reasons. The first reason is the name. It is called *Swiss* because someone at first thought it was launched from Switzerland, but the last time I heard of people searching for the source, they thought it was from Germany or Canada. Nothing is quite as exciting as closing right in on a perpetrator.

To understand how this particular virus works, you have to understand how Amigas work. Not the technical aspects, but rather how people share information when they use Amigas. Amigas have very strong user groups. For example, it's not unusual for an Amiga user group to have hundreds of people, with meetings twice a week. So they have several hundred people meeting twice a week, exchanging disks with each other, giving talks, and doing all sorts of computer related social activities. Sharing is very prevalent under these circumstances.

This virus enters one of the system files on an Amiga, and eventually destroys the information on the disk in a similar way to the PC-based viruses we have discussed. When I first heard about this virus, I called up the person at Commodore (the manufacturer of the Amiga) in charge of defending against it, the chief systems programmer. He said "I have it under control; it's no big deal," and he wrote a program that looked for the first byte of the virus in that particular file. If the first byte of that virus was present, it said "this is an infected program, restore from backups to repair the problem" or some such thing.

So, he sent this defense out, and about a week later there was a new version of the virus that started with a different first byte. So I called the guy up and said "Wouldn't you like to do something better?" He said "No, no, we have it under control...," and then he sent out a program that looked for either of those two first bytes. The third round involved a copy of the virus that evolved through any of ten different first bytes, so I called him again and he said "No, no, I've got it under control..." This time he wrote a program that checked to see whether the first byte was not the legitimate byte of the Amiga program. About a week later, there was a version of the virus that had the same first byte as the legitimate Amiga program, but a different second byte. That was the last time I bothered calling this guy up. I figure that by now, they're up to about the tenth or eleventh byte, and still battling it out.

### 2.3.7  The Mainframe Christmas Card Virus

In 1987, we also had the Christmas card virus that spread throughout mainframes of the world by way of computer mail. It was created by a student in Germany as a Christmas card. In order to understand how this virus worked, you have to understand that part of the corporate culture in IBM was for people to send each other Christmas cards via computer mail. As a result, when someone you knew sent you a Christmas card you would normally read it without hesitation.

So this person in Germany created a Christmas card and sent it to the only two people he knew. The first recipient looked at it and said "I don't know this guy, I'm not going to look at this Christmas card." It was Friday afternoon, and the second recipient went home. On Monday, he came in and read his Christmas card, and it put a fairly poor looking Christmas card on the screen and said "Merry Christmas." But, unbeknownst to the recipient, it also did something else. It looked through his list of outgoing mail recipients (the people he normally sends mail to), and sent a copy of this Christmas card in his name to everybody on that list. Naturally, when they got this Christmas card from their friend, they said "Oh great, I'll read it" and they read it, and it sent copies to everybody on their outgoing mailing lists in their names, and on and on.

At its peak there were something like 500,000 copies per hour. It brought down most of the computers in the European Research Network (ERN), the IBM internal network (VNET), and the American version of ERN (BITNET). It brought them down for about 2 hours and then, because of a limit in the network protocol, brought the network down again. For about 8 weeks afterwards, they had what the people at IBM called minor "aftershocks." That's when a couple thousand copies appear here or there in the network.

### 2.3.8   The MacMag Virus

In 1988, the MacMag virus was the first computer virus to be used for advertising purposes, which I guess means that the technology matured. MacMag is (was?) a Canadian magazine for MacIntosh users, and in 1988, they apparently commissioned a professor from a university in the United States to write a computer virus for them. The press, in keeping with the wishes of the computer security community, did not reveal the name of this particular professor, and I understand the professor was rather upset, because he figured this was his way to fame and fortune. The security community took the position that to reveal the name would glorify the attacker, and the press went along at this time. Of course today, it could be the road to jail and ruin, because it is now illegal to covertly introduce viruses into systems in most places.

The MacMag virus modified a system file on the Mac II computer so as to put a message on the screen on a particular date saying something like "Happy 2nd Anniversary to the Mac II, our wishes for world peace," and it was signed "MacMag." In order to launch the attack, MacMag placed a copy on "CompuServ." Compuserv is one of these service networks in the United States where you can make airline reservations, look up bibliographic database information, et cetera. You can also store programs there for other people in the network to retrieve if they wish to do so.

Within 2 days somebody that picked up a copy of this virus, detected its presence, and notified the people at CompuServ. At about that time, I found out about this attack, so I called up CompuServ and said "Gee, would you like some help to get rid of this virus?" They said "No, no we have it under control" and they had their favorite contract software house write up a special-purpose program to delete this virus, announced it on the bulletin board, and told everyone to use it. As punishment MacMag was kicked off of CompuServ "forever," which I guess is as big a punishment as they can come up with. CompuServ and most of the rest of the community thought the attack was all over, until...

About two months later (so the story goes), a man was visiting his friend, who was a contract programmer. He showed his friend a copy of a game called "Frogger." The programmer tried Frogger once, and said "This is really a dumb game, in fact, this is the dumbest game I've ever seen. I'm never going to run this game again." However, once was enough.

This particular programmer, it just so happens, wrote training software for several companies, including such industry leaders as Lotus, Ashton-Tate, and Aldus. Over the next couple of weeks, he distributed copies of his newest training software to one or more of these companies, and the virus that came in Frogger spread. Aldus subsequently released about 5000 copies of their newest program, "Freehand," which were infected. This was the first (but not the last) time that a virus was released in a legitimate, shrink wrapped, commercial software distribution.

### 2.3.9   The Scores Virus

The so-called "Scores" virus operates on Apple MacIntosh computers, and was apparently written by a disgruntled ex-employee of Electronic Data Systems, a Texas firm that does computer security work worldwide. The reason we believe this is that it directs its attacks against programs written by particular programmers from EDS, and through an anonymous source, I heard some further details that were convincing.

The Scores virus does absolutely nothing for about 4 days after its initial infection. For the next 4 days, it infects, but does no other damage. The 4-day time period may be because of a procedural defense at EDS, which a 4-day wait bypasses, but nobody is certain of this except the attacker. From then on, whenever you run an infected program, it operates as follows:

> For the first 15 minutes of operation it does nothing.
> For the next 15 minutes, it prevents saving anything,
> Finally (mercifully), the system crashes.

So if you are running an editor written by one of these authors at EDS, for the first 15 minutes everything works great. After that, when you try to save the file, it says (in effect) "Sorry, I can't save that." The user typically responds with something like "What do you mean you can't save it? Save it," and for the next several minutes, a frantic effort to save the file is made, until finally the system crashes, and the changes are lost. Needless to say, it is a very disconcerting experience for the user when it happens the first time, but things get worse...

It takes about 2 hours to completely get rid of the Scores virus from a MacIntosh with a hard disk (from the details I have heard), but as I have mentioned, there is another side effect. Over the 4-day period of reproduction without damage, the virus tends to get into floppy disks and backups, spread over networks, et cetera. As a result, many organizations have the Scores virus for a long time. One administrator from a government agency described curing this virus from all of the computers in one network once a week for a year.

### 2.3.10   The Internet Virus

The "Internet virus," commonly called the "Internet worm" (it turns out that worms are a special case of viruses), was launched in 1988 in the Internet. The Internet is a network that, at that time, interconnected about 100,000–200,000 computers around the world, is used by universities and other research organizations, and provides connectivity to many other networks. I can't remember the names of half the networks it is connected to, but among the connected networks in 1988 were the ARPA-net (Advanced Research Projects Agency) and the DOD-net (U.S. Department of Defense).

In the Internet attack, a graduate student at Cornell University designed and launched a computer virus that replicated and moved from machine to machine in the Internet. It entered about 60,000–70,000 computers, but was designed only to replicate in 6000 of them. In a matter of a few hours, it spread throughout the network, causing widespread denial of services. According to the author, it was not intended to deny services, but due to an error in programming it replicated too quickly.

This virus was designed specifically to work in a particular version of a particular operating system and, even though it would be very simple to make it work on other versions, special code was in place to prevent its undue spread. It replicated by "fork'ing" processes and tried to move from system to system by exploiting a (de)bug in the computer mail protocol. It turned out that if you had debugging turned on in the mail protocol on your machine, then if somebody wanted to, they could issue commands as if they were the "Superuser" on your computer. It also turns out that most of the systems in the Internet had this switch turned on at compile time, and in many cases, they could not turn it back off because they didn't have the source code to the mail program for recompilation, and the designers didn't provide any mechanism for overriding the debugging mode.

This particular virus also crossed the boundaries between the ARPA-net and the DOD-net, which were supposedly secured against all such intrusions. In the next few days, several viruses apparently crossed this boundary, and the link was then severed.

### 2.3.11    The AIDS Disk

In late 1989, a well-funded group purchased a mailing list from a PC magazine, and distributed between 20,000 and 30,000 copies of an infected disk to the people on this list. The disk was a very poor virus, but it caused a great deal of damage because there were so many copies mailed, and the recipients used the disk widely despite procedural policies in place prohibiting such use.

The disk was advertised as a program to evaluate a person's risk of getting AIDS based on their behavior. Included in the distribution was a description of the fact that this was a limited-use distribution, and that it would cause damage to the system if it was used without paying royalties.

The disk infected the host system by adding a line to the "AUTOEXEC.BAT" system startup file which, although it appeared to be a comment, was actually a peculiar program name. After running this program a number of times, the virus would encrypt directory information so that file names became unusable. If you continued to use the system it would eventually try to convince you to put in a floppy disk to make a copy for a friend.

The alleged perpetrator was eventually caught by tracing the mailing list purchase process back to the buyer. The last I heard, the person they caught was in the middle of extradition hearings to England, where the virus caused enough damage to warrant prosecution.

### 2.3.12    The Datacrime Virus

The "Datacrime" virus was the most widely announced and least widely spread well-known virus in recent memory. It was rumored to exist as early as 6 months before it was to cause damage, and was eventually the subject of the first NIST National Computer Virus Alert in the United States. This virus only caused minor damage in a few instances in Europe, and never took hold in the United States. Perhaps coincidently, IBM introduced its antivirus program to the world on exactly the same day as NIST announced its first national computer virus alert. Not a single incident was reported or detected in the U.S. as far as I can tell, but IBM sure sold a lot of virus detection software.

### 2.3.13 Early Evolutionary Viruses

In late 1989, the first seriously evolutionary virus to appear in the real world began spreading in Europe. Earlier viruses had evolved in minor ways, simple self-encryption had been used before, and experimental viruses with no association between evolutions had been demonstrated, but this virus was the first one to be released into the world with many of these properties.

This virus replicates by inserting a psuedo-random number of extra bytes into a decryption algorithm that in turn decrypts the remainder of the virus stored in memory. The net effect is that there is no common sequence of more than a few bytes between two successive infections. This has two major implications. The first problem is that it makes false positives high for pattern-matching defenses looking for the static pattern of this virus, and the second problem is that special-purpose detection mechanisms were simply not designed to handle this sort of attack.

Since the first evolving real-world virus appeared, authors have improved their evolution techniques substantially. One author even created a set of evolutionary subroutines called the "Mutating Engine" (often referred to as MtE), which can be integrated with other viruses to form a highly evolutionary form. After over a full year of analysis and response, the best virus scanning programs still hadn't achieved a detection rate over 95% on a sample of several thousand mutations created by Vesselin Bontichev (a well-known Bulgarian malicious virus defender) to test their quality. This brings up an important point about virus detection rates that I will defer to our discussion on epidemiology.

### 2.3.14 Simulation (Stealth) Viruses

The simulation virus that appeared in late 1989 represented a major step toward attacks meant to bypass virus defenses. In essence, this virus simulates all of the DOS system calls that would lead to its detection, causing them to return the information that would be attained if the attack were not present. It is presently spreading widely throughout the world. and because it does no obvious damage, it is generally going undetected. Since that first simulation virus, researchers have decided to use the term "stealth" to indicate viruses that use sophisticated hiding techniques to avoid detection. The term "stealth" is derived from the U.S. "stealth" aircraft that were so successful at avoiding radar detection in the Gulf War in the early 1990s.

Hiding techniques have their biological analogy, the most commonly known example being the chameleon which changes its color to match the background. Many insects blend into their background and thus avoid predators, and a common feature of invasive micro-organisms is the presence of chemical sequences identical to those of their hosts, which enable them to pass as if they were native cells instead of invaders.

Now there is a very important difference between biological stealth techniques and the techniques of modern malicious viruses that I think I should mention before you get any misimpressions. There is a tendency to anthropomorphize hiding techniques as if to indicate that a conscious effort is made by an organism to hide by creating matching chemical sequences. In biological systems, except for higher forms of animals, there is apparently no evidence that there is intent behind the hiding techniques. Rather, random variations caused some color differences or chemical sequences, and it just happened that those creatures didn't die as often as others because of their stealthy characteristics, and so they survived to reproduce.

The stealth techniques we see in modern computer viruses are quite different in that they are intentionally designed to hide by exploiting weaknesses in the operating environment. For that reason, all current stealth viruses are designed to attack PC and MacIntosh operating systems, which are inherently vulnerable. Against the stronger defense techniques now available, current stealth attacks fail completely when operating system protection such as that provided in Unix, MVS, and VMS is in use.

There are ways of hiding in most modern timesharing systems with these protections in place, but none of the real-world viruses we have seen have done this yet. For example, an infected program could start a background process to perform infection so as to reduce the time effects associated with infection, and give the memory resident process a name similar to the name of other common memory resident programs so that it would not be easily differentiated when looking at operating processes.

### 2.3.15  The Bulgarian Viruses

In early 1990, a research institute in Bulgaria released a set of 24 viruses to the rest of the world research community. They had not previously been known outside of Bulgaria. Astonishingly, none of these had been detected in Western Europe until these samples were provided. With the fall of the

Iron Curtain, the flow of people and information between the former Soviet bloc countries and the rest of the world dramatically increased. Along with this openness came the open exchange of viruses, and a whole new set of problems were created for defenders on both sides of the former partition.

### 2.3.16   Some Trends

Although many of these viruses have not spread widely, the number of widespread viruses is on the increase, and the incidence level is increasing quickly. For example, in a recent visit to Taiwan, I was surprised to learn that of 50 companies represented at a seminar, on the average they experienced about 10 viruses per year! This is particularly important in light of the fact that most[3] of the world's PCs are manufactured in Taiwan, and several incidents of widespread dissemination of viruses from manufacturers have been reported.

Another interesting trend is that only about 10% of the known viruses are responsible for 90% of the incidents. According to several minor studies, this has been true for several years, and according to a recent larger-scale study of Fortune 500 companies done by IBM, only 15% of the known viruses were detected in the real world. They also report that 33% of incidents are caused by the two most prevalent viruses ("Stoned" and "Form"), and the 10 most prevalent viruses are responsible for 66% of incidents.

### 2.3.17   Virus ToolKits and Automated Evolution

These numbers represent very substantial growth, but don't reflect the recent advances in attack technology. Several virus-generating programs are currently available, both from semilegitimate software houses and from other less identifiable sources. Some of these virus generators are capable of generating millions of different viruses automatically. Some even allow the user to select different infection techniques, triggering mechanisms, and damage using a menu. Even simple evolution is available in some of these generators.

A far more interesting program has been developed to perform automated evolution of existing programs so as to create numerous equivalent but different programs. This program exploits knowledge of program structure, equivalence of large classes of instructions, and sequential indepen-

---

[3]The figure 80% appears in their official government documents.

dence of unrelated instructions to replace the sequence of instructions comprising a program with a behaviorally equivalent instruction sequence that is substantially different in appearance and operation from the original. In one of the appendices, several examples of evolutionary and hiding techniques are shown, and a good case is made to show that detection by looking for viruses is quite difficult and time consuming if these techniques are applied.

### 2.3.18   Cruncher

The "Cruncher" virus is a real-world version of the compression virus described earlier, but with an interesting twist. For the decompression process, it uses a very common decompression program and the virus is added to the file being infected before compression. The net effect is that when we look at the file, it looks like a legitimate compressed executable program. If we try to scan for this virus, we are in great difficulty because the compression algorithm is adaptive in that it generates codings for subsequent bits based on occurrence rates earlier in the file. Since this particular virus is placed at the end of the file, we can't detect it until we decompress the entire file! No finite number of "scan-strings" exist for detecting the virus because the virus is compressed with the adaptive compression algorithm.

This virus first appeared in January 1993, and as of this writing is not detected by any virus scanners. It is not likely to be reliably detected by them soon, unless run times are dramatically increased.

### 2.3.19   What's in a Name?

Many people seem to think that researchers have a good way of keeping track of viruses, but we really don't. In fact, there isn't even a common naming scheme for viruses or a common method of counting them. The count of 2200 viruses is according to the CARO counting and naming scheme, and the names of the viruses I describe in this book are fairly common, if somewhat simplified. On the other hand, if you buy 10 different virus-detected products, you can bet that there will be at least 5 different naming schemes.

It seems that in the rush for market share, many companies took to listing their detection programs by how many viruses they detect. This became a game of one-upsmanship, and at one point, we even saw simultaneous advertisements for three different products, each claiming to detect *all n* known viruses, where *n* ranged from 80 to over 200. The counting problem stems from a number of problems, but the most common difference is over how to count nearly viruses with only a text string changed. I am still waiting for someone with generic virus detection to advertise "∞ viruses detected."

One real problem with the numbers game was accurately pointed out in an article in the "Virus Bulletin." They rightly noticed that in their haste for high detection rates, many companies don't bother to detect evolutionary viruses or viruses that are hard to find for one reason or another. Instead, they detect the most easily detected viruses, claim very high detection rates, have very fast products, and don't worry about the hard-to-detect viruses. Their position is aided to a large extent by the poor evaluation techniques used in the computer industry, which commonly publishes detection rates against a small percentage of known viruses and evaluates products based on beauty of user interface and speed of operation rather than accuracy.

The "Virus Bulletin" recently proclaimed that the Cruncher virus may be the first truly benevolent widespread virus, but I should note that this may be used as an excuse by many virus defense producers to avoid the difficulty in detection. They will simply claim it is benevolent, and therefore that they don't have to detect it. Eventually an attacker will create a variation that does serious damage, and that will end that excuse, but it won't cause the defenders to defend against it.

The companies that ignore hard-to-catch viruses and spend resources on flashy user interfaces win in the evaluations, sell more product, and put the companies with strong detection out of business. Because their products sell at retail, they are never up to date, and because the computing industry is more interested in profits than in accuracy in reporting, the products sold at retail are not widely called on their detection failures. If a detection failure comes up, they use the failure to sell an updated version of the product, which in many cases still doesn't detect the particular virus very well. Thus, it is a winning strategy for the vendor to provide a product that works poorly but looks good, runs fast, and detects a large number of relatively unimportant viruses.

# Chapter 3

# TECHNICAL PROTECTION FROM VIRUSES

## 3.1 PERFECT TECHNICAL DEFENSES

There are three and only three things you can ever do to absolutely and perfectly prevent all computer viruses from spreading throughout a computer system or network: limit sharing, limit transitivity, or limit programming. This has been proven mathematically.

### 3.1.1 Limited Sharing

The first thing you can do is limit sharing. So let me give you an example of what we mean by limited sharing. Figure 3.1 shows a picture of a Bell-LaPadula–based system where a user at a given secrecy level cannot read information that's more highly classified, lest information might be leaked to them, and can't write information to an area that's less classified, lest they could leak information out.

Similarly we have the Biba integrity model (see Figure 3.2). If you are at a given integrity level, you can't read information of lower integrity, lest it might corrupt you, and you can't write information of higher integrity, lest you might corrupt it.

If you want both secrecy and integrity, all you have to do is eliminate all the sharing, since as you can see, putting these systems together yields a system in which you cannot read or write up or down (see Figure 3.3).

It turns out that this is only one specific case of limited sharing. Let me show you what you can do more generally to limit sharing. The best you can ever do (i.e., the most general structure for limiting sharing, in a general-purpose transitive information network with sharing), is to implement a policy based on a structure called a POset, a partially ordered set.

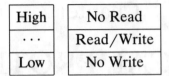

**FIGURE 3.1**   The Bell-LaPadula security model.

**FIGURE 3.2**   The Biba integrity model.

| No Read | | No Write | | No Access |
|---|---|---|---|---|
| Read/Write | + | Read/Write | = | Read/Write |
| No Write | | No Read | | No Access |

**FIGURE 3.3**   Combining secrecy with integrity.

Mathematically, a partially ordered set follows these rules:

$$\forall \text{ domains } A, B, \text{ and } C \in \text{ the POset}$$
$$1—A \le B \text{ and } B \le C \to A \le C$$
$$2—A \le B \text{ and } B \le A \to A = B$$
$$3—A \le A.$$

Basically, a POset can be pictured as a bunch of boxes with lines between them, and a rule that says information can only flow up (or left to right if you turn it on its side) as shown in Figure 3.4. Here's how it works.

Suppose somebody in $A$ writes a computer virus. Well, let's see, it could spread to $B$, $C$, $D$, $E$, and $F$, but it could not spread to $G$, because there is no path for any information in $A$ to ever get to $G$. If no information in $A$ can ever get to $G$, then no virus in $A$ can ever get to $G$.

Similarly, if somebody in $H$ is trying to leak information, they could potentially leak information from $I$, $J$, $K$, $L$, $M$, $N$, $O$, and $P$, but they could never leak any information from $Q$, because there is no path for information in $Q$ to ever get to $H$.

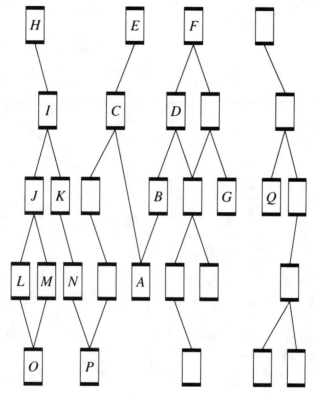

**FIGURE 3.4** A POset.

In other words, we are limiting the flow of information, and the most general structure for doing this is a POset. So let me put this into more familiar terms by using a picture of a POset that describes some of the operation of a typical business (see Figure 3.5).

You might get *letters* in the *mail*. The *letters* might generate *orders* or *payments*, and if they generate *orders*, that generates *shipping* and *invoicing*. *Invoicing* and *shipping* go to the *customer*. *Shipping* and *invoicing* copies also go to *file1*. When a *payment* comes in, it gets mixed with *file1* to generate a *deposit*, the *payments* independently generate a *commission*. That's how information flows through some parts of this organization.

What we can then do is associate individuals with these areas. Say Joe is a programmer who works in *letters*, Mary programs in *file1*, Jill programs in *shipping*, et cetera. We assign individuals to the operational aspects of each of those areas and we have thus structured the flow of information in our organization. Let me point out some advantages of this technique.

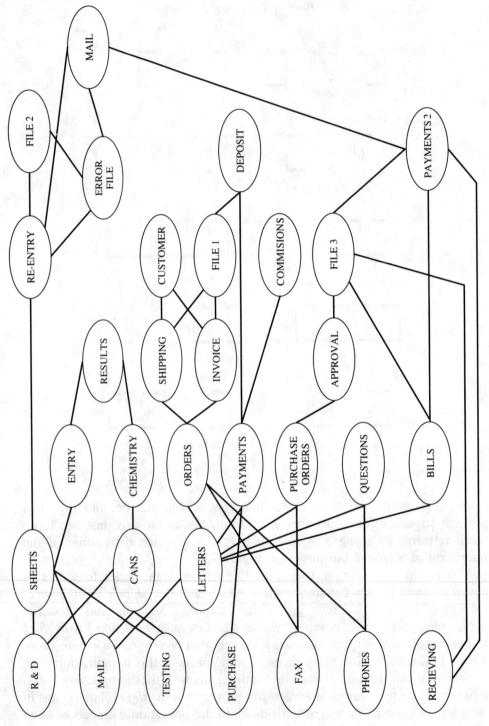

**FIGURE 3.5** An example business's POset.

One of the advantages is that if somebody launches a virus, it only spreads to a subset of the organization. For example, if Joe launches a virus from *letters*, it could potentially get to *letters*, *orders*, *payments*, *purchase orders*, *questions*, and *bills*, and then indirectly from there to *payments*, *file1*, *approval*, *commissions*, *deposit*, *file2*, *invoice*, *shipping*, and *customers*. It could not get to any of the other domains, so the worst-case damage is limited.

But there is more to it than that. Suppose we somehow find that there are things going wrong in *shipping*, *customers*, *file1*, and *deposits*, and we suspect it is a virus. Where could that virus have come from? If it came from *orders*, it would probably also get to *invoicing*. Therefore, it probably didn't come from *orders*. Could it have come from *invoices*? No! It could not have gotten from *invoices* to *shipping*. We have isolated it very quickly to *shipping*. In other words, structuring the flow of information allows us to track down the sources of corruption efficiently.

Similarly, we can track down where information might be leaked. For example, if we are getting information leaks from *shipping*, *invoice*, and *customer*, the only place that could have leaked all of that information is *customer*.

So this structuring, besides limiting the ability of viruses to spread and limiting the ability to leak information, also allows us to track down the possible sources of corruptions and leaks.

There are some other significant advantages to this approach to protection, in that it substantially reduces the complexity associated with protection management, and it makes the implications of protection decisions immediately evident. For example, a POset-based protection system for a typical timesharing system has only a few hundred bits of protection information, whereas a standard timesharing system has on the order of 1,000,000 bits of protection information. Just as a side note, this type of system has been successfully implemented and is in use in several organizations.

### 3.1.2   Limited Transitivity

The second of three possibilities for absolute prevention is limited transitivity, as shown in Figure 3.6. Here's how it works.

*A* might be able to give information to *B*. In fact, *A* could give information to *B* and *B* could give information to *C*. But it's against the rules for *A* to give information to *B* which *B* then passes on to *C*. With this scheme, if *A* writes a virus it could get to *B*. But if *A* wrote a virus that got to *B*, it could not be passed on to *C*.

Prevention

• The Limited Transitivity Approach

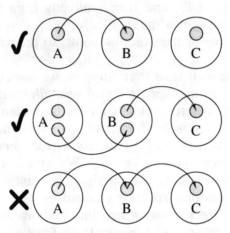

**FIGURE 3.6**   Limited transitivity.

If you can implement limited transitivity you can prevent a virus from spreading more than a certain distance from its origin. The only problem is there is no feasible way to use this in a real computer system. It is feasible to implement limited transitivity, but when you try to use it, almost everything spreads as far as it can spread very quickly, and then sharing is almost entirely halted. The problem is that viruses are just like any other information, so whatever you do to restrict viruses has to apply to all other information as well.

### 3.1.3  Limited Function

The third of three possibilities for absolute prevention of computer viruses in a computer system or network is limited function. We could, for example, have a system that allows you to enter data into a database, selectively put it into a spreadsheet, analyze it, put the results into a pie chart, pass the pie chart to a word processor, and print the result in two-column format in color on a laser printer. We can do all of that without giving users general-purpose functions.

Unfortunately, today you can't buy a database that doesn't have macros allowing general-purpose function. So you can write a database macro that replicates and spreads from database to database. In fact, you can write a database macro to infect databases and spreadsheets. Similarly, you can't buy a spreadsheet today that's any good without having macros such that the user can enter a spreadsheet macro that spreads from spreadsheet to spreadsheet, or from spreadsheet to database, or even over to word processors. Similarly, word processors have macros that tend to be general purpose, so it's fairly straightforward to write a word-processor macro that spreads from document to document.

There are some situations where we do have limited function in the real world. For example, most EFT (Electronic Funds Transfer) networks are limited in their function. The way EFT networks normally operate, any information on the network is treated as a *from* account, a *to* account, an *amount* of money, and a *check* string. It doesn't matter what you put in that network; you can send a Basic program, and the network will treat the first so many bytes as *from*, the next so many bytes as *to*, the next so many bytes as *amount*, and the next so many bytes as *check*. If *check* doesn't match, the network will ignore the transaction and report it as an error.

The reason you can't infect one of those networks is not because the information being sent over the network can't contain viruses. It's because no matter what information you send over that network, it cannot be interpreted so as to reproduce. In other words, the limited function does not come from the information, but how it's interpreted. Let's think of it another way. Information only has meaning in that it's interpreted. So unless you interpret it with a method that allows its meaning to be a virus, you can't have viruses. That's what we mean by limited function.

Now many of you may have menu systems for your secretaries and data-entry people, and you may think they are limited in function, but they aren't necessarily. Let me give you an example.

I was at a computer conference in California in 1985, and for one reason or another, my invitation included the proviso that I had to evaluate all of the computer security systems at this conference.

r So I walked around to the first booth, where I   came across a limited-function interface. I asked if I could do a little experiment to see if we could break into their system, and they said:

"There is no way you are going to break into this system. It's absolutely safe." So, I said: "Really?!? That's great; then you shouldn't mind a little experiment, right?"

So they gave me the least privileged account they could. This was an account that was only supposed to let you store a file on the system or retrieve that file back. That was all you could do with this account. So I said, "Okay, let's try it." I went over to the expert and I asked for the name of the user login "profile" file that describes how the system first interacts with the user upon login. I told the system to store into that file. The system obliged, and stored a command to run the system command interpreter in that file.

Lo and behold, the next time we logged in, instead of putting us into the limited-function interface, it put us into the command interpreter, and because the designers were so sure that this was limited function, they didn't provide any of the normal operating system protection. We were logged in with Superuser privileges.

So we walked over to the next booth, and by the time we got there, the guy at the second booth said "Don't bother, it will work against our system too." We went to the 3rd and 4th booths, and they said the same thing. Just because it says *limited function* doesn't necessarily make it so.

## 3.2   TECHNICAL DEFENSES WITH MAJOR FLAWS

So those are the three and only three things you can do for absolute prevention, and given that you are able and willing to do those things, you can limit the ability of viruses to spread in a computer system or network. If those are inadequate for your needs, you might like to look at other types of defenses, in particular, detection and cure.

These defenses are all in the class of imperfect defenses, so we can't expect them to be flawless, but in order to see their flaws, it will be helpful to look at a couple of questions first. We'll start there.

### 3.2.1   Can We Detect All Viruses?

Is this program "*CV*" a computer virus?

```
Program CV :=
  { ...
  main-program:=
    {if D(CV) then goto next;
     else infect-executable;
    }
next:
  }
```

Suppose you had somebody that wrote a program *D* to detect computer viruses. It would look at any other program *P* and return TRUE if *P* was a computer virus and FALSE if *P* was not. So let's take a look. See program *D* being called from *CV*? If your program says *CV* is a virus, then *CV* will not infect an executable. So if *D* says *CV* is a virus, then it is not. But if *D* says that *CV* is not a virus, it infects an executable, and is thus a virus. So no matter what your detection procedure *D* says, it's guaranteed to always be wrong. That means you cannot write a program *D* that correctly determines whether or not other programs are viruses, unless that program:

> runs forever without a result in some cases–OR–
> has an infinite number of false positives[1]–OR–
> has an infinite number of false negatives[2]–OR–
> has combinations of these three problems.

### 3.2.2 Can We Find Resulting Infections?

Let's go a step further. Suppose we have a known program "*EV*," and we have determined that *EV* is definitely a virus. The question is, if we have some other program, say "*EV_2*," can we write a program "*D'*," that looks at *EV* and *EV_2* and tells whether *EV_2* is an evolution of *EV*, and therefore, whether *EV_2* is also a virus?

```
Program EV:=                   Program EV2:=
  {...                           {...
  main-program:=                 main-program:=
    {if D'(EV,EV2)                 {if D'(EV2,EV)
      then goto next;               then goto next;
      else infect-exec             else infect-exec
          with EV2;                    with EV;
    }                              }
next:                          next:
  }                              }
```

Well, let's take a look. Decision procedure *D'* is supposed to tell us whether *EV* evolves into *EV_2*. If *D'* says *EV* does not evolve into *EV_2*, then *EV* evolves into *EV_2*. If *D'* says that *EV* does evolve into *EV_2*, then *EV* does not evolve into *EV_2*. So again, you cannot determine all of the evolutions of all known viruses, at least not systematically with a program.

---

[1] Cases where a virus is detected when no virus is present.
[2] Cases where no virus is detected when a virus is present.

## AN EVOLUTIONARY VIRUS

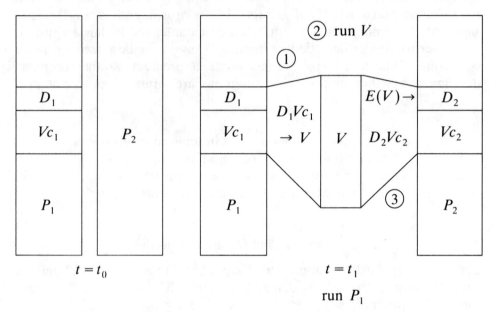

**FIGURE 3.7**   An encryption virus.

Let me clarify this, because it is a bit obscure in mathematical form, and I want to put it into as solid a basis as I can. I'm going to do that with an example. Figure 3.7 shows an example of an evolutionary virus and I'm going to tell you how it works.

At time $t = t_0$, we have an infected program $P_1$ and a clean program $P_2$. If, at time $t = t_1$, we run $P_1$, the following steps take place:

1. $D_1$, a decryption algorithm, decrypts $V_{c_1}$, the encrypted version of $V$, into the original $V$.

2. $V$ is run.

3. $V$ selects a different encryption algorithm $E_2$, re-encrypts itself with $E_2$, giving us $V_{c_2}$, and places a decryption algorithm $D_2$ (designed to decrypt things encrypted with $E_2$) into program $P_2$ along with $V_{c_2}$.

Except for the probability of random sequences coinciding, no common sequences of bytes exist between $P_1$ and $P_2$ due to this virus.

Let me give a more specific example. Suppose $V_{c_1}$ was encrypted with a DES encryption. When we run $P_1$, $D_1$ decrypts $V_{c_1}$ using the DES to get

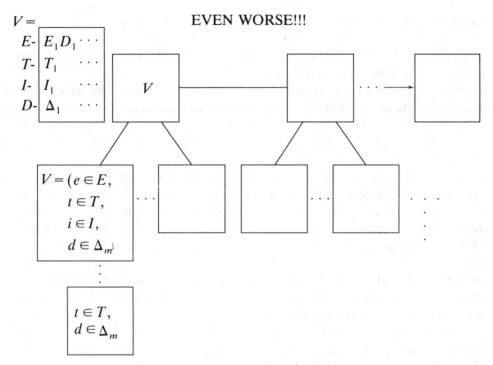

**FIGURE 3.8**   An even worse virus.

the original virus $V$. Then virus $V$ chooses the RSA cryptosystem and
encrypts itself with the RSA, leaving $V_{c_2}$. It then puts an RSA decryption
algorithm $D_2$ along with $V_{c_2}$ in program $P_2$. So what do you say? Does
anybody here think that they are going to be able to write a program to
automatically, given any $D_1$ and $V_{c_1}$, figure out that $D_2$ and $V_{c_2}$ are an
evolution of it? Does anybody see even a little hope for doing this
automatically?

Well, if you thought that was bad, you haven't seen anything yet!

In Figure 3.8, we have a new version of that evolutionary virus, where $V$
has a whole set of encryption algorithms $(E_1 \cdots E_m)$, decryption algorithms $(D_1 \cdots D_m)$, triggering mechanisms $(T_1 \cdots T_m)$, infection mechanisms $(I_1 \cdots I_m)$, and damage mechanisms $(\Delta_1 \cdots \Delta_m)$.

We have already mentioned two encryption algorithms, and there are
certainly thousands more that can be automatically generated. There are
also key-customized algorithms that can be automatically generated.

Triggering mechanisms might include a wide variety of time, use, and
logical conditions, perhaps generated pseudorandomly from a large class of
such algorithms. Infection might include such variations as "put it at the

beginning of the file," "put it at the end of the file," "put it in a bootblock," "put it 23 instructions from the beginning," "put it 25 instructions before the middle of the program," "put it at a pseudorandom 'return from subroutine' statement," et cetera.

A large number of damage mechanisms are also easily generated. For example, "change the 5th bit in the 7th byte of the program," "change the 25th through the 29th byte in the 7th program you find," "look for data files with the 123 extension, and modify the first cell in the spreadsheet," et cetera.

The virus evolves and spreads through programs in your computer system for a while just as the evolutionary virus above, but then it replaces itself with a subset of the encryption and decryption algorithms, triggering conditions, infection mechanisms, and damage mechanisms. It then repeats the whole process, spreading and evolving for a while, then replacing itself with a subset, et cetera. As time goes on, you may have a very wide variety of different variations, all looking very different from each other in terms of the sequence of the bytes that appear in your system, all spread throughout your computer and backup systems.

One day, you will start having minor damage; a file gets deleted, or maybe some bits get changed in a random data file. Suppose you identify those things right away, you work real hard, and you figure out which Trojan horse caused the damage. You search your entire system and you find no other copies of that Trojan horse, so you figure you're safe. About 5 minutes later, two things start to go wrong, then three, then four, then five. Over the next couple of days, you probably get to the point where hundreds of thousands of these simple things are starting to go off in all sorts of ways.

So what do you do? You go to your backups, right? You go back a week in the backups, you search for all these different patterns and you find none of them. There is no indication that anything there is corrupt, but it starts happening again. You go back two weeks, three weeks, four. You go back as far as you want, there is never any way to be sure that this isn't happening again. This points out the problem with evolution, the problem of tracking down viruses once they are throughout a system, et cetera.

Several questions usually come up here. For example: "How do you keep these from reinfecting the same program repeatedly?" You don't have to, of course, but there are a variety of ways to limit infections. For example, never infect anything larger than a given size, or with a modification date ending in the digits 1, 2, or 3. Some of the examples later will point this out more clearly, but let it suffice to say that no universal recognition mechanism is necessary in order to operate such a virus successfully, so the virus doesn't have to be able to detect itself.

### 3.2.3   The Tail Chasing Problem

The tail chasing problem comes when you try to remove a virus from a system while that system is in active operation (see Figure 3.9). Suppose we have an infected system, and it's operating as we are detecting and eradicating viruses. In this example, $P_1$ and $P_2$ are infected. When we detect a virus in program $P_1$ we cure it, but in the meanwhile $P_2$ is run and it infects program $P_3$. No problem, we find that $P_2$ is infected and cure $P_2$, but in the meanwhile someone runs program $P_3$, which goes and reinfects program $P_1$! We are now chasing our own tail.

Whether almost everything is almost always infected, or whether almost everything is almost always clean depends on the relative rates of infection and cure. This follows the biological theory of epidemics. Basically, the number of infected programs times the frequency of use gives the number of new infections per time. If this exceeds the rate of cure, then the chances are that almost all programs will always be infected. If the rate of cure exceeds the rate of new infection, as time goes on, the system will become completely devoid of infected programs.

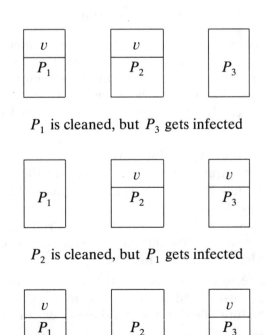

**FIGURE 3.9**   The tail-chasing problem.

Under certain conditions, you can even get an equilibrium situation. As an example, when the number of already infected programs slows the infection rate to near the cure rate, more cures will cause more infections, while fewer cures will cause fewer infections, and thus we may be in a stable condition.

Currently, our cures, except in the rarest cases, are very slow. Our viruses, on the other hand, are very fast. So for the most part, in current situations, it's rational to deny services while performing cure. There are some advantages in a well-structured system. For example, in a POset network, once a virus is detected, we know the extent of where it could have come from and gone to, and thus which portions of the system may be operated unhindered while cure is performed. So you don't have to deny services to the whole system, you just deny services to those areas that might be affected.

There is one well-known computer security consultant in the United States that says: "If you get a virus, the first thing you should do, is turn off your computer and call in an expert." Of course he is a consultant, so he is one of the experts you might call in.

### 3.2.4   Instrumentation

Viruses are normal-user programs. That means that whatever statistic you use to determine whether something is a virus, it's always possible for a virus to slip below it if other programs can be written to slip below it. As you lower the threshold to try to catch more viruses, eventually you will lower it enough to catch some legitimate software, and then you have a choice.

- You can throw it away, in which case, if it had a virus, you eliminated that copy of the virus, but you also threw out the program. If it was legitimate, you just threw out a legitimate piece of software, and you still don't know if you are safe. So you keep lowering the threshold, throwing out more and more software, until you are completely safe. All you have to do is throw out all your software. Then your system is completely safe, but it is also useless.

- You can decide to trust it because it is an important program. But if you decide to trust it and it has a virus in it, you've just trusted the virus and therefore allowed it to continue to exist in your system.

- There is only one other possibility. When you detect a possible infection, you try to determine whether or not there is an actual infection. So how do you do that? Well, we have already shown that

**FIGURE 3.10** A vaccine.

it's undecidable to tell whether a program is infected. In other words, trying to look at it to tell whether it's infected doesn't work, because you can't ever be sure one way or the other.

That's why instrumentation has problems. Instrumentation comes down to verifying all the software in your computer system, which we cannot do. By the way, that doesn't mean that you should not ever use instrumentation. For example, you could reasonably have a set of normal operating parameters on your system, detect when the system goes outside those parameters, and take appropriate action. It just isn't perfect.

### 3.2.5 Vaccines

If you have a virus that looks for itself in another program and does not infect the other program if it has already been infected, then a vaccine might fake the indicator used by the virus to determine whether the program has already been infected, so that, thinking this file is already infected, the virus won't bother to reinfect it (see Figure 3.10). Let me point out some problems with this.

The first problem is that, in order to be effective, you have to vaccinate against a large number of viruses. In other words, you have to modify existing programs to have all of the various indicators of the 2200 known viruses, and every day you have to modify these programs several times to include the indicators from new viruses. Perhaps there is a 1 at location 8 and a 7 at location 15 for one of the viruses, and a 12 at location 3 for another virus, and so on. If you try to do that to your programs, it's going to be very difficult to keep your programs working.

The second problem is that not all viruses can be vaccinated against. For example, the Jerusalem virus cannot be vaccinated against because it doesn't look to determine if programs have already been infected. Even for some of the vaccinable viruses, vaccination might be quite expensive. For example, suppose we have a virus that only infects programs smaller than 30K bytes. Small programs would have to be made large in order to prevent infection, thus dramatically increasing disk usage. This may be the only side effect of the virus, and thus we are doing more damage by defending in this way than the virus causes in the worst case.

The third problem is that vaccinating against one virus may permit another virus to enter. This comes from the concept of competing pairs in the population.

Suppose we have virus $V_1$ which works like this:

> If location 4 is less than or equal to 24, do an infection.

The vaccine is to make location 4 greater than 24, so that $V_1$ will not infect a given file. But suppose we have another virus $V_2$ that works like this:

> If location 4 is greater than 24, do an infection.

To counter $V_2$, we have to make location 4 less than or equal to 24. Since you cannot make location 4 less than or equal to 24 and also greater than 24, you cannot vaccinate against both. Vaccinating against one of them only reduces the occurrence of that one in the population, and thus provides more food for the other virus. If you vaccinate against $V_1$, you increase the population of $V_2$ because you are providing a lot of food for it. $V_2$ eats all the new food, but as $V_2$ eats more and more, it provides more food for $V_1$. The system eventually returns to a stable population ratio.

This same principle can lead to a method of self-control for benevolent viruses. By portioning the space of legitimate values between different members of the population, you can effectively secure a stable population ratio even as some viruses are eliminated and others become errant.

### 3.2.6   Virus Scanners

A "Virus Scanner" is a program that examines systems for the occurrence of known viruses. Modern virus scanners are fairly fast. They can typically scan something like 10 executable files per second for any of a few thousand viruses on a 20-MHz PC-AT with 60-ms hard disk. The main performance factor in our experiments was disk access time, so a fairly fast modern computer could be scanned for most known viruses in a few minutes.

Scanners are sometimes used as a BOOTSTRAP check for known viruses in personal computers. They have some major problems that make them expensive and ineffective in most circumstances, even though they are currently very popular in the marketplace.

A first problem is that they are only good against known viruses and other known attack patterns, so they won't work against a virus that the organization did not know about ahead of time. Any organization worried about intentional attacks against them or internal attackers should be aware that no scanner is likely to help them against this threat.

A second problem is that they tend to take a noticeable amount of time to scan a system or network for these patterns. In a normal PC-based installation, a scanner used daily costs about $1 per day per system, or about $250 per year per system. This is the cost associated with a "quick scan" (i.e., where we look at only a few bytes to detect a virus at a known location in the infected program), but not all viruses can be detected by this approach. For example, the Cruncher virus described earlier cannot be detected by this technique, and it is fairly easy to design a virus that requires all bits of a file to be examined for reliable detection. The time associated with examining all of the bytes on a disk is far longer, even on the fastest systems available. For example, a "read" test that reads all of the bytes on a 200-megabyte disk on a 50-MHz 486DX processor with a 12-ms hard disk takes over 15 minutes, and that test doesn't do any substantial processing of the data it reads. Even some nonevolutionary viruses may be quite difficult to scan for, since they may place themselves in a nonfixed location in the infected program. The speed of current scanners comes mostly from knowing where to look in a file for a known virus. This is also why scanners are ineffective against viruses in nonexecutable programs. These programs (e.g., spreadsheets, databases, et cetera) don't typically store the virus in a fixed location.

A third problem is that in order to remain effective, a scanner must be updated often. Otherwise, by the time you detect a relatively new virus, it will have spread throughout your organization, and you will have a massive cleanup problem on your hands. Suppose you only update 4 times per year, and the cost of sending out and installing an update is $5 per copy. That comes to another $20 per system per year. New viruses appear at a rate of several per day, so keeping up-to-date is literally impossible. Even the companies that spend all of their time and effort updating scanners are commonly 4–6 months behind. In June of 1993, for example, most of the scanners tested for viruses that were well known and widely published in January of 1993 were unable to detect them. One of those viruses was distributed to 60,000 subscribers of an electronic information service after the information service had scanned for known viruses using several of the best available scanners.

A fourth problem is that scanners are not very good against evolutionary viruses, some of which have begun to appear in the real world recently. No current scanners detect "Cruncher," which has been available for several months, and until several years after the MtE was spreading in the world, no scanner was able to pick up over 95% of the infections. Several other evolutionary viruses are not detected well by existing scanners after several years of effort by the manufacturers.

A fifth problem is that some scanners produce false positives. That is, they tend to indicate the presence of some viruses when that virus, in fact, is not present. It is not unusual for a new version of a program to have a pattern similar to a known virus in it, and for several scanners to begin indicating false positives in response to a program update. The better scanners are very unlikely to get a false positive, but it's hard to tell which ones those are from the advertising. In one case, a lawsuit was filed against a major scanner manufacturer for shipping product that falsely identified a legitimate product as infected, thus costing the manufacturer substantial lost revenues.

A sixth problem is that people don't use scanners reliably. Just yesterday, I was contacted by a consultant with a virus, and she described how she scanned for viruses. She had a 2-year-old scanner, she only scanned incoming disks and often failed to scan them for various reasons, and she had a virus that the scanner didn't pick up. She suspected it came from a disk that had "virus" scribbled on it, which she thinks was placed in her system by someone who used her computer for a while when she wasn't there.

### 3.2.7  Software Self-Defense

The idea of self-correcting code came up a number of years back. Basically, it works by having a program with some redundancy built into it, examine itself and automatically remove corruptions. When you run the program, it checks itself using that redundancy, and if it detects errors, uses the redundancy to correct them (see Figure 3.11). There are a couple of problems with this scheme.

The first problem is that the virus may modify the redundant part of the program $P_1$ to accept or even propagate the virus. Here's an example:

- There's a program called "Mirror" that runs on the PC. Mirror makes an exact bit-for-bit copy of a program, except that all the "1"s are changed to "0"s and all the "0"s are changed to "1"s. It stores this "mirror image" on disk. Whenever you run the program, the operating system compares the original to the mirror image. If they aren't exactly opposite, it mirrors the mirror image to give you a clean original.

- Somebody wrote a virus that infects the mirror image with a mirror image of the virus. When you run the program, the system compares the original to the mirror. They disagree, and the mirror image is mirrored, giving a new, cleanly infected version of the program.

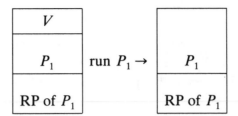

**FIGURE 3.11**   Software self defense.

The second problem is that detection may fail. If you use a simple checksum, we have already shown you how to make that fail with a compression virus. If you use the size and modification time or a CRC code, or any combination of those, you have the same problem because they can all be attacked by fairly simple algorithms in a short period of time.

Product designers do a lot of things to increase performance while trying to compromise as little protection as possible. One of them is to only check the first and last block of a file. Another is to only check the "header" information of a file. Some select five or six blocks from the file to check, or some such thing. There are all sorts of schemes to make checking very fast by not checking all the information, but they tend to fail because it is easy to intentionally defeat them. For detection to be reliable it must be hard to forge an illegitimate change.

The third major problem is that by the time the program gets hold of itself, it may look clean. It turns out this is really the death blow to self-defense. Let's see why that is.

Figure 3.12 shows a generic attack against any self-defense mechanism. It's generic in that, if you launch this attack without knowing what self-defense the defenders are using, only that it's a self-defense technique, it's guaranteed that this attack will work. One attack fits all.

Initially the infected version $P_1'$ of program $P_1$ is infected with the virus $V$, and the clean version of the program $P_2$ is uninfected. If at time $t_1$, we run $P_1'$, the following sequence of events takes place:

$t_1$–$V$ infects some other program $P_2$.

$t_2$–$V$ replaces $P_1'$ with the original $P_1$.

$t_3$–$V$ runs the original $P_1$.

$t_4$–After $P_1$ finishes, $V$ reinfects $P_1$.

Between times $t_3$ and $t_4$, $P_1$ looks at itself and determines that it is clean, because indeed it is clean at the time it is run. The same thing can

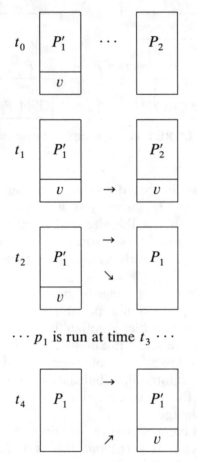

**FIGURE 3.12**    Generic attack on self-defense.

be done by simulating operating system calls when $P_1$ looks at itself, but this particular variation only works when operating system protection can be bypassed, which is normally limited to DOS and MacIntosh systems, or in sophisticated attacks against multiprocessing systems with protection.

### 3.2.8    Boot Locks

When you turn on most computers, they go through a start-up process wherein a "bootstrap" program is run in order to load and begin interpreting the rest of the operating environment. On most systems, in order to allow for installation and recovery from faults, an external bootstrap device is checked for a bootstrap program before using the computer's internal disks. In an environment where the first program to run has total control of the computer, in theory, it cannot be bypassed. It could, for example, simulate the rest of the computer, and thus avoid any technique for defense that a defender could put in place.

This is the mechanism attacked by so-called boot-block viruses, and it forms a fairly universal attack that could be applied to almost any current operating environment. In fact, some of the common PC viruses don't depend on having the DOS operating system on the disk, and operate with any other operating system in place.

In addition to containing the first instructions to be executed on system startup, the "partition table" on most systems includes information on how the disk is structured. This information is commonly used by viruses to attack a system before it begins operating and turns on its defenses. A "bootlock" is a program that replaces the normal bootstrap program and the data describing the structure of the disk so that the disk structure information is not readily available to the attacker. In essence, it is a way of recoding the disk so that without the right decoding algorithm, accessing the disk is more difficult.

Some current viruses directly access disk hardware, and they can thus corrupt the physical partition table, but they still cannot be used to examine or modify the logical contents of the DOS disk if it has been locked well enough. This means that unless attackers use defense specific attacks, they cannot reasonably be expected to infect DOS files. Thus bootlock protection prevents all but low-level viruses from entering the system when bootstrapped from the floppy disk.

Most boot locks can be easily bypassed, which means that it is normally possible to attack these defenses without a great deal of effort, but it also means the attacker has to have access to the defense or find a set of attacks that happen to bypass it. In general, we can do quite well by increasing the difficulty of decoding the disk information. This technique is sometimes taken to the extreme of disk encryption, and recent theoretical results show that in general we can make low-level attacks such as this NP complete.

### 3.2.9 Snapshots

The "snapshot" defense makes a copy of the memory, registers, and other critical operating information at first use, and replaces the memory state of the machine with the stored state on subsequent uses. This has the effect of removing any corruption from memory at system startup, and thus provides an uninfected initial state for checking and repairing the remainder of the system, including the boot block and operating system critical areas and files. Assuming this mechanism gets control, it can defeat any attack that tries to prevent the normal startup process, and bypass even the most clever simulation virus. The only ways around this defense are a defense-specific attack or a high-quality system simulation by the attack.

### 3.2.10   System Call Interception

There are several weak defenses that exploit assumptions made by attackers to make substantial numbers of current viral attacks fail. For example, we can prevent "executable" programs from being modified in-place by limiting "open" calls on files with particular names. It turns out that this defense prevents infection by over 90% of current PC viruses, while consuming only about 20 instructions on each file "open," and not impacting most normal operation. This is a weak defense because, for example, the attacker could rename the file, perform infection, and rename it back after infection, without impacting this mechanism. We can limit renames, but this is also easily bypassed. If we make this protection too effective, the system becomes too constrained for normal use.

Another weak defense is a mechanism that prevents tracing through operating system calls. It turns out that many DOS viruses trace calls into the operating system to determine internal operating system addresses which are then used to bypass protection. We can stop most of these attacks by turning off tracing at an appropriate point in the defense. This attack can be defeated by a sufficiently clever attacker by simply checking defense operations to determine if they turn off tracing, and simulating the instructions that turn tracing off. The DOS debugger does this to some extent, and the techniques it uses can be augmented to cover more clever trace trapping defenses.

Several other weak defenses are now in common use, and to the extent that they consume very few system resources while defending against substantial portions of the existing attack techniques, they are cost effective, particularly in the short run. For the most part, these very weak defenses have utility in operating systems with no real protection. With sound operating system protection, many of these defenses are unnecessary.

### 3.3   TECHNICAL DEFENSES THAT WORK WELL

The defenses we will now discuss work in the sense that they provide a very high degree of protection, but they are not perfect in that they do not make viruses mathematically impossible. One of the defenses we will discuss (the "Integrity shell") is extremely practical in the current environment, while the other two have some rather serious limitations that make them inapplicable for all but the rarest of circumstances.

### 3.3.1 Software Fault Tolerance

There are two general ways to reduce the impact of component failures. We can harden components to reduce the number of failures (i.e., fault intolerance), or we can use redundancy to tolerate component failures (i.e., fault tolerance). Fault tolerance can be done in hardware or in software. Let me give you an example. On the United States space shuttle, when they enter the atmosphere, this thing is going awfully fast. It's going way faster than the speed of sound, and to slow down, it goes through a series of hypersonic S curves, slowing down so it doesn't burn up in the atmosphere. It turns out that during those hypersonic S curves, the shuttle is dynamically unstable. That is, if the computer system that controls the space shuttle stops working for more than 1 ms, the shuttle will crash and burn, and there is no way any person or computer can recover after that 1 ms of failure. The shuttle will flip over, the wings will fall off, the tail will fall apart, and the whole thing will crash and burn.

So what they do is use redundancy, because they know that computers fail, especially when you are shaking them madly, they are at high temperatures, et cetera. They have five computer systems connected together to work like this:

- Three of them vote with each other.
- If one of the three disagrees with the other two, they kick the bad one out and insert the fourth computer in its place. They then again have three computers voting.
- If one of those fails, they kick that one out, and then the remaining two vote against each other.
- If these two disagree with each other, they are both thrown out, and the fifth computer is used in their place.

The reason they go to the fifth computer is that it is running a different program for the same task, so if a software problem is causing the failures, this computer will not have the same problem. The first time they ran the shuttle, several computers failed.

It turns out that you can do the same thing in software as you can do in hardware. It's called *n*-version programming, and it's done by having redundant copies of programs, as shown in Figure 3.13.

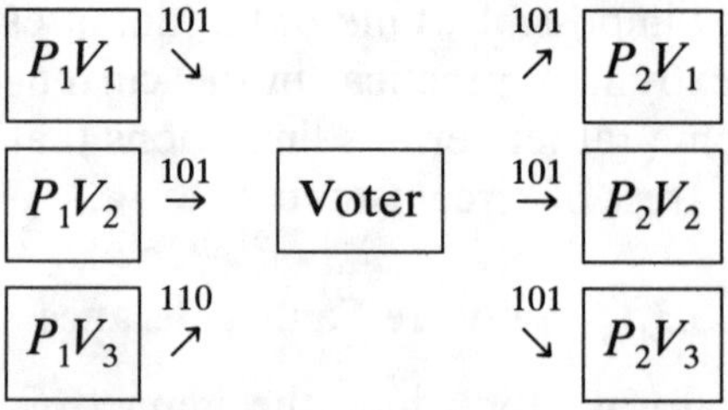

**FIGURE 3.13**   *N*-version programming.

We have here a picture of a system with three versions $(V_1, V_2, V_3)$ of two programs $(P_1, P_2)$. $P_1V_1$ is infected with a virus, and therefore, produces wrong output under some circumstances. Since the output goes through a voter, when this happens, the voter disregards the bad output, making all three outputs identical, and the system continues unhindered. Thus $P_2V_1$, $P_2V_2$, and $P_2V_3$ all get correct inputs, even though $P_1V_3$ produces wrong results. If the whole system is redundant, subsequent stages cover voter errors and any single error is automatically covered. So what are the problems with *N*-version programming?

- It's expensive. It takes three times the number of computer programs, and therefore three times the number of computer programmers. Also, you need three times the computing power to get the same performance. So it is somewhat more than three times as expensive to write a redundant program as it is to write a single program, and that's quite expensive. The high expense means it only applies in rare circumstances like the space shuttle.

- It's hard to do. How hard is it? Well, there was an experiment done in the early 1980s at UCLA. The experiment involved 100 computer programmers who had just passed a programming course. They were all asked to write a program to add a column of numbers together. Every one of those programs worked, but no two of them worked the same. Let me give you an example:

  - Suppose we have an overflow level of 100 and we are adding 75, $-60$, and 75 together. If we first add 75 and 75, we get an overflow. When we then subtract 60, we may have a meaningless answer. But if we add them in another order (e.g., $75 - 60 = 15$, followed by $15 + 75 = 90$), there is no overflow, and we get the correct answer.

A great deal of work has been done since this experiment, and we now know that improved specification, verification, and testing is vital to getting

*N*-version programs to work. More work is underway and the cost of *N*-version programming is coming down, but it is not yet cost effective for most applications.

- This defense is not guaranteed against intentional attack. That is, this defense will work well if the problem comes from random Gaussian noise, but it may not apply to an intentional attack. An intentional attacker, for example, might use the legitimate modification mechanism to modify both $P_1V_1$ and $P_1V_2$. Then the voter would then kick out the legitimate results from $P_1V_3$. So this defense, at least in this simple form, it's not guaranteed against intentional attack.

### 3.3.2 Sound Change Control

Sound change control is a quality assurance process that keeps corruptions from passing a "guard." Normally, we have two environments: a "Research and Development" (R & D) environment, and a "Production" (P) environment. The R & D environment is where we make and test out changes. The P environment is where we use systems day to day. So how do we do sound change control? Very poorly for the most part.

In sound change control, there is an area between R & D and P called "Change Control" (CC), and a set of rules about how the system works (see Figure 3.14). These rules are typically supported by technical safeguards and administrative controls. The rules for sound change control usually go something like this:

1. CC can only approve or reject a proposed change; it cannot make a change on its own. In other words, you make changes in R & D and pass them through CC. All CC can do is say, "This is acceptable!" –OR–"This is not acceptable."

2. CC can only pass sources from R & D to P. It cannot pass binary libraries, executables, or other such things, because we can't reliably determine what non-source programs do.

3. CC is done via human and automated verification methods. What do we verify about changes?

   - We verify that the change is necessary. We don't allow changes to take place for no reason.

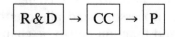

**FIGURE 3.14** Change control.

- We verify that the change is appropriate to the goal. In other words, we say we need a change for a particular reason, and we have to make sure that the change relates to that reason.

4. The change has to be tested on sample data from the P environment to make certain it works properly.

5. The operation of the change must be clear and obvious. Unclear or inobvious software can often be easily modified to include subtle attacks.

6. The change may not have any unnecessary code or data. Any unnecessary code or data might contain corruptions, and is expensive to handle.

That reminds me, does anybody here use change control in their environment? Do you do it this way? No. I've done a pretty thorough survey, and I only know of about three places in the world that do sound change control. One of them is the people that design nuclear missile control systems. I am very pleased that they do sound change control. Another one is the Federal Reserve Bank in the United States. At least they claim to do sound change control. There are probably a few others that do this, but I am sure there are very few.

Why doesn't everybody else do this? There are four major problems with sound change control that keep it from being used in most environments, even those where some form of change control is used.

1. It's quite expensive. According to the places that really do it, you need twice as many people doing change control as programmers making changes, so it triples programming costs.

2. It's quite slow. If you have a serious problem in your computer system, you can't just go and fix it, you have to go through change control. You have to fix it, test it out, show that it's appropriate, and make sure that it is just what it's supposed to be. Then the change goes into affect, and not before.

3. It's rarely done right. From my informal survey of several thousand organizations, almost nobody follows all the rules all the time.

4. Sound change control must cover all changes! If we only cover changes to the things that are compiled into binary executables, that's not good enough. We have to cover changes to spreadsheets, databases, other macro processors, and all sorts of other things. Everything that isn't limited function has to be change controlled, and this, of course, is intolerable. Almost nobody can afford to do this properly.

### 3.3.3 Integrity Shells

An integrity shell uses redundancy to detect changes, and is thus a form of automated fault tolerance and change control. We know just when to check and what to check, and we can even, in certain cases, do automated correction. So let's look at how this works.

We begin by restating the problems with software self-defense, because integrity shells came about by fixing all of the problems with self-defense techniques. There were three problems:

1. A virus may modify the redundant part of the program.

2. Detection may fail.

3. By the time a program gets control, it may look clean.

The first and second problems have to do with the fact that we need a reliable way to detect corruption in the presence of intentional attack. The only way we know of to accomplish this goal is with a hard-to-forge cryptographic checksum (CCS). So what's that?

I'll start with the checksum. It's like a fingerprint. We take a fingerprint of a file. If we subsequently modify the file, its fingerprint changes. So when we look at the file the next time, it will have the wrong fingerprint, and therefore we will detect the change. But, we still have to do the fingerprint in a reliable and uncircumventable fashion.

So imagine that we do a CCS by encrypting the file using a secret key, and then performing a checksum on the encrypted file. If the cryptosystem is good enough, and the key is kept secret, we have a hard-to-forge fingerprint. To be more precise, we have a set of triples $[(F_1, k, S_1) \cdots (F_N, k, S_N)]$, where each $F$ is a file, $k$ is the secret key, and each $S$ is a CCS. An attacker can see only $F$ and $S$.

If the cryptosystem is "good enough", you cannot cost-effectively modify $F$ so that under the same $k$ you get the same $S$, you can't modify $F$ and $S$ so that under the same $k$ they will match, and you cannot guess $k$ by looking at $F$ and $S$. That's what makes it a sound CCS technique for this particular purpose.

It turns out that there are a couple of techniques like this that seem to be very good, and the cryptographic community has analyzed these to a certain extent. Let me take a moment to list some of the other properties of CCS techniques, so we can understand their virtues.

- The CCS can be independent of the operating system. That is, we can have a CCS, so that even if the operating system is modified by an attacker, even if a system's manager, a system's operator, and/or a system's programmer, collude to make the system work differently without telling anyone, a CCS could still pick up the change.

- A CCS is also independent of other users, so that each user can independently detect changes. Each user can have a different key, so that even if an attacker can make a forgery that works properly under one key, it is unlikely to work under all the other keys.

- Multiple, independent checks are possible with a CCS. That means that an external auditor can do an audit and detect changes. They can use their own CCS with complete independence.

- A CCS can work on all information, not just binary executable files.

- A CCS can work over networks. You can verify the integrity of information during network transmission, storage, and retrieval, and you can use the same CCS technique, regardless of the system it's used on.

- There is a trade-off between performance and protection. We can usually get better protection by sacrificing some performance. That doesn't mean that lower performance always gives you better protection. For example, you might have a slow cryptosystem that isn't particularly good. Nevertheless, you can typically improve the level of protection by using a larger key, storing a larger CCS, et cetera.

The last problem with software self-defense was that, by the time a program gets control, it may look clean. Recall that there is a generic attack against any self-defense mechanism. How do we get around that problem? The only solution is to check the program before it gets control. We do that using something called an integrity shell. Here's how an integrity shell works:

```
The user says ``Interpret X'':
    If X and everything X depends on is unchanged
      then interpret X
      else Accept -OR- Trust -OR- Forget -OR- Restore
```

Let's start by describing what I mean by interpreting $X$. I don't mean that $X$ is an executable binary program that is run on the hardware, although that is an example of interpretation. It might be that I have a spreadsheet that is interpreted by a spreadsheet program. The spreadsheet is interpreted, but it depends for its proper interpretation on the spreadsheet program. The spreadsheet program may in turn depend on a variety of other information. The same is true for a source program that is translated by a compiler or interpreted by an interpreter, a database that is interpreted by a database program, et cetera.

When the user says "interpret $X$," if $X$ is not changed (i.e., if $S_X$ for $X$ has not changed) and everything $X$ depends on for its proper operation has not changed (i.e., their $S$'s have not changed), then we know that we have an unchanged environment. In other words, the environment has not been corrupted since the last time a CCS was done. So we can simply interpret $X$ with a degree of assurance that it is what it is suppose to be.

If either the information being interpreted or the information it depends on for its interpretation has been modified, we cannot trust that the interpretation will operate properly. In this case, we have choices to make:

- One option is to "accept it" in its new form. That is to say, use it, even though you know it is corrupt. For example, if I am on the space shuttle and I am going through hypersonic S curves and I find a corruption in a program, and it's on my last computer, I don't want to shutdown the computer because it has a corruption, because then I will certainly crash. I would much prefer to run the program until I land (if I land), and fix it then. This is a "fail-safe" mode because in the case of a failure, it fails in the safest mode available.

- Another option is to "trust the change." For example, if I just made a legitimate change, I would want to tell the system that this change was appropriate, and have it identify further change afterwards.

This is often the case during program development and maintenance.

- Another option is to "forget it." For example, if I'm in the nuclear missile business, and I send a nuclear missile out, and the program to control that nuclear missile goes bad, and that corruption is detected by the system, I personally would make the decision: "Don't blow up, fall to the ground, turn off the engine, don't blow up!". This is also called "fail-safe" because it fails in a "safe" mode. Obviously, "safe" means different things in different circumstances.

- The last option is "restore it." If I have a backup and I know where it is, I can go and get that backup and automatically restore the corrupt information to its previous state. With on-line or LAN-based backups, the system fixes the corruption and proceeds normally with just a slight delay. In most systems, this is the safest default. In the better systems, after restoration the process is repeated, and if corruption persists, another option is selected.

At this point, in a short course, we normally demonstrate an integrity shell operating with a number of different types of corruption. We begin by turning off integrity protection so we can show a virus as it would operate without integrity present. It spreads from program to program, displaying its progress along the way. We then turn integrity protection back on and repeat the demonstration, only this time, the corruption is detected immediately, and further spread is prevented. Demonstrations are normally done on a portable DOS or Unix system, but they are fairly generic and do not depend on features or limits of particular operating systems.

Now most of these examples are against viruses, but it turns out that integrity shells are very general-purpose mechanisms. Let's look at an example. We go into the DOS directory, where all of the DOS programs are stored, and we find a program called "FORMAT.COM," which is an operating system program. We run FORMAT to show how it appears on the screen, and then we exit without doing anything of interest.

```
C:>FORMAT A:
Insert new diskette for drive A:
and strike ENTER when ready ^C
```

The next thing we do is type a command like:

```
C:>ECHO No way Jose > FORMAT.COM
```

This replaces the contents of FORMAT.COM. We then type FORMAT.COM to show that it has indeed been corrupted, and do a directory which shows that FORMAT.COM is only 14 bytes long.

```
C:>TYPE FORMAT.COM
No way Jose
C:>DIR FORMAT.COM
FORMAT    COM       14  3-01-89  12:01p
C:>
```

In the DOS environment, if you ran such a program (and I wouldn't advise you to do it without an integrity shell in place), the system would normally crash. That is because the operating system simply loads the file into memory and starts executing instructions at the first byte of the file. So let's run FORMAT.

```
C:>FORMAT A:
Insert new diskette for drive A:
and strike ENTER when ready ^C
```

The integrity shell detected the corruption, replaced FORMAT.COM using an ON-LINE backup, and ran the corrected FORMAT program, taking only a bit of extra time.

If you want to restore from an on-line backup, you need to have the backup on-line. You can do the same thing with off-line backups, but it takes a lot longer. Thus, you get a time/space trade-off. On-line backups take more space, while off-line backups take more time.

### 3.3.4   Integrity Shell Limitations and Features

Integrity shells deserve special attention both because of their strength as a defense and their increasing application. Just to give you an idea of their impact, in 1986 they were proven optimal in untrusted systems. One integrity shell product has now successfully defended against all viruses for over 3 years (over a factor of 20 increase in attacks with no impact on defense).

### A "Good Enough" Cryptosystem

The first limitation is that the cryptographic system must be "good enough." So what does "good enough" mean? Well, what it really means is that no attacker will get around it, and that's not very easy to predict ahead of time. But, there are some other issues that may be considered. For example, the performance versus integrity trade-off. Let me give you an example from the integrity shell we use in our demonstrations. It has different cryptosystems depending on how you want that trade-off placed. You decide whether you want it to take 10 seconds, 1 second, 0.1 seconds, or 0.01 seconds to check the average program. If you take 0.01 seconds, you're not likely to get much in the way of integrity. If you take 100 seconds, it's probably going to be too slow to justify. So normally, people set a performance level, and have the system do the best it can for that performance.

You need a sound basis for believability of any cryptographic system. For example, many people come to me and say, "we have a great cryptographic system, it's been approved by the NSA.[3] It must be great." I usually say "Approved for what?" If they say it's been approved for selling overseas, that means the NSA can break it, right? Cryptosystems are usually not

---

[3]The U.S. National Security Agency.

approved for export unless the NSA can read them. So you need a basis for believability, and in terms of cryptography, there are only three systems in general use that are credible at this time.

One of them is the "perfect system" (aka the One Time Pad), analyzed by Shannon in the 1940s. It is provably unbreakable, but it is not practical for the integrity shell application.

The second cryptosystem that is relatively sound, and I use the word "relatively" loosely, is the "DES."[4] This system withstood a fair amount of attack, and although I have heard from several governments around the world that they are able to break DES codes in a matter of days (or in some cases hours), the typical attacker is not likely to break DES codes in order to launch a virus, and if they did, it would take a long time and a lot of space to perform an infection.

The third system is the "RSA."[5] In the RSA system, we can break any code, but the amount of time it takes to break the code can be varied by changing the key size. For example, a 100-digit RSA takes hundreds of years to break using the fastest algorithms on the fastest supercomputers today. A 200-digit RSA signature takes hundreds of trillions of lifetimes of the universe to break with the best systems available today, but it also takes more time to generate signatures.

How do you determine whether a system is sound? It's very difficult, but there are some indicators of unsound systems. For example, if you have a cryptographic system that doesn't take longer to check things that are bigger, chances are it's not checking everything, because it takes more time to encrypt more information. There are a couple of products that check 50-kilobyte files in a tenth of a second on a PC-XT. This is certainly not sound, because it takes over a second to read 50-kilobytes on a typical PC-XT. Another example of unsound cryptographic practice is the use of an unchangeable cryptosystem key. If we all have the same key, the attacker has it too, and can forge modifications without a problem.

### A Trusted Mechanism
The second limit is that the mechanism itself has to be unalterable. If you can't secure the mechanism, an attacker can modify it to allow corruptions

---

[4]The Data Encryption Standard specified by the U.S. government some time ago for encryption.

[5]Rivest, Shamir, and Adleman published a paper defining this cryptosystem, which was the first dual public key encryption algorithm, and is currently the most widely used hard-to-break public key system available.

to pass unnoticed. You can use the CCS to check the integrity shell, but if we can alter the mechanism, we can bypass any defense.

In virtually every system, there is a way to use hardware protection to defend the integrity mechanism. Even on a PC, you can have hardware write protected floppy disks that provide a fair degree of hardware protection against corrupting the integrity mechanism. You run an integrity check from the floppy disk to check the integrity mechanism on the hard disk, the operating system on the hard disk, and all the other critical parts of the operating environment, and then you have some assurance that they are sound. You can then start to use them as a basis for running other programs on the system.

Let me just mention something about write-protect tabs on 5.25-in. PC floppy disks. If you protect a floppy disk with a black plastic write-protect tab, it might not work. It turns out that many PCs use infrared to detect the presence of a write-protect tab, and those little black stickers don't block infrared light. So even though you use the write-protect tab, the disk may not actually be write protected. So you might say "let's get all metal stickers," which we certainly should do, but even with a metal sticker, the disk isn't always write protected properly. On some systems, a little metal finger comes down to check for the presence of a write-protect tab. If the write-protect tab gets a little bit dented, the disk drive may not detect it. Microfloppy (3.5-in.) disks, by the way, don't have these problems.

An alternative trusted mechanism that is becoming more popular is a hardware device inserted into the computer. This tends to be quite expensive (i.e., manufacturing costs on the order of 25–50 U.S. dollars) relative to software solutions, is harder to update, and once bypassed, cannot be easily reconfigured for successful defense. Although it is theoretically possible to devise a secure hardware device for this purpose, most current hardware devices of this sort can be easily bypassed by a sufficiently knowledgeable expert, and the expense becomes far greater for a secure system (i.e., several hundred U.S. dollars each, and each is tied to specific hardware configurations).

Another alternative that is currently the most cost effective of the available options is the combination of a bootlock, a snapshot, and disk encryption, all implemented in software. The bootlock prevents many attacks, the encryption makes it difficult to use a defense-specific attack, and the snapshot eliminates simulation attacks. Even though any such defense can eventually be bypassed, the goal is to drive up attack complexity with a minimal impact on performance and cost. This combination seems quite effective.

### A Trusted Path for the Key

The third thing we need is a trusted path for the key. If the attacker can watch the key as we type it in, they can use that key to forge a CCS. Normally, a trusted path is generated by forcing the integrity shell to run before other programs in the environment, so that nothing can insert itself between the system startup and the integrity shell's operation.

In most systems, it is inconvenient or infeasible for users to remember keys. One alternative is to provide a hardware key device, but that is also expensive and inconvenient. The most common alternative is to store a key on the system disk and use the stored key for defense. The problem is that an attacker could exploit this key to implement undetected changes by resumming files after alteration under the available key. This implies the requirement for access controls that prevent an attacker from accessing the key, and/or some form of obscuration that makes it difficult to identify or apply the stored key. The latter is very insecure in almost all cases, because the information must be usable by the defense in order to allow authorized changes.

### The Granularity Issue

The fourth limitation is really more of a trade-off than anything else. It's called the granularity issue. If we are trying to cover a 500-megabyte database, and we check the whole database every time we read, and resum it every time we make a change, it becomes inconvenient and slows performance dramatically. For things like large databases, it's probably much more appropriate to have checking at a lower granularity level than the file level. In that case, you would like to have the database program verify the CCS associated with each record as it is read, and update the CCS every time a record is written. It is not adequate in all cases to use a command interpreter based integrity shell. In fact, anything that interprets something else should really have built-in integrity protection.

### The Problem of Intent

The final limitation of integrity shells is a fundamental issue, in that the legitimacy of change is a function of intent. That is, we can't tell whether a change is legitimate or not unless we can somehow determine what the intent of the user is, and compare that intent to the actual change. In most current systems, most users don't know what part of the system should change when they make a change to something on their screen. They have no sense of that. So ultimately, we have no way to assure the legitimacy of the change in any such system. Integrity shells can detect change and act as they are told, but they cannot determine the intent of the user and map that into the actions of the system.

## Optimal Protection

The basic feature of an integrity shell, and the reason the integrity shell was devised the way it was, is that it is optimal. That is, in an untrusted computer system, by definition, you cannot prevent infection. Since you cannot prevent infection, the best you can hope to do is to detect it and limit its further spread. That's just what an integrity shell does.

- An integrity shell detects all primary infection (infection by a trusted program), and prevents all secondary infection (further infection by a program infected through primary infection). Furthermore, this is the best we can ever do in such a system.

## Efficiency

The second feature of integrity shells is that they are very efficient. When I say efficient, I mean that for optimal protection, integrity shells use the minimum overhead:

- They don't perform any checks that don't have to be performed in order to prevent secondary infection, and they only check the things that have to be checked when they have to be checked. So, they are efficient in the sense of minimal overhead.

- They are also efficient in the sense that they can automate the repair process. Without this automation, the cost of getting rid of a virus once found is potentially enormous. For example, if you have 5000 computers and a virus spreads throughout your organization, you will have a Herculean task cleaning them up. With automated cure, you don't even have to interpose yourself in the process. It is completely automatic and transparent.

- Finally, they are efficient because they are easy to use. That is, from the standpoint of a user, integrity shells can be transparent if you automate all the decisions based on your policy.

I want to mention one other thing about this optimal situation. Some people use a CCS without an integrity shell. For example, they might perform a CCS to detect changes every morning. The problem with that scheme, and one of the reasons integrity shells are optimal and this is not, is that a virus could be designed to only infect programs modified in the last day. This sort of virus is commonly called a "slow" virus, and in this case, only legitimate looking changes would be picked up by the CCS and the virus would spread undetected. That is why an integrity shell must check information just before use, and automatically resum it after use if there are legitimate changes. It shuts the window for illicit changes being treated as legitimate. There are, by the way, real-world slow viruses that work this way.

## Product Issues in Integrity Shells

There are three major product issues in the design of integrity shells.

*Basic Capabilities:* Some systems have on-line backup capabilities; others do not. The soundness of the CCS is vital to proper operation of an integrity shell. Other features are required in various environments, and their existence and quality are critical to the value of the product.

*User Interfaces:* You probably need a different interface for the systems administrator than for a typical secretary. Integrity shell capabilities must be able to integrate into existing interfaces as easily and transparently as possible, and be relatively easy to deal with. For example, an interface that doesn't integrate with a windowing environment is inappropriate if that is the dominant environment, since it will not be effective most of the time.

*Automated Decision Making:* Because there are so many different ways to use integrity shells in different environments, and because different decisions are appropriate under different conditions, it is appropriate that decisions be configurable for the environment. A typical issue is whether we should automatically trust new programs in the environment in order to make new program installation simple, or prevent running new software to keep from trusting a program that should not be trusted. Automation should help automate organizational policy to as large an extent as possible.

## Future Developments

The major things we lack now are more comprehensive tools for refining the automation of integrity maintenance. We would like to have a language for expected behavior so that, for example, if we have a spreadsheet that's supposed to modify other spreadsheets with the same first three characters of the first name, the process of checking and summing can be automated.

A language that specifies intent is not as simple as it may sound. The closer we can get to specifying our intent, the better job we can do at determining whether our intent has been met or not, but that also implies that we have to know a lot about the way systems work and be able to impart that knowledge to the computer effectively.

Another problem with trying to describe intent is that it is different for different environments, uses, and people. We cannot automatically figure out what's intended. We can get close, however, and the closer we get, the less of a difference there's going to be between the actual intent and the specified intent, and the smaller the window of vulnerability we will have.

## 3.4  DEFENSE-IN-DEPTH AGAINST VIRUSES

Defense-in-depth redundantly combines techniques that are individually less than ideal, to provide a whole defense that is, presumably, stronger than any of its components. For example, all of the techniques we have discussed in this book can coexist without difficulty.

### 3.4.1  The Moated Wall

To explain synergistic effects, I want to tell you about one of the great technological innovations of all time. It's called the moated wall, and it is a wonderful example of synergy.

It seems that since before history was kept, there have been cliff and cave people who used walls to defend themselves against animals and other people. The walled city was present in biblical times, and walled fortresses were widely used in feudal times to protect the city from assault. Unfortunately, walls have a major failing in that they can be approached from the outside and battered until they fall. Molten liquid is commonly used to prevent these attacks, but it's not all that effective on a simple wall, because it's easy to move before the liquid hits you. Similarly, holes in the walls used for spears and arrows work as a defense, except that spears and arrows go in as well as out, and you have to have people at all of the holes all of the time or risk assault.

Now it is also true that water has been a natural and later an artificial defense as long as we can remember. The Bible describes God parting the ocean to allow the Israelites to cross, and it was common for rivers to be used for defense thousands of years ago. Water has its weakness in that it can be crossed, and with the support of arrows, a beach can be secured and then expanded upon. You also have to defend the entire waterfront all of the time, because a small lapse can be exploited to form a beach head, and off you go.

Well, I'm sure I am wrong about the details, but at some point in the middle ages, somebody figured out that combining water with walls provided advantages that neither had alone. With the moated wall, a castle could be defended by far fewer people, because you couldn't form a beach head on the face of the wall, and you couldn't very easily break down a wall when standing in a moat full of crocodiles. Arrows were ineffective, and so was assault by force. Thus the synergism of these two defenses made the moated wall stronger than either of its parts.

Now, before going on, I should mention that a powerful attack on the moated wall is the siege. You surround the wall, forcing the occupants to starve to death. However, proper castles had their own wild stock and deep wells, and could withstand sieges of several years if necessary. Some without this capability had secret tunnel entrances, but like the computer's back door, this can be exploited for attack.

### 3.4.2   Synergistic Effects of Defense-in-depth

Defense-in-depth against computer attack also leads to synergistic effects that may cause each of the defense to operate with more strength than it could operate with alone. For example, it turns out that the combination of access control with an integrity shell is particularly synergistic. Without integrity protection, we have seen that access control becomes ineffective. The Bell-LaPadula example detailed earlier should make this very clear. On the other hand, without access control, integrity protection is subject to corruption of the defense mechanism, which we also described earlier. Notably, when integrity and access controls are combined, they offer both integrity for the access control scheme and access control for the integrity mechanism, thus making each defense stronger than it would be alone, and the combined defense stronger than the sum of the strengths of each defense implemented independently.

Now in that last sentence, there was a major problem. The problem is that in order for the synergistic benefits to occur, it is not adequate to simply implement each of a set of different defenses and throw them together. That would be like having a moat on one side of your fortress and a wall on the other side. It allows either weakness to be exploited. They have to be properly integrated in order to achieve the synergistic effects. For example, access controls normally allow or prevent a user from accessing information. But integrity protection must be able to apply the CCS key to detect changes. If the key is accessible, then an attacker can exploit it, but if it is not accessible, the defender cannot apply it! The solution is an integrated defense that permits access during legitimate operations and prevents access during illegitimate operations. This can only be done if the legitimacy can be determined by the access control scheme, which means it has to be integrated into the access control scheme in order to achieve the synergistic effect.

There are a lot of other synergistic effects between mechanisms, and I just want to review some of them here both for your understanding of how they impact the virus defense issue and for their broader implications toward protection. I only cover a particular set of techniques in this discussion. Please be aware that other techniques and synergisms exist.

Any access control scheme must have a means of identification and authentication in order to differentiate between (at a minimum) systems administrators and users. Without access control, stating an identity doesn't limit user actions, but without identification and authentication, access control can't differentiate between different users.

Access controls are rarely perfect, and even if they were, it would be important to know when someone tries to bypass protection in order to eliminate other attacks. Audit trails don't protect against anything, but they do provide the means for analysis after the fact, and if well implemented can indicate an attack before it succeeds. Without access controls, audit trails cannot be protected against tampering, while without audit trails, you may never know that people are trying to find ways around your access controls. Eventually, either mechanisms will break down. When put together, the audit trails can indicate an access attack before it succeeds, while the access controls protect the audit trails from being tampered with.

Audits and authentication work well together too. For example, audit trails without authentication can't prevent an illicit user from modifying the audit trails. But without audit trails, we can guess at authentication information forever without much risk of detection. When we combine them, we not only prevent audit trail modification by requiring authentication, but we also prevent password guessing by detecting attacks before they succeed.

### 3.4.3   Limits of Synergism

The list goes on and on, with every form of defense acting synergistically with other forms of defense to one extent or another, either directly or indirectly. In effect, we can make a matrix of interactions describing how defenses act synergistically, which would be an interesting research project, but not one that I am prepared to complete right now.

It's not that I couldn't list many synergisms. Rather, the problem is that outside of indicating the existence of synergism and giving a few special cases, we don't have any systematic way of evaluating the phenomenon. Without a system of analysis, we could play around forever without coming to a real understanding of the full impact of synergism.

We do know that the impact of synergism can be quite stunning. For example, up until 1983, most of the knowledgeable computing security community was almost certain that the existing "secure" systems were very hardened against any kind of attack other than physical attack. Then, with the advent of computer viruses, the whole understanding of protection shifted, and we now understand that the most trusted systems of that era are easily bypassed with an almost trivial attack. This "house of cards" fell down because of the synergism of viruses with covert channels.

More to the point, we have no real reason to believe that the same sort of impact could not happen again with another novel sort of attack. We simply have no accurate way of modeling overall protection from a mathematical viewpoint at a high enough level to be practical, and therefore no way to understand the true nature of the problem or the solutions.

### 3.4.4   Other Effects

One other advantage of defense-in-depth worth mentioning is that it permits defenders to compensate for new attacks before they succeed in completely penetrating the defense, even when they are partially successful. For example, a previously unknown virus will bypass a virus monitor, but may be detected by an integrity shell. We can then augment the virus monitor to defend against this attack without undue exposure during improvements. As new viruses are detected and defended by the combined defense, each of the component defenses are improved, so similar viruses don't penetrate as far in the future.

This is essentially an issue of brittleness. By brittleness, we mean that, even though the protection structure looks solid, a fairly small amount of pressure properly applied yields an utter collapse of protection. This is normally because attacks are only covered by a single defense mechanism. It is the way of nature that things fall apart, and when some protection feature fails for one reason or another, if the system is brittle with respect to coverage of the failed feature, the whole protection system fails.

Eventually, any defense can be defeated, but the use of defense-in-depth seems to provide far more effective protection than any other current alternatives because it covers each attack with multiple layers of defense. The increased coverage provides some redundancy for fault tolerance. A well-designed system of defense-in-depth should provide coverage against brittleness.

# Chapter 4

# NONTECHNICAL DEFENSES

Although technical defenses are central to success against computer viruses in the modern environment, history has shown that no technical method alone is effective for information protection. Any system must be used by people, and people must make decisions about what methods to use and how to use them. In nontechnical defenses, we address policies and procedures for human behavior, limitations of the techniques due to the way we use them, and legal action as punishment, deterrent, and compensation.

## 4.1  LIMITED SHARING

Limited sharing is both a technical defense and a procedural defense, because in the vast majority of modern computing environments, people can cause sharing even when technical defenses attempt to prevent it. Furthermore, many organizations use forms of limited sharing in a nontechnical way without providing any technical capability to enforce the policy.

Limited sharing effectively limits the spread of viruses if it is used properly, but almost no organization uses it properly. As an example, this is the basis by which the U.S. DoD network was (supposedly) separated from the Internet. Unfortunately, these controls were not properly implemented or used, and thus the DoD network was infected through gateways that were supposedly secure. Once the Internet virus got through, the DoD decided to use better isolation. Unfortunately, this makes it still harder for the newest technologies to be integrated in to DoD systems. This is called the chilling effect.

### 4.1.1  Isolation During Attack

One common limited sharing strategy is isolation during attack. IBM says when an attack is detected in the network, they "pull the plug." That doesn't mean they are safe. If a virus has been spreading for six months and causes damage today, pulling the plug in the network isn't going to help. On the other hand, if the attack is not a slow or subtle one, pulling the plug might help.

So let me ask you, who here knows where the plug is? Do any of you operate a computer network? Do you know where the plug is to disconnect yourself from the rest of the world? Let me tell you that IBM did not know where the plug was. When the Christmas card attack took place, they just didn't know how to immediately disconnect from outside networks. Now they know.

In many organizations there isn't one plug; there are 50 or more of them. If you are going to go to isolation, you have to know how to do it. There has to be somebody that knows where the plug is, and there has to be a contingency plan in place to assure that the plug can be pulled effectively. In most large organizations today, diconnecting from the global network would be disastrous from a denial of services standpoint, so there is a trade-off between utility and safety.

### 4.1.2  Separation of Function

One form of limited sharing that is somewhat effective and is in widespread use, is the separation of R&D from Production. We pointed out many of the problems and features of this method earlier under the heading of change control.

### 4.1.3  The AIDS Disk

Another common form of limited sharing is a policy not permitting external floppy disks or tapes into a facility, requiring all incoming programs to be checked through a central clearinghouse, or other similar procedural methods. This brings us to the story of the AIDS disk.

In 1989, one of the widest scale extortion attempts ever made was initiated when tens of thousands of infected floppy disks were mailed to people on a computer magazine's mailing list. Many of those subscribers were in organizations with a "no external disks" policy in place. Despite the administrative control, there were organizations where hundreds of users put these disks into their computer systems and got the bug. It cost these organizations several man-months of effort to get rid of the problem, because the employees didn't follow the policy.

The perpetrator was caught in this case because the people who rented the mailing list kept track of the renters, and eventually the process of elimination yielded the source. Unfortunately, catching the perpetrator didn't limit the damage or result in compensation for the victims.

### 4.1.4   No External Disks

Let me give you another example. An employee showed up at one door with a floppy disk. The guard said "Didn't you read the memo? You can't bring in external disks." The employee responded "This isn't an external disk, it's an internal disk. I took it home last night, and I'm bringing it back today." The problem is that the employee did not understand what the policy meant when it said "No External Disks." If you are going to use administrative and procedural controls, you have to educate your employees on what they mean and why they are in place. Typically we don't do that. We make a regulation, don't bother to explain it, and they interpret it in their own way, or just ignore it.

### 4.1.5   Clearinghouses

Another common technique is to require all software to go through a central clearinghouse before internal use. This is a sensible policy, if only to assure that new programs interact properly with the existing environment. It is not an effective defense against unknown viruses, but it is a rational place to use scanning technology. Even though it won't pick up new viruses, it will be effective against some known viruses, and it will be very low cost because it is only used at one central site. Ultimately, such systems fail because in practice, such systems fail occasionally, and one slipup can be disastrous if this is the only defense in place. It is just too brittle to depend upon.

### 4.1.6   Limiting Information Sources

Eliminating bulletin board access is inexpensive and fairly common as a procedural defense. Some bulletin boards have a reputation for posting Trojan horses, but for the most part, bulletin boards that provide valuable information are worth subscribing to. A more common policy is the "no shareware" policy. Let me give you some historical facts. No legitimate distribution of public domain software or shareware has ever contained a virus as far as we can tell, but almost every major manufacturer of commercial software has distributed a virus in a legitimate software distribution. Several hardware manufacturers have distributed disks with preloaded operating systems containing viruses. A PC magazine has distributed several thousand copies of a virus in a distribution to its readers. One major electronic software distributor in Europe distributed 60,000 copies of a virus to its customers because the virus went undetected by their virus scanner. So if we are going to make a sound decision based on historical fact, we should have a policy to only buy shareware and public domain software if we want to avoid viruses, and to never buy "legitimate" shrink-wrapped software.

There are probably some good reasons that shareware and public domain software have never been infected with viruses. When you get shareware or public domain software the author's name is attached. There is a human being whose name is attached to that software, and therefore they have a very good reason to make sure it's right, because it's their reputation that's at stake. On the other hand, if you work for Microsoft and you put in a virus, nobody will ever know who did it and your name will not be on the copyright anyway. So why should you care if it causes problems? Finally, trying to manage protection protection in an environment where you one person writing a piece of software is very easy. Trying to maintain protection in an environment with thousands of programmers is not so easy. The probability of a virus getting into Microsoft is much higher than getting into a small software manufacturer's operation.

## 4.2   CHANGE CONTROLS

Administrative controls tend to be very inexpensive and very ineffective. The problem seems to be that a single error or omission in the application of a policy can cause widespread collapse. Despite this problem, the low cost of administrative controls makes them justifiable as a supplement to technical defenses.

A classic administrative control is the "Changes Should Be Approved" policy. Note the wording. It doesn't say we should use sound change control. It says changes should be approved. There is a person with a rubber stamp that says "Approved," and this person stamps every change that goes by. Maybe in a highly sophisticated organization, once a month, the person says "Not Approved—Resubmit," but the vast majority of the changes are simply approved.

This is ineffective as change control, but it is effective in one sense. If you are an officer of a public corporation, you may be personally liable for failing to take prudent action. You now have somebody to fire.

## 4.3 AUDITING

Auditing has been almost completely ineffective in virus defense, and has been minimally successful in tracking down attackers. The first problem is that the available audit trails don't keep enough information to track the progress of a virus.

Many systems have access control facilities that report attempts to violate the access controls, but a virus doesn't have to do anything that's not authorized, so that sort of tracking is ineffective. It only detects attacks that aren't very well written.

Then, there's postmortem (i.e, *after you're dead!*) analysis, which works just great, except that it's too late. You know, call the auditor, who comes in and tells you that your computer system is indeed not working, and tries to determine everything that was corrupted in the process. It may be the only way to restore the system to its proper state, but in some cases it takes months to resolve, and it doesn't keep you in business while the repairs are under way.

Recent innovations in auditing technology have led to more and more automated audit trail analysis, and there are some systems available today that detect anomalies in real-time. None of these systems are yet able to detect viruses with any degree of reliability, but the day may come when they are able to do so.

## 4.4 PEER NETWORK PROBLEMS

We have already mentioned that procedural methods tend to fail, but sometimes these failures can be quite subtle. One example is the problem in so-called "Peer Networks." A peer network is a computer network where two "peers" at different physical places in the network have equivalent access rights. The problem with peer networks is that by making peers in distributed locations equivalent, you also make all of the protection mechanisms related to those peers equivalent. Since the protection "chain" is only as strong as its weakest link, you distribute every weakness at any location to all of its peers.

Say, for example, that in one location (Pittsburgh) where people have access to facility *A*, a specific set of procedural controls are strictly enforced (e.g., no floppy disks are allowed in, all incoming software is checked for propriety, no physical access is allowed by unauthorized personnel, and all personnel are well trained). Meanwhile, in another location (Melbourne), people also have access to facility *A*, and a different set of procedural controls are strictly enforced (e.g. all software goes through sound change control, all personnel are well trained, only listed vendors are used, and only authorized software is executed by the operating system). Each is a good set of techniques, but they don't match well. For example:

- A virus accidentally brought from another site by a printer maintenance person in Melbourne can't infect Melbourne computers because they won't run unauthorized software. It can, however, move over the network to Pittsburgh where, acting as a peer program from Melbourne, it will be trusted to operate. Once the virus infects programs in Pittsburgh, it can then spread back to Melbourne because it comes in authorized programs.

Note that both Melbourne's policy and Pittsburgh's policy, when acting alone, would have prevented infection from the virus. In Pittsburgh, the physical security would have kept the infected disk out, while in Melbourne, the technical defense would have prevented infection, but in concert, the defenses didn't match. It is the combination of peer equivalence and unmatched policies that results in this vulnerability.

We have seen one incident of this sort in a large U.S. government department. Uniform standards were in place across the organization, but one site had very tight procedural defenses, and the other had more technical defenses. As a result, a virus entered into one site, and through the network, transmit into an equivalent area in the other site. Once infection took hold, it returned via peer infection.

The Internet virus and the Christmas card were both effective because they operated in peer networks with very similar problems, and most viruses that operate on a single system operate over peer networks because the networks are designed to make peer operation transparent.

In order for defenses to work, especially in peer networks, the methods and procedures must be uniform or properly matched. This in turn presents a problem in that procedures are things that people do. It is very hard to get people in two physically different locations to do the same things because of cultural and personal differences.

## 4.5 TRACKING DOWN ATTACKERS

I have mentioned that auditing techniques are very poor for tracking down viral attackers. To support my contention, I would like to discuss the few successes of EDP audit techniques in catching virus authors.

### 4.5.1 Tracking Down the Christmas Card Attacker

The Christmas card was first detected when it put an end to processing and network communications for about 500,000 users around the world. Since many of these users had Christmas cards on their screens, and all of the time and space was being consumed in the same activity, the immediate source of the problem was self-evident. The virus was in source form, and was only a few lines long, so it didn't take very long for the administrators to find it, determine what it did, and create a special-purpose defense against it.

The Christmas card was soon tracked to an attacker in Germany through the use of EDP audit, which was certainly a magnificent feat in light of the fact that it involved literally millions of transmissions through a global network. It turns out that the networks where the virus was launched kept track of each file sent over the network by sender, receiver, file name, and transmission time. Since the Christmas card did not do any infection, the file name used for transmission was always the same. The organizations involved coordinated the effort through the network after the defense was in place, and found the earliest time of transmission. This was the first copy sent, and identified the user who sent it.

### 4.5.2 Tracking Down the Internet Attacker

Another example of an auditing success was the Internet attack. In the Internet attack, there were some rather obvious behavioral changes. In particular, 6000 users could do almost nothing with their computer systems. It took a very long time for users of those 6000 computers to even log in, while 60,000 other users effectively couldn't use the computer network. Various individuals decided that something was going wrong, and one of the first things they did was to look at the process table (a simple way to look at all the active processes under Unix, the operating system being affected).

What they found was thousands of processes on their computers. One of the people that took part in tracking this attack down said "I was really impressed, I didn't know this computer could have that many processes" (or some such thing). Over the next day or so, a wide variety of attempts were made to stop the virus from acting, and eventually some of the defenders found defenses. They had considerable difficulty in communicating the defenses because most of the people involved only knew each other by computer mail addresses, and the network was too overloaded to communicate effectively, but eventually they got the word out. By the end of the second day, the network was operating again, and many of the sites had installed defenses.

They then traced packet quantities over time by looking at network statistics gathered by one of the sites in the network as a matter of course, and found that there were an abnormally high number of packets being sent in two regions of the country. One region was in the area between San Francisco, California, and San Diego, California, within about the first 50 miles from the west coast of the United States. That's an area of about 20,000 square miles (60,000 square kilometers). The other region was on the east coast of the United States, between New England and Southern New York, as far in from the coast as Philadelphia. That's another 20,000 square miles.

A large percentage of the population of the United States is in those areas, so what they did was search every computer system that was on this network, 60,000 systems or so, in both of these large areas. Imagine if you will, somebody saying there is a carrier of the "Bubonic Plague" either in the New York area or the Los Angeles area, so we are going to go door to door and search every room in Los Angeles and New York to try and find this person. That's what we are talking about in terms of these searches.

Nobody challenged their constitutional right to search all of these computer systems without a warrant. I guess that means that in the United States, we don't have a reasonable expectation of privacy in our computer systems. They did the massive searches and they found a likely source. In the meanwhile, two graduate students at MIT and two graduate students at Stanford University were "uncompiling" the binary executable program that was determined to be the cause of this problem. It took each team about two days to create a "C" program that compiled into the identical binary executable program as the 60-kilobyte binary part of the virus (which is quite a feat).

They tracked it down to a particular person, found physical evidence to support their contention, tried him, and found him guilty in federal court in the United States. Even though he pled innocent to the criminal charges, he admitted to having written the virus.

### 4.5.3   When a Success Is Not a Success

In some sense these were tremendous auditing successes, but I see them in another light.

One important point is that out of about 3000 viruses in the world, only about 5 that did not list their authors have been tracked down to a source. Furthermore, none of the other attacks in the environment today will likely ever be tracked to a source. This is partially because there are no audit trails provided as a normal part of the operating system on personal computers, but a far more important aspect of this issue is that modern computer systems do not log the information that would be required to trace the progress of a virus. If we included this sort of audit trail, it would take enormous amounts of time and space, we would have to find new types of tools to allow us to analyze the audit trails, and it would not significantly reduce the difficulty of tracking down an attacker.

A far more important problem, in my opinion, is that in every case, audit has failed to detect the presence of the attack until the damage became evident due to massive widespread damage. In other words, it was behavioral changes in the system identified by users that caused detection. That's pretty disconcerting to me.

### 4.5.4   Needed Improvements in EDP Audit

In order to be effective, our audits should pick up viruses before behavioral changes take place, and the tools available to the auditor until recently were simply inadequate to the task. Change control is inadequate in most cases. Dependencies are rarely considered in an EDP audit. In an EDP audit they will almost never tell you that your mailing list could become corrupted and that might cause all your bills to go wrong. Those indirect things tend to be the things that cause big problems on computers. We generally think of it as subtle little bugs, but they are not really that subtle. If we kept track of what was going on, we could predict this ramification. That's why understanding the risk analysis we will discuss later is very important.

### 4.6   BACKUPS AS A DEFENSE

Backups are often touted as an important aspect of virus defense, and we certainly agree that without other defenses in place, backups are helpful against most attacks, but they are not without their problems. As we pointed out earlier, backups are safe harbor for viruses, and thus they present a major spreading and cleanup problem, but there are several other problems with backups in the current environment.

### 4.6.1   They Don't Always Work

One of the major problems is that backups don't assure the propriety of what's backed up. I like telling stories, so let me tell you a story about backups.

AT&T has a set of computers that run the Unix operating system, and when you use these systems to do backups, the backup menu asks what you would like to backup:

Backup which file structures? ALL / /usr /usr2

The natural choice is, of course, "ALL," but it turns out that if you chose "ALL," you can't restore from backups. As bizarre as that may seem, all of their maintenance people know this, and know how to get around it. If you are not under an AT&T maintenance contract, this can be very expensive.

DOS has historically had the same problem. If you do a full backup including system files using the default DOS backup program, when you restore, the restore program tries to overwrite the system files in the root directory. Unfortunately, in versions of DOS prior to 1992, the system files are required to be stored contiguously on disk and must be the first two files in the root directory. When you do a restoration using the DOS restore program, these special system files are replaced by normal copies that aren't necessarily contiguous or first in the directory list. The restored system no longer operates properly, and it is somewhat inconvenient to resolve this problem without special knowledge.

Let me give you another example of why backups may not be restorable. There is something called head skew, where the tape head used for backups is off at an angle. When you write the tape on a tape drive with a skewed head and use another tape drive to read the tape back, it doesn't work. I had an experience where a tape drive was realigned and then couldn't restore from backups because the tape head was now aligned differently. To restore the backups, I had to misalign the head, adjusting it while trying to read from the tape until the tape started to read correctly. Then I could restore from the backups, after which I had to realign the tape heads and write the backups again with proper tape alignment.

Another problem is with heat. What happens when you put the backups in the back of your car on a sunny day? Well, it doesn't take very long for your backup tapes to become useless. There are many other such problems with the backup tape technology in widespread use today.

So let me ask you, who here has ever had a problem restoring a backup? About 50% of every audience I talk to has experienced a failed backup. If this is your only safety net, you're not very safe, because we can't be sure that the backup works, much less assure that what we backed up was what we wanted to backup.

### 4.6.2   They Aren't Kept Long Enough

How long should you keep backups? Well, it's a function of what you are doing.

People in the banking industry say that if they have to go back one day, they will be out of business. In this circumstance, week-old backups of transaction data are essentially useless except under the rarest circumstances. The reason is that a typical bank transfers its entire assets in electronic fund transfers (EFTs) about twice a week. The "Federal Reserve Bank" of the United States transfers the entire GNP of the United States every day in EFTs. If you lose one day's transactions, can you go back to yesterday and reasonably expect your system is going to work right? Your entire assets will be wrong. So there's no sense in which you can really ever go backwards in that sort of system without an enormous EDP audit effort.

For a software manufacturer, the situation is much different. Backup copies are very often used to repair old versions of software, to determine why errors are occurring in a particular application, and to assure that new versions don't introduce new problems. In this environment, even external backups can be quite useful for both operational and legal purposes.

### 4.6.3   They Act as Safe Harbor for Viruses

The final problem with backups is that they provide safe harbor for viruses. We discussed this in some detail earlier, but we have not discussed how to resolve it.

### 4.7   RECOVERY FROM VIRAL ATTACK

So how do you recover from a virus attack? It turns out that if you are prepared, it's rather straightforward. Fighter pilots have a saying that goes:

"See it, kill it, and get away quickly." That's how you survive as a fighter pilot, and it's about the same for computer viruses.

### 4.7.1　See It

If you are going to get rid of a virus, you have to see it. If the virus is in your backup system over a 6 month period, evolving and changing and dropping off little time bombs all over the place, it's going to be too late by the time everything starts failing. If you can't detect it ahead of time, you simply can't get rid of it in the long run. Detection is critical.

The best method of detection at this time is the proper use of cryptographic checksums in integrity shells. Good change control is also a feasible way to enforce integrity. You can, for example, periodically compare change control logs with actual changes on the system. This can be very expensive because it involves repeated manual reexamination.

### 4.7.2　Kill It

How do you kill it? If you can see it, you can kill it pretty easily. The simplest thing to do is find all the infected programs and delete them. For example, if you are using cryptographic checksums, you can very easily find everything that has changed, restore them from backups, and the virus is exterminated. The reason this works is that, if you can see the virus right away, and if you have done a good job in verifying the propriety of backups, you know the backups are correct, and you can restore them safely.

Well, okay, so how do I assure the propriety of the backups? I got interested in this problem because I have had backups go bad from various mundane problems, and I am the careful sort. What I do to make sure that I have good backups is to restore from the backups onto another computer, and verify their cryptographic checksums. Restoring on another system assures that the backup worked, that the tape can be restored, and that the subsequent checking operations are independent of the system being backed up. Verifying the change control information provides assurance that the information on the tapes corresponds properly to expectations.

As we discussed earlier, when you try to remove a virus during normal processing, you have a race between the cure and new infections, but if you stop all processing, the virus cannot spread, while the cure can eradicate it. In systems with hardware-based protection, you can often do a better job at recovery because you don't always have to stop all processing in order to remove the virus. For example, if we know that the virus is only in a few domains in a POset-based system, we can continue processing in areas the virus cannot reach with a high degree of assurance that the virus will not spread even though other processing is ongoing.

### 4.7.3   Get Away Quickly

Each organization has to make its own decisions about prioritizing which of these things to do first and how quickly to do them, but as a rule, each of them should be done. I prioritize them as follows most of the time, but there are exceptions.

1. Isolate the infected systems to prevent further spread.

2. Get copies of the attack code, and send it off to an expert for analysis. If you have a good defense product and it picks up something that nobody has ever seen before, the copy will help find any side effects that may have to be corrected. If you have a poor product, it is unlikely to come up with anything new, but you should probably try to get a copy just to be certain.

3. Search out and destroy the virus on your backup media, floppy disks, tapes, and other related systems.

4. Get the system back up and working. You do that by killing all of the copies of the virus, restoring from backups, and restarting user operations.

If you have good detection in place, you don't usually have to do all of these steps because you pick up attacks before they can spread.


### 4.8   CERT TEAMS

CERT (Computer Emergency Response Team) teams are groups with responsibility for preparing an organization for emergency response to computer problems, typically including viruses. The CERT team is typically responsible for educating the organization in the area of viruses, training individuals for the actions they will be required to take, determining appropriate technical precautions, and assuring that human and technical systems operate properly. When an actual emergency takes place, these teams usually coordinate the defensive effort.

In the current environment, good CERT teams are almost entirely proactive in their role. This is because there are sufficient technical defenses to make response to the vast majority of attacks completely automatic. The well-prepared CERT team spends its time evaluating protection improvements, educating employees, preparing for disaster recovery, and assuring that policy is aligned to needs.

Less well-prepared CERT teams end up in a very different circumstance. They spend anywhere from hours to months cleaning up after attacks, they have to deal with rampant reinfection, and they sometimes have to reenter massive amounts of data from original copies. In one case, a company had to reenter 3 years worth of data because their employees weren't properly educated in how to respond to an attack. They put in backup disk after backup disk in an attempt to recover, only to find that the virus destroyed their backups because they were not write protected. A well-prepared CERT team would have prudent methods in place to prevent this problem.

### 4.9   REACTIVE AND PROACTIVE DEFENSE

One dimension of the defense problem is the proactive versus reactive issue. Historically, reactive defenses have been widely used in computer security. The problem with reactive defenses is that they depend on people noticing the side effects of an attack without computer assistance, and then correcting the problem with a lot of hard work. As we have seen, many of the viruses that may come up don't have easily identifiable symptoms, once corruption is detected the source isn't always obvious, and there may be a great deal of effort required to undo the damage once it is detected. Let me give a few examples.

- The Internet virus was in an environment where, even though substantial security controls were in place in much of the network, the entire network was unusable for several days, because there were no proactive integrity controls in place.
- The mainframe Christmas card attack brought down thousands of mainframes for several hours and left aftershocks for weeks. Again, good computer security controls were in place, but there were no proactive integrity controls.

The major disadvantages of reactive defenses are that they take a lot of time, systems fail during the reaction time of the defense, and they don't anticipate problems that may not be recoverable without prior preparation. The major advantage of reactive defense is that is costs nothing unless an attack takes place (at which time it usually costs a great deal).

Special-purpose proactive defenses have been in place for quite some time, but they tend to be relatively ineffective. For example, there is a product called CA Examine (by Computer Associates) that works on ACF2-based mainframes. It "knows" the operating system, so if somebody writes a virus that gets into the operating system of ACF2, CA Examine may pick it up. The same is true of virus scanners and monitors. Although they are successful against well-known attacks, they are generally ineffective against new attacks, attacks without obvious side effects, hard-to-track viruses, and evolutionary viruses.

General-purpose proactive defenses have been in place since 1985, and they are the only automated defenses that have ever "discovered" a new virus. Without these defenses, no subtle virus would likely be discovered, because there would be no behavioral change for users to notice.

## 4.10  MANAGEMENT TOOLS

Although basic technical safeguards are important, you need adequate management tools to deal with protection at any level. Let me give you some examples of how inadequate our management tools are.

A typical PC has about 10,000 bits of protection information, a typical engineering workstation has about 100,000 bits of protection information, a typical LAN-based file server had about 1 million bits of protection information, and a typical mainframe computer system has about 10 million bits of protection information. Right now, the way we manage all those protection bits is one bit at a time!

Well, guess what, nobody is able to handle 10 million bits of information properly without good tools. Two surveys were done in 1988 of large MVS shops. One was done by the Office Management and Budget in the United States, the other one was done by a major CPA firm. The results were reported in the New York DPMA Computer Virus Clinic.

- In industry 80% of the systems, and in the government 90% of the systems, did not adequately use the protection mechanisms in place. In other words, they had protection mechanisms there to use, but they just couldn't manage them. Now, I don't believe that's the fault of the system administrators. I think it's because they didn't have adequate tools.

At the same conference, there was somebody there from Computer Associates (the company that maintains ACF2, a security packages for MVS), and they said it's no problem to properly manage protection in MVS. All you have to do is properly manage the 15 protection related modules and not make any error in any of those 15 modules and you will be safe from attack. Well, let's see, in a typical MVS shop you might have 100,000 users. With 100,000 users, how often does somebody get hired or fired? One hundred employee changes per working day would mean that 25,000 changes per year, or an average employee turnover time of 4 years. How many people shift jobs a day? Oh, probably another 200, that's a promotion or job change every two years. How often do we add or remove access to a given user? You get the idea.

In a typical day in a typical MVS shop, you have 1,000,000 or more bits of protection state changing. That's why a big MVS shop has a lot of people working on protection. In one very efficient MVS shop discussed in a short course, there were 8 people dedicated to protection for 500 users. That's 1.6% of the computing personnel, or 1600 full-time people for a 100,000-user system, and an average of about 1000 bits set per protection person per day, or several protection bit changes per person per minute. That's too much overhead just to set all these bits, especially if they still can't set all the bits right all of the time. What we have to do is devise tools to manage these protection systems, otherwise it's a hopeless case.

## 4.11   LAWS AGAINST MALICIOUS VIRUSES

One of the ways we defend against viruses as a society and as individuals is through the creation and vigorous application of laws. Since computer viruses became a substantial threat in the late 1980s, state governments in the U.S. and national governments throughout the world have created laws against the introduction of malicious computer viruses into computer systems without the consent of the owner.

One of the people who has tracked laws about computer viruses, Jay BloomBecker, wrote a good article on the subject in 1992. In his article, he described and quoted several laws against malicious viruses. Most laws that address viruses, address them through the use of words like "self-replicating programs," and do not use the word "virus" Those that do use the term "virus" define it in strange ways.

The conclusion that I have drawn from these laws that three components are required in order for the launch of a virus to be considered a computer crime. To constitute a crime, a virus has to be launched intentionally, maliciously, and without authorization. All three elements must be present in order for a crime to exist, but of course these issues are not necessarily cut and dried in all instances. That's why we have juries to determine the facts based on the evidence.

### 4.11.1  Intent

Legislatures have followed the long legal tradition of "mens rea," which means reasoned mind (literally from the Latin), or as it is used in legal circles, "criminal intent," or alternatively, "guilty mind." In other words, in order to commit a criminal offense, the perpetrator has to have acted maliciously and intentionally, as opposed to stupidly and accidentally.

If you accidentally place a virus into a system because you didn't know it was there, you are not guilty of a crime. As you move away from that position, you are increasingly moving toward a criminal activity.

For example, if you knowingly work with malicious viruses and through forgetfulness, but without explicit intent, release one of those viruses to the world, you may be found guilty because you didn't take reasonable and adequate precautions in light of a known risk. If you place malicious viruses in peoples systems because you disregard reasonable precautions, you may be acting with a wanton disregard for others, in which case you may be liable under the law. If you intentionally place a malicious virus in a system without explicit permission from the owner, you will almost certainly be guilty of a crime.

Now to understand this just a bit more fully, I should mention that in the case of Robert Morris, who created and launched (perhaps accidentally) the Internet virus, the question of mens rea was brought up. It seems that while Robert Morris intended to create the virus, and perhaps even intended to launch it, he did not intend it to disrupt computers throughout the world. The impact was accidental, but the concept of mens rea was applied so as to find him guilty of intended damage. In other words, there is legal precedent to the effect that you can be held responsible for the unintended side effects of committing a computer crime, as long as you had mens rea for the illegal actions you took.

### 4.11.2  Malice

Fortunately, the law does not generally restrict the use of benevolent viruses. A benevolent virus that gets out of hand might be prosecuted on the basis that it is malicious to wantonly disregard the safety and well being of others, assuming that inadequate precautions are taken to prevent unauthorized operation.

For example, if we launch a "benevolent" virus without any restriction on where it can spread, the mere fact that there is no restriction may be held as evidence that it is malicious. On the other hand, if we take effective precautions against unauthorized spread, it is unlikely to be found malicious on that basis. As an example of how easy it is to commit a crime, removing safeties from a benevolent virus that are designed to prevent its unauthorized spread is an intentional and malicious act that may cause unauthorized spread, and it is likely that you would be found guilty of a computer crime if you were caught doing this.

On the other hand, even a virus that is restricted in its spread can be found malicious if it does some tangible harm. Thus restricting spread is not adequate to remove malice from the equation.

### 4.11.3 Unauthorized

If you intentionally create malicious viruses but keep them under control in your own or other authorized environments, you are not likely to be found guilty of a crime, because you acted with legitimate authority.

This third key is important to researchers more than anyone else, because if we can't have malicious viruses intentionally placed in authorized systems, we can't examine them to create defenses. But I am quite certain that the research potential did not drive the legal process in this instance. Rather, I believe it was property law.

The history of computer law is based on property law because as physical objects, computers are bought and sold as property in the same way as any other physical object is treated as property, and the information stored in computers is property because it is covered under the heading of intellectual property as either copyrights, patents, or most usually, trade secrets.

Laws regarding "entry" into computers are treated as other types of "trespass" laws, and like other kinds of trespass, there is a concept of authorized use. If I authorize you to come into my house without further restriction, I cannot reasonably have you arrested for sitting on my chair or walking in the upstairs hall. If I authorize your entry only for the purpose of fixing my entrance way, it may be trespass if you walk in my upstairs hall. If I don't authorize you to enter my house, it is definitely trespass for you to enter my house.

It is very similar for computer entry. If you place a virus in a computer system without authority to do so, you are trespassing. If you create a program to perform unauthorized entry for you, it is not very much different than if you create a robot to illegally enter homes. Thus, a virus that enters unauthorized systems is likely to be illegal under most interpretations of the law.

### 4.11.4   Other Factors

Without a very thorough understanding of the law, it is not easy to determine what is legal and illegal. In fact, even the best lawyers in the world cannot reliably predict the outcome of a trial. In addition, ignorance of the law is no excuse. In effect, the only safe policy is to be very conservative.

I should also say that just because something is illegal doesn't mean we can prove it. In fact, it is unlikely that you will even be able to get anyone from the police to listen to you when you call and tell them that someone introduced a virus into your system. This is a changing situation, and in cases where "federal interest computers" are involved, the FBI may often respond if you can show damages in excess of $5000. These are, of course, U.S. laws, but while laws may vary widely around the world, the basic principles and problems are often the same.

Let's suppose you get the police to listen. Now you have some other problems to consider. Unless you know who committed the crime, it is often impossible to trace the virus to its source because of inadequate controls and audit trails. Even knowing who did it is not the same as proving it in court. A third problem is that it is hard to explain computers to the average jury, and even harder to convince them that enough damage has been done to warrant putting someone in jail. Of course jail is almost never the result of a conviction under a computer crime statute. Robert Morris only got a fine and community service as punishment for bringing 60,000 computers down for 2 days with the Internet virus. Frankly, this punishment seems appropriate to me in light of the minimal punishment that goes with assault and other crimes against people in our society.

### 4.11.5   Civil Recourse

Civil recourse has only barely started to be considered in the computer virus arena. For example, nobody has sued a major manufacturer for accidentally including a virus in a distribution. It seems like a reasonable expectation that someone who is selling you software will have precautions in place against corruptions. The software companies hide behind their legal wording that proclaims they are not responsible for the proper operation of their products, and explicitly voids any implied warranty of merchantability, but that doesn't mean they can act in wanton disregard for your safety or ignore standards of practice.

Another thing we haven't seen is suits against computer criminals for recovery of monetary damages. In this case, we could create a lot of long-term financial distress for people even if they aren't punished by being sent to jail.

Finally, I would personally like to see a law that prohibits people convicted of a computer crime from getting a job working with computers for 7 years. It seems that a popular occupation for computer criminals is to help those they have attacked find better defenses. Unfortunately, most computer criminals are not very good at devising defenses, and even more to the point, legitimate experts who don't break the law are denied jobs because we hire the criminals instead. That's one way to guarantee a constant stream of new computer crimes and limit the number of legitimate protection experts.

# Chapter 5

# SOME ANALYSIS

So much for the introductory material. Now that you know enough about viruses and virus protection to make intelligent mistakes, it's time to learn how to assert those mistakes with authority. That's what the rest of this book is about.

## 5.1  RISK ANALYSIS

There is a tendency to embrace interesting defenses as a strategy for virus protection. This may be a pleasant way to learn about different defenses, but it may also be disastrous from an operational standpoint. I take an analytical perspective on defense because I have specific goals I wish to achieve in my application of defenses. Generally speaking, my goal is to reduce costs associated with viruses.

My first specific goal, and one that is not achieved as often as we would like, is that the cost of attacks and defenses combined does not exceed the cost of attacks with no defenses. It may seem hard to believe, but probably the majority of current virus defense users use defenses that are more expensive than the cost of recovering from the attacks without those defenses.

This falls generally into the category of risk analysis. In risk analysis, the classic technique is to assess costs in terms of the probability of events and the costs associated with those events. You multiply the cost of an attack by the probability of that attack, and that gives you an "expected loss." For each proposed defense, you then multiply the attack probability with the defense in place by the cost of attack with the defense in place, subtract it from the undefended cost, and get the reduction in expected loss. If the cost of the defense is less than the reduction in loss, the defense is "cost-effective."

The typical procedure for applying risk analysis is to analyze all known attacks and all proposed defenses, and to implement all cost-effective defenses beginning with the one that is most cost effective. This technique works well for well-understood situations. For example, we have very good statistics on electrical component failure rates of various sorts, and we can easily assess costs and effects associated with using redundancy in different ways to reduce those risks. All we have to do is associate costs with negative outcomes, and we can "plug and chug" to find the optimal solution.

Unfortunately, virus protection issues are not as cut and dried as system failure rates based on component failure rates. Let's look at it blow by blow.

- We have very good statistics on component failure rates and well tested models on their impact on system failure rates. We have very poor statistics on computer virus incidents and even worse statistics on their impact on organizations.

- We have very good analysis of the costs and effects of specific redundancy techniques on reducing system failure rates. We have fairly poor analysis of the costs and effects of virus defense techniques, and two seemingly identical products may have very different characteristics under actual attacks.

- We have a small set of well known redundancy techniques to reduce risks of component failures. We have a large set of poorly understood virus defenses and no systematic way to evaluate them.

- We have good models of component failures and a limited number of corruptions to consider in any given component. We have no good models of protection problems and no specified set of protection impacts to consider in evaluating virus defenses.

So we know everything necessary to analyze risk in circuits, but almost nothing necessary to analyze risks in computer viruses. So much for the analytical approach! Well... not quite. Now that we know what we are missing, we can seek it out systematically.

## 5.2  PRODUCT COMPARISON BY TYPE

There is a hierarchy of defensive techniques in terms of their quality and assurance. The soundest defenses are hardware based with software assistance, while the least sound are pure foolishness. We list them here from most sound to least sound, but please understand that soundness is not the only criterion used in making rational decisions about viral defense.

### 5.2.1   Defense-in-Depth

Generally speaking, properly combined defenses do better than the individual component defenses do, so as a general principle this is better to have than to lack.

### 5.2.2   Perfect Defenses

The best kind of protection is a POset, but you can only buy POset structured protection for PCs, where the hardware limits its effectiveness. You can get computers with Bell-LaPadula secrecy, Biba integrity, and compartments, and try to configure them to act like a POset, but this is pretty difficult to do. You can try limited transitivity, but you can't buy any systems that provide it. You should apply limited functionality wherever you can. For example, if you have someone doing data entry, there's no reason for them to have general-purpose use of the computer system. It's a perfectly reasonable thing to do.

### 5.2.3   Integrity Shells

In theory, integrity shells are not quite as sound as limited sharing and limited function, but from a practical standpoint, sound protection can only limit viral spread, so integrity shells are probably still a necessary component of a rational defense plan.

### 5.2.4   Cryptographic Checksums

Cryptographic checksum systems are effective against most common attacks, but they are vulnerable to a number of theoretical and real-world attacks, and they have serious limitations. Furthermore, they cost about the same as integrity shells, so there is really no good reason to use a cryptographic checksum when you can get a full-fledged integrity shell for the same cost.

### 5.2.5   System Call Detection and Prevention

Some popular defenses try to limit viral spread by intercepting system calls and forcing the user to make protection decisions. These tend to create numerous false positives and false negatives, are very hard for the average user to understand, and only protect against a limited number of attacks. Ultimately, these sorts of systems can be used to simulate hardware-based protection. For example, the POset structured PC protection system is based on this technology.

### 5.2.6   Known-Virus Detectors

Virus scanners and monitors are technologies for searching for known viruses, and are a fairly popular defense, even though they are quite expensive to operate and maintain, and are ineffective against attacks the designer was not aware of at the last distribution. They tend to produce an expensive and false sense of security.

### 5.2.7   Special-Purpose Defenses

Special-purpose defenses only make sense under real and present attack. If you have a local university that has the Scores virus, and if you have MacIntosh computers, and if you have employees going back and forth to that university, it makes a lot of sense to get a Scores virus defense product in house right away. In fact, it probably makes sense to buy a site license for the university so they can clean up and you don't have to keep worrying about the Scores virus. But once that attack is gone, it's time to stop using that defense all the time. The reason is, it's just for one specific attack. It takes time and space, and if you did that for every attack, you would have 30 00 or more different special-purpose programs running every time you turned on your computer, checking for these attacks, taking up space, and taking up time. You don't want to end up with thousands of these defenses taking up all your disk space and computer time.

### 5.2.8   Looking for Questionable Instructions

Some defensive products look through files for known damage routines to try to detect programs that will cause significant harm, but in practice, this defense is ineffective and produces many false positives and false negatives.

### 5.2.9   Examining Printable Strings

The one ineffective defense that is considered worth using by many people is a program that searchers for printable strings in programs. If the program has a string that says, "ha, ha, I got you, I'm deleting all your files," you probably shouldn't run that program. On the other hand, just because a program doesn't state that it deletes all your files, doesn't make it safe to use.

## 5.3 EPIDEMIOLOGY OF COMPUTER VIRUSES

We have discussed how it is that viruses can spread at the mechanical level, but we have not yet considered how viruses spread from the standpoint of an organization or the global computing community. That's what epidemiology addresses.

### 5.3.1 Virus Vectors

In biology, we discuss the spread of diseases by taking about "vectors" through which "diseases" spread between "hosts." A typical example is the spread of malaria between people through the mosquito. In this case, people are the hosts, malaria is the disease, and the mosquito is the vector. A person with malaria is "bitten" by a mosquito, which in turn carries the diseased blood to the next person it "bites."

When we analyze the spread of disease in humans, we usually start at the macroscopic level by categorizing people as sick, well, susceptible, or immune. Disease is then traced in terms of infected members of the population rather than in terms of the number of infected cells in each person. In the epidemiological study of computer viruses, the same tactic has been taken. At this level, we are concerned with the vectors through which infections spread between computers, and the overall health state of machines, rather than which files are infected at what moment in time. Let's take a quick inventory of the vectors through which viruses spread in the world today, how they operate, their performance, and their connectivity characteristics.

- **Sneaker Net:** The so-called sneaker net is the vector formed by people carrying floppy disks and other media between computers. The key properties are that people are slow in terms of the number of machines reached per unit time, but they spread between organizations (e.g., through maintenance people, between work, school, and home, etc.) and are not centrally controlled or monitored.

- **LANs:** "Local Area Networks" typically include EtherNets, RS232 networks, Token Ring networks, X25 networks, Star networks, etc. The key properties are that they are local to an organization or an office, and they permit very fast communication and file sharing between computers within the local area.

- **Wans:** Wide Area Networks" (under our definition) include such varied examples as Internet (which connects hundreds of thousands of computers in a real-time manner), BitNet (a less real-time network of similar magnitude), publicly accessible bulletin board systems such as ComputServ, and all other networks that provide remote access over large distances. The key properties here are that remote access is generally point-to-point from a user point of view, and systems are effectively connected from any one place in the world to any other place in the world.

- **Software Distribution**:  These vectors are typified by a central site that distributes from thousands to millions of copies of a particular piece of software to thousands of distribution points over a wide geographic area. The key properties are that identical information is introduced into thousands of widely distributed sites over a period of weeks to months.

- **Hardware Distribution:** These vectors are typified by a central site that distributes from tens of hundreds of copies of a particular hardware/software system to points over a nationwide geographic area. The key properties are that similar information is introduced into hundreds of sites usually in one country over a period of weeks to months.

- **Combined Vectors:** Depending on the nature of the disease, several of these vectors may be combined sequentially or in parallel to form the effective vector set of a disease.

To understand how vectors interact with disease, a few examples may prove fruitful. We will start with examples that travel through only a few vectors, and go on to more complex cases from there.

Sneaker net was the only significant vector involved in the spread of the Brain virus. This is normally true of all "partition table" viruses (i.e., viruses that only infect the programs used to initialize a computer) because they can only vector naturally between devices that are used to bootstrap computers. In the case of PCs, this route goes from floppy disk to hard disk to floppy disk, et cetera. Since the only bootstrap vector between machines is usually floppy disks, only physically carrying floppy disks between computers normally causes this virus to spread naturally.

LANs typically spread "file-infecting" viruses very quickly. The main reason for this is that LANs are often used to permit file sharing between file server machines and numerous remote computers. LANs typically simulate virtual "file systems" in which remote files can be accessed as if they were local files. Since the remote access is transparent to the program performing the access, viruses that infect programs on a local disk using normal file system operations can infect remote files transparently. Once a file on the file server is infected, users on the other remote machines accessing the infected file may infect files on their own machine. A typical example is the "Jerusalem B" virus, which spreads very quickly on (among others) Novell networks. In this particular case, it is not unusual for nearly every PC on the network to become infected in a matter of hours. The success of this particular virus in this particular network is because the "login.exe" program normally stored on the file server and used by all users to gain access to the server can be infected by the virus when an infected administrator gains access to the server. Once this happens, all other computers in the network will become infected as they gain access to the server.

WANs typically allow long-distance movement of select files and remote login with terminal support only. Furthermore, there tends to be less and less communication as the distance between sites increases (i.e., within a country as opposed to between countries as opposed to between continents). The CompuServ incident that led to the widespread distribution of the MacMag virus described earlier serves as a typical example.

Software distribution is the most common method by which viruses become very widespread very quickly, and the most typical example I can recall is the case of an upgrade provided by Novell. Novell had fairly strong programs in place for detecting viruses in software distributions before they went to the duplication facility, but despite their efforts, they managed to distribute tens of thousands of copies of a virus. The culprit was their people's failure to follow procedures, which is another way of saying inadequate procedures. Disks ready for duplication were literally on the way out the door when it was discovered that a critical file was missing. They took the disks to an infected computer attached to their internal network to add the missing file, and the computer infected their master disk. They then duplicated the disk, packaged it, and shipped it out without any further quality controls. Some suggestions for Novell? Check sample disks after duplication, put distribution files on permanently write-protected disks, train your people better, provide virus protection for all of the users in your environment, seal the distribution disks between the distribution center and the duplication facility, and put a quality-control step at the duplication site.

Typhoid Mary had nothing on hardware distribution systems either, and one of the prime examples is the Michelangelo virus. Now I should begin by saying that this virus was nowhere near as widespread as some of the people who market antivirus software would have you believe. In the end, under 1 of every 10,000 computers was found to have this virus in the year the media made a big deal of it, while the "Stoned" virus infected from 2 to 10 times that number of computers in the same period. On the other hand, this virus was practically identical to several other viruses that only reached that level of infection over a period of several years. The reason for this was that a major manufacturer of joysticks distributed the virus on the disk containing the software needed to use their product. One of the side effects of this "Typhoid Mary" incident was that the U.S. and european community (E.C.) had proportionately more incidents than Mexico. The apparent reason  is that Mexico is a poor country in which computer games are too expensive for the average citizen, so very few joysticks are sold there.

In many cases, viruses spread through multiple vectors. For example, file-infecting viruses tend to spread through all of these media. A special class of viruses commonly called "multipartite" viruses are designed with multiple infection methods, which results in their being spread through multiple vectors. As an example, several viruses combine file infection with partition table infection. The point of stating this is to indicate that analyses may involve combined effects more complex than current models provide solutions for.

### 5.3.2   General Trends and Time Factors

Now that we know about some typical vectors, it may be handy to get an idea of how quickly infection spreads through these vectors. In this particular area, science has done a very poor job of providing raw data. This stems, among other reasons, from the hesitance of companies to report incidents and gather data on them, a lack of central reporting and analysis similar to that provided by the U.S. Centers for Disease Controls (CDC), and an unwillingness of companies to provide even the limited data they have to other companies or researchers. You will find that I make these estimates without very much substantiation and certainly without citation, but I think that once people start to look more deeply into this, they will find these results reasonably accurate (see Table 5.1).

The interpretation of this table is that for a given type of vector, it will typically take the stated amount of time between the first infection through that vector and when numerous infections will be found throughout the specified area. For example, from this table you would expect that a LAN-vectored virus would spread throughout an organization in a matter of hours, but that the LAN vector would not cause spread throughout a country, a continent, or the world. Hardware and software distribution only vector viruses to specific machines, so except in cases where whole organi-

**Table 5.1**

| Sneaker net | In org—days |
| --- | --- |
|  | In country—1–6 months |
|  | In continent—3–12 months |
|  | Global—12 + months |
| LANs | In org—hours |
|  | In country—n/a |
|  | In continent—n/a |
|  | Global—n/a |
| WANs | In org—n/a |
|  | In country—weeks |
|  | In continent—weeks |
|  | Global—months |
| Hardware distribution | In org—widespread but scarce |
|  | In country—widespread but sparse |
|  | In continent—rarely |
|  | Global—very rarely |
| Software distribution | In org—widespread but scarce |
|  | In country—weeks |
|  | In continent—weeks |
|  | Global—weeks-months |

zations purchase the same infected package and install it throughout, infections are widespread but sparse.

The combination of vectors dramatically alters the result. For example, if a software distribution of a file infecting virus goes to large numbers of organizations with LANs, it is likely that the initial widespread sparse distribution through a continent will quickly (i.e., within days of arrival) turn into a widespread and deeply embedded infection in each of the organizations impacted.

### 5.3.3   Susceptibility of Modern Systems

Given the empirical results for PCs, we might be misled into believing that all environments act similarly. It turns out that one of the major reasons PCs are so susceptible to so many different sorts of viruses is that they were designed to provide no protection of any sort. Operating system protection was commonly applied at the time PCs were first introduced, and it seemed strange to me that there was no protection in PCs. In 1988, I discussed this with members of the team at IBM that designed the original IBM PCs and the PC/M and DOS operating systems, and were at that time working on the design of OS/2. They said in no uncertain terms that they intentionally left protection out and intended to continue to do so. Their explanation was that a PC was a "Personal Computer" and that since people don't want to be protected from themselves, no protection would be put in. I put it to them that most people are not programmers and get software from other sources, that PCs are widely used in business, and that most people occasionally make mistakes and would like to have some protection against disastrous errors and omissions. Their response was essentially a repeat of their previous statement.

Time has told, however, and we are now beginning to see the rudiments of protection being put into even PC operating systems. They are still poorly designed and easily bypassed, but nevertheless, they are becoming somewhat hardened against accidental damage. But IBM PCs are not the whole story of the modern computing environment. A very substantial number of systems are Apple MacIntosh based; the Unix operating system is starting to become the system of preference as PC-based operating environments begin to approach it in terms of function, disk usage, and memory requirements; mainframe computers are slowly departing from the market but still have a substantial impact on operations of large corporations; Novell-, 3-Com-, Banyon-, and Unix-based LANs are quite popular; and global networking is already connecting over 1% of the world's computers.

Most of these systems provide far better performance and more capabilities than the DOS operating environment, and many are already far more cost effective than DOS because they provide most of the software that DOS users have to buy separately. In addition, some have substantial protection capabilities to prevent accidental and even malicious attempts to corrupt information, leak private data, deny other users services, and account for user actions. A natural question is how the protection capabilities of these environments impact susceptibility, and, as a result, how they affect the threshold of epidemic.

In August and September of 1992, I had the chance to perform a series of experiments with Sanjay Mishra at Queensland University of Technology to assess the impact of built-in protection in Novell and Unix LAN environments on their susceptibility to viruses. These experiments consisted of an exhaustive test of protection settings wherein we created enough files and directories to set one file to each of the possible protection settings in each directory, and to set the protection of directories containing these files to each of the possible directory protection settings.

Under each protection setting, we tried to cause infections with each of a set of viruses chosen or created to test different methods of file infection.

What we found was that while it is possible to configure these networks so as to reduce levels of susceptibility, the vast majority of networks are not configured in this way. The reasons seem to be that protection in these networks is hard to administer well, the safe configurations limit the utility of file servers, and the designers of commonly used programs stored on file servers design their programs without protection in mind, so that they often don't work with protection in place. Our susceptibility results were essentially that file-infecting viruses using standard I/O calls are not substantially limited by the LAN environment, while non-standard programs that infect systems by modifying directory entries, memory buffers, and other parts of the operating system cannot spread in these environments.

Similar results can eventually be derived for any virus of interest operating in any environment of interest by a similar technique of exhaustive test. Unfortunately, I don't have the personal resources to do this analysis for all of the viruses in all of the environments of the world, but other researchers are examining this in more depth, and it is fairly easy to estimate these results without doing detailed experiments.

### 5.3.4 How Defenses Impact Epidemiology

Now that we have discussed infection vectors and susceptibility, we have the background needed to examine epidemiology. In 1984, we knew that epidemiology would help lead to better understanding of the spread of viruses in the environment, but we had insufficient statistics to derive any useful results, and our feeble attempts at modeling were not good enough to publish anything substantial. We were left with the simple suggestion that this line might be useful in the future.

Probably the most detailed theory on computer virus spread was first published in 1989 by W. Gleissner. This theory appears to accurately parameterize the problem and its solution, but is widely ignored (probably) because it requires more mathematical sophistication to apply than most people are willing to use, and the parameters required for the analysis are hard to derive. It also makes some assumptions about uniformity that may not reflect the real-world situation.

In 1990, Peter Tippet proposed the "Tippet" theory of viral spread that assumes exponential growth and uniform global sharing. According to the Tippet predictions, we should have far more viruses today than we actually have, and most serious researchers discounted this theory early as being too simplistic. Exponential growth is an obvious characteristic of replicating systems which was suggested in the first virus papers, but there are limits on this growth that must be considered for a realistic theory.

In about 1990, Bill Murray began studying this subject in earnest, and started to publish results based on Baily's mathematical analysis of biological epidemics, which is commonly used in medical circles. A research team at IBM's High Integrity Computing Laboratory began to look seriously into that subject, and in 1993, an excellent article appeared in *IEEE Spectrum* by Jeff Kephart, Steve White, and Dave Chess of that research group. In this article, they pointed out quite accurately the connection between the large-scale (i.e., macroscopic) behavior of computer viruses and biological viruses, and performed simulations of some vectors to determine how the spread of viruses is impacted by network topology and the application of defenses. To get the whole picture, we should start as they do with a historical perspective.

The first statistics on the spread of disease were apparently gathered in the 1600s in London, and as a result, during the 1854 cholera epidemic, statistical data led physician John Snow to understand the link between dirty water supplies and disease. The water source was shut down, the epidemic ended, and the first victory for statistical epidemiology was in hand. Considering that the microscopic view of diseases involving bacteria and viruses wasn't developed until after that time, it is clear that we don't need to understand how infection works at a detailed level in order to effectively defend against it or analyze its operation. Smallpox was wiped out by the combination of the microscopic development of a vaccine and a macroscopic analysis of how to properly apply it. The cost of defense was dramatically lowered by the fact that only susceptible members of the population in areas where vectors could reach them were inoculated. It makes sense that select computer viruses might be cost-effectively controlled by a similar combination of technical defenses and epidemiological understanding.

Biological disease is normally modeled by considering each individual in a population as being in one of several "states." For example, an individual may be healthy, sick, dead, susceptible, immune, or a carrier. Vectors are modeled statistically by assuming a contact probability between individuals and an infection probability associated with the states of the individuals making contact. As a simple example, the likelihood of a healthy individual being infected by another healthy individual on any given contact is 0, while the change of a sick individual infecting a susceptible individual might be 1 in 3 for each contact. A table can be made for the likelihood of infection, and a state-transition diagram can be drawn to model the situation for any individual as Table 5.2 exemplifies.

**Table 5.2   Likelihood of infection.**

|          | Healthy | Infected | Immune |
|----------|---------|----------|--------|
| Healthy  | 0       | 0.5      | 0      |
| Infected | 1       | 1        | 1      |
| Immune   | 0       | 0        | 0      |

This table indicates that when an individual currently in a state indicated by the row name meets an individual currently in the state indicated by the column name, the likelihood of the individual whose state is indicated by the row name will be infected is as indicated. In this simple example, immunity is perfect, and the vectors used for the meeting cause infection 50% of the time. Similar tables can be produced for the effectiveness of known cures, the immunity provided by known defenses against known viruses through known vectors, and all other aspects of this problem. We can then produce a statistical simulation wherein each simulated system follows the tables to determine next states from current states and random numbers, and run those simulations enough times to get a good statistical model of what happens when infections arrive.

The same approach was taken at IBM. They modeled each computer as being susceptible to, immune from, or infected by any given virus. They call the rate of transition from susceptible to infected the "birth rate" of the virus ($b$), and the rate of transition from infected to susceptible the "death rate" ($d$) of the virus, and in keeping with the biological analogy, rediscovered that if the birth rate exceeds the death rate, "epidemic" is reached with a probability of $b/(b + d)$ and that the epidemic stabilizes at $b/(b + d)$ of the population infected. In the remaining $d/(b + d)$ cases, the infection will die out without ever reaching a substantial portion of the population. In numerical terms, if we have 3 births for every death, epidemic will occur in $\frac{3}{4}$ of the incidents, and on the average, $\frac{3}{4}$ of the population will be infected after the situation reaches equilibrium. In the remaining $\frac{1}{4}$ of the cases, epidemic will never occur, and the infection will subside after only a small portion of the population is infected and cured.

A major difference between the most common biological analysis and the recent innovations in the study of computer viruses is that topology is now being considered in the computer virus case. Topology is a fancy word for "how things are connected," and as we discussed above, there are a number of different methods of connecting computers that act as virus vectors in quite different ways. At IBM, substantial experiments were performed simulating networks with different topologies. The claim is that real computers are connected in a variety of different topologies, and that this will impact the spread of viruses. Indeed, their results show that, whereas systems assumed to have global homogeneous connectivity have infection growth rates that are exponential and approach the predicted ratios rapidly, systems with other topologies either approach the same ratios more slowly, approach lower ratios, or never become stable at all.

The components required in order to perform accurate analysis include a topological description of the vectors, their bandwidth, and the viruses they support; a characterization of the susceptibility of members of the population to different viruses due to defenses in place; a rate of introduction of viruses into the environment; a cure rate associated with the ability of defenses to cure members of the population; and a death rate associated with the rate at which systems become so damaged from disease that they are no longer able to cause infection through vectors.

One key to analyzing virus spread and the global impact of defenses is clearly indicated through this epidemiological approach. The same techniques are already used to a limited extent in biological epidemiology, and with the addition of topology and simulation, we may be able to improve both the biological and the information disease situation at a global level.

This having been said, I feel it is important to note that our study of epidemiology is still in a very rudimentary state. We don't yet have a good enough model of any of these factors to allow very good analysis, and the computer time required in order to get statistically valid results is quite significant. On the other hand, simulations such as those done at IBM can easily be done by any company or individual to get a good picture of their own situation and to analyze the effects of various defenses on their operation.

### 5.3.5  Another Vital Result

Perhaps the most important result of the IBM work in this area is their study of the impact of central reporting and response on incident size and duration. We had strong reasons to believe that rapid response dramatically impacted incident size and duration based on the difference between the behavior of the Lehigh virus and the Brain virus, and theoretical epidemiology clearly shows that the sooner you start to implement a cure with increased frequency, the less likely you are to have an epidemic. But the real test of any theory comes in practice, and that's just what IBM did.

In their study, they began a program of central reporting and response for large corporate customers. During the first months of their study, implementation was just beginning, and their statistics showed that 12% of the incidents spread beyond 5 computers. Once procedures for central reporting and response were well established, only 2.5% of incidents spread beyond 5 computers. The best defense they found in the response stage was to help users clean machines with known infections, and then check neighboring machines for infection.

### 5.3.6   The Impact of Evolution on Epidemiology

Earlier, I mentioned an interesting side effect of imperfect detection of the MtE and similar evolutionary viruses. Now I want to address it. The problem stems from the fact that some current evolutionary viruses are particularly hard to identify with virus-specific detection methods. Vessellin Bontichev, the well-known Bulgarian virus researcher, performed a series of experiments over a period of years testing the best virus scanners in the world for their detection rates against evolutions of viruses they claimed to detect. The results were somewhat upsetting. Even the best available known-virus detection systems picked up only 90–95% of the infections from such a virus after the defenders had access to the virus for more than a year. What would the effect of 90% detection be on the epidemiology of a virus in the environment? To answer that, I will begin with a scenario that assumes that mutations are random with respect to the detection mechanism in that each one has a 10% chance of going undetected.

A virus enters a system with 100 susceptible files and infects them all. The detector detects 90 of those cases, we clean them, and then resume normal operation with 10 undetectable infections remaining. These mutations reproduce and infect the remaining 90 files. The detector detects 81 of them (90% of the 90 new viruses), we clean them up, and leave 19 undetected infections. As the scenario proceeds, we have 27, 34, 41, 47, 52, 57, 62, 65,... and eventually, 100 undetected infected files after about 50 generations ($0.9^{50} < \frac{1}{200}$). At that point, our detector will tell us the system is clean, when in fact, every susceptible file is infected.

Now let us imagine that evolution is relatively nondramatic over a small number of generations, and therefore that there is a form of locality in the evolutionary process. Assuming that the detector fails because it misses some localized evolutionary characteristics, we might get a very different situation. Suppose that the characteristic that causes detection failure (let's call it the invisibility gene, or "IG" for short) generates 90% progeny retaining IG and 10% progeny not retaining IG, and similarly that 90% of infections not containing IG will not create progeny containing IG, and 10% of them will produce progeny with IG. After initial infection, we have 90 visible and 10 invisible viruses. As the invisible viruses reproduce, 90%

of the new infections retain IG, leaving only 9 progeny without IG. These 9 are detected, and in the next generation, only 1 infection fails to have IG. Finally, in the fourth generation, we are unlikely to detect any infections, even though all 100 susceptible files are infected.

In the larger community, the situation is even worse because the computers that get infected first will quickly weed out the evolutions without IG, so that as the virus spreads to neighboring machines, all of the viruses that spread will have IG. We would therefore expect that the neighbor of a system that first got infected and cleaned would start with 90% infections containing IG, and after one or two cleanings, IG would be successful throughout.

In addition to all of this, viruses with IG will spread without competition from those without IG because those without IG are killed by the defense. If it weren't for killing of those without IG, those with IG would not have places to reside, and might be unable to survive well. The presence of the imperfect detector will assure that the detected evolutions are killed off quickly, while the evolutions with IG will thrive. The net effect is that the defense will select the strains containing IG for widespread survival.

For those of you that don't recognize the analogy, this is exactly what is happening in the biological world with antibiotics. Our use of antibiotics has decreased the population of easily cured diseases, leaving a ripe breeding ground for the harder-to-kill ones. By defending against weaker stains, we have effectively created an environment where tougher strains have less natural competition, and therefore spread more widely. The surviving strains are the so-called superviruses that resist antibiotics and are becoming more and more widespread.

In effect, by widespread use of weak defenses, we kill off some viruses by driving them into extinction, but we also leave a ripe breeding ground for epidemics of what might otherwise be rare strains that our defenses miss. Furthermore, some forms of evolution have far different ways of adding or removing genes. Suppose that only 1 in $10^{12}$ evolutions of viruses without IG generate infections with IG, but those with IG generate infections without IG in only 1 in $10^6$ cases. As soon as one case of a virus with IG occurs, it will thrive, yielding a detection rate of only 1 in $10^6$ infections. I should note that Bontichev's virus samples involved only a few thousand samples, so it is very possible that this situation already exists with MtE.

This brings to light a possible flaw in the IBM analysis that I feel should be considered. In effect, one of their conclusions is that each individual or organization that protects itself also protects the rest of the global community. I would add a caveat that each individual or organization that uses inadequate detection techniques and thereby fails to detect select strains is doing a great disservice to the rest of the world by providing a ripe breeding ground for exotic strains that might not survive in either a more or less defended environment.

### 5.3.7  How Good Is Good Enough?

With this new understanding, the obvious question that comes to mind is how good must our detection be in order to prevent the widespread evolution of exotic strains. I regret to inform you that I have no closed-form solution, but I also have some very good news. The good news is that it is very likely that cryptographic checksums will not be susceptible to this problem of localized evolution. Here's why.

The reason select strains of viruses thrive with imperfect detection in the model just described is because they have some characteristic gene that makes them undetectable by the imperfect detector. This drives the evolutionary process toward a select gene pool. In the case of cryptographic checksums, the ability to detect the virus is essentially random with a probability related to the size of the checksum and the shape of the checksum's probability space. It is this randomness that prevents genetic niches from forming.

Suppose that we have an effectively random cryptographic checksum with 10 possible checksum values that depends on the entire state of a file. It then follows that any random change produces a 90% chance of detection, and thus a 10% chance of nondetection. Unlike the example above, it is not some special characteristic gene of the infection that causes one variation to go undetected, only the random probability that the detector will fail. Because of the randomness, even an exact copy of an undetected virus placed into a different file has only a 10% chance of going undetected. We return then to the first analysis wherein it takes 50 generations to inundate a system with 100 susceptible files.

But it turns out that things are quite a bit better than that with cryptographic checksums. It is quite simple to produce a cryptographic checksum system with a nondetection likelihood of 1 in $2^{32}$ by simply using 32 bit words in the checksumming mechanism. This means that only one out of about $2 \times 10^{10}$ infections go undetected. In a system with 101 files, if one undetected virus is in place, each time it infects 100 other files, the likelihood of one of those infections going undetected is 1 in $2 \times 10^8$. Put another way, it will take on the order of $10^8$ rounds of infection followed by cure before there will be 2 undetected infections in place. If we have a full system infection and cure it once a day, it will take almost 300,000 years before the second undetected infection will take place.

This of course leads us to a direct analysis of how good a random detector has to be. We select a desired average time between infections, and derive the size of the cryptographic checksum required to meet this goal. But it turns out that the situation in the community is even better with random detection of this sort because in any given environment, there may be multiple keys used by different checksumming systems and/or users. Multiple keys effectively increases the size of the checksum to the combined size of the keys, which has an exponential benefit on driving up the time between undetected infections.

I have one last parting shot. This analysis is true of systems that approach randomness in terms of their detection capabilities. Any simple pattern-based technique will not act this way. For example, a CRC-based checksum will have pattern-specific failures. If it turns out that a strain of a virus has a genetic component that leads to pattern specificity and that pattern coincides with detection failures in a CRC-based coding scheme, all bets are off. The CRC scheme will act just like any other nonrandom detector, and specific strains of a virus will find a niche. It may in fact be a fairly simple matter to design an evolutionary virus intended to evolve so as to find these niches. This returns us to the issue of attack complexity and the quality of cryptosystem design.

### 5.3.8  Epidemiology and Strategic Planning

The technical aspects of epidemiology provide a framework for analysis, but they don't provide a workable plan for strategic defense. Like experiments in the scientific method, epidemiology alone cannot provide progress. In science, we develop theories, test those theories with experiment, and use the results to improve our theories. In the same way, strategic planning for virus defense consists of developing strategies, testing those strategies with analysis and (where appropriate) simulations and experiments, and using the results to improve our strategies.

We will attempt to use our epidemiology as a guide to analysis, but because of the limits of our knowledge, it will not always provide the answers we seek. At this stage, it is more of a test of rationality that eliminates strategies that are likely to fail without asserting that they will succeed.

### 5.4  EXPOSURE ANALYSIS

Computer risk analysis has changed in two basic ways since the advent of computer viruses. The first change is that integrity corruption is now being considered. The second change is that we now have to consider transitive information flow in our analysis. There are also several historical assumptions about defenses that have now become outdated. For example, backups alone don't remove the risk from computer viruses.

Unfortunately, standard risk analysis makes the assumption that we can associate probabilities with events. Since we don't have any significant amount of reliable data on the factors that contribute to viral attack, it's hard to assess probabilities. Since inadequate detection is the norm, we cannot hope to get significant amounts of reliable data in the near future.

One alternative to risk analysis in this case is exposure analysis. Exposures are essentially the worst-case possibilities for loss under a given scenario. We can "cover" exposures by using appropriate defensive techniques, decide how many simultaneous failures of coverage to tolerate before coverage breaks down, and provide appropriate redundancy to reach that goal.

### 5.4.1  The Information Flow Model

I will start the discussion by showing a "subject/object" matrix commonly used to represent access control in modern computer systems (see Table 5.3).

In this model, there are sets of subjects (i.e., Joe, Alice, Bob, and Lam), objects (i.e., DB1, FILE1, BUP, FILE2, FILE3, and DB2), and a set of access "rights" [i.e., $r$ead and $w$rite ($r$ and $w$)]. The matrix is supposed to describe what's allowed and not allowed, but as we will now see, it doesn't quite do that.

Our subject/object matrix says, for example, that Joe can $r$ead or $w$rite DB1. If Joe can $w$rite DB1 and Joe can read DB1, Joe can *flow* ($f$) information to himself. I'm going to put that result in a different picture that describes how information flows in a system. Table 5.4 is called an information flow matrix, and it is used to describe the flow of information.

In this matrix, instead of dealing with "subjects" and "objects" and "rights" of subjects over objects, we deal with information "domains" and

**Table 5.3  A subject / object matrix.**

|       | DB1 | FILE1 | BUP | FILE2 | FILE3 | DB2 |
|-------|-----|-------|-----|-------|-------|-----|
| Joe   | *rw* | *r*  |     |       | *r*   | *r* |
| Alice |     | *rw*  | *rw* |      |       | *r* |
| Bob   |     |       | *r* | *rw*  |       | *rw* |
| Lam   |     | *r*   | *w* | *w*   | *rw*  |     |

**Table 5.4   An information flow matrix.**

|       | Joe | Alice | Bob | Lam |
|-------|-----|-------|-----|-----|
| Joe   | *f* |       |     |     |
| Alice | *f* | *f*   | *f* | *f* |
| Bob   | *f* | *f*   | *f* | *F* |
| Lam   | *f* | *f*   | *f* | *f* |

the flow of information between them. Joe can "*f*low" information to Joe, so we put an *f* at the intersection of Joe and Joe in the flow matrix. Let's look at Alice. Alice can *w*rite something that Alice can *r*ead, so Alice can *f*low information to Alice. Alice can *w*rite something that Joe can *r*ead, so Alice can *f*low information to Joe. Alice can also *f*low information to Bob and Lam.

Instead of using these sentences, we can abbreviate the wording by writing equations like this: "Bob *f* Joe" will mean "Bob can *f*low information to Joe," "Bob *w* Joe" will mean "Bob can *w*rite something that Joe can *r*ead," and "Bob *r* Joe" will mean "Bob can *r*ead something that Joe can *w*rite." Let's try it.

$$\text{Bob } w \text{ Joe} \Rightarrow \text{Bob } f \text{ Joe}$$

$$\text{Bob } w \text{ Alice} \Rightarrow \text{Bob } f \text{ Alice}$$

$$\text{Bob } w \text{ Bob} \Rightarrow \text{Bob } f \text{ Bob}$$

$$\text{Bob } f \text{ Alice AND Alice } f \text{ Lam} \Rightarrow \text{Bob } f \text{ Lam}$$

That last one is a bit tricky; Bob can *w*rite information that Alice can *r*ead, and Alice can *w*rite information that Lam can *r*ead, so Bob can *w*rite information that Lam can *r*ead indirectly via Alice. This shows the "transitivity" property of information flow that was not widely recognized until viruses demonstrated it so clearly by spreading from user to user. In the flow matrix, we use *F* to differentiate indirect flow as an aid to the reader. Let's press on.

$$\text{Lam } w \text{ Joe} \Rightarrow \text{Lam } f \text{ Joe}$$
$$\text{Lam } w \text{ Alice} \Rightarrow \text{Lam } f \text{ Alice}$$
$$\text{Lam } w \text{ Bob} \Rightarrow \text{Lam } f \text{ Bob}$$
$$\text{Lam } w \text{ Lam} \Rightarrow \text{Lam } f \text{ Lam}$$

**Table 5.5   An information flow matrix.**

|   | *a* | *b* | *c* | *d* | *e* | *f* | *g* | *h* |
|---|-----|-----|-----|-----|-----|-----|-----|-----|
| *a* | *f* | – | – | – | *f* | *f* | – | *f* |
| *b* | *f* | *f* | – | – | – | – | *f* | – |
| *c* | – | *f* | *f* | – | – | – | *f* | – |
| *d* | *f* | – | *f* | *f* | – | – | – | – |
| *e* | *f* | – | – | – | *f* | – | – | – |
| *f* | – | – | – | *f* | – | *f* | – | *f* |
| *g* | *f* | *f* | – | – | – | *f* | *f* | – |
| *h* | *f* | *f* | *f* | – | – | – | – | *f* |

So what's the real situation? Everybody except Joe can send information to everybody else. Joe can only send information to himself. If you look at the access matrix, you might think that Alice cannot read or write F2, but it's not true. So what this access matrix seems to mean, isn't what it really means at all.

Let's look at another example. I'm going to use the *flow* (*f*) description from now on, because it's a lot easier than "*r*ead's" and "*w*rite's." Table 5.5 shows another flow matrix with a few flows marked, and we are now going to determine all of the flows implied by this matrix. Here we go:

$$a \, f \, a \text{ (Given)}$$

$$a \, f \, e \text{ (Given)}$$

$$a \, f \, f \text{ (Given)}$$

$$a \, f \, h \text{ (Given)}$$

$$a \, f \, h \text{ and } h \, f \, b \Rightarrow a \, f \, b$$

$$a \, f \, h \text{ and } h \, f \, c \Rightarrow a \, f \, c$$

$$a \, f \, f \text{ and } f \, f \, d \Rightarrow a \, f \, d$$

$$a \, f \, b \text{ and } b \, f \, g \Rightarrow a \, f \, g$$

$$a \, f \text{ everyone!}$$

So *a* can flow information everywhere in the system! This was certainly not clear from the initial picture. Let's see what else we can see.

*a f a* (Given)

*b f a* (Given)

*d f a* (Given)

*e f a* (Given)

*g f a* (Given)

*f f d* and *d f a* $\Rightarrow$ *f f a*

*c f b* and *b f a* $\Rightarrow$ *c f a*

Everyone *f a*!

So now we know that everyone can send information to *a*. Well, if everyone can send information to *a* and *a* can send information to everyone, everyone can send information to everyone else!! Table 5.6 shows the real picture.

The chances are, whatever the system you have today, this is the case. You have "*r*ead" and "*w*rite" access controls over information, but if you really look at what they imply, chances are that everyone can send information to everyone else. Anyone in your system could damage or leak any and all information.

**Table 5.6  The real picture.**

|   | *a* | *b* | *c* | *d* | *e* | *f* | *g* | *h* |
|---|---|---|---|---|---|---|---|---|
| *a* | *f* | *f* | *f* | *f* | *f* | *f* | *f* | *f* |
| *b* | *f* | *f* | *f* | *f* | *f* | *f* | *f* | *f* |
| *c* | *f* | *f* | *f* | *f* | *f* | *f* | *f* | *f* |
| *d* | *f* | *f* | *f* | *f* | *f* | *f* | *f* | *f* |
| *e* | *f* | *f* | *f* | *f* | *f* | *f* | *f* | *f* |
| *f* | *f* | *f* | *f* | *f* | *f* | *f* | *f* | *f* |
| *g* | *f* | *f* | *f* | *f* | *f* | *f* | *f* | *f* |
| *h* | *f* | *f* | *f* | *f* | *f* | *f* | *f* | *f* |

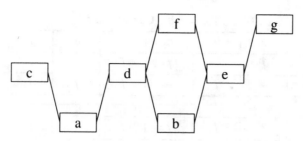

**FIGURE 5.1**   Another POset.

Let me just point something out for the more mathematically minded among you. If you have a POset, you have an upper triangular matrix. All POsets can be written as upper triangular matrices, and all upper triangular matrices can describe POsets (although they don't necessarily describe all of the implied flows) (see Figure 5.1).

Suppose we are concerned about what happens if two people collude to corrupt or leak information. For example, we might like to assure that no three people in our organization can collude to corrupt more than 20% of the organization's information. It turns out that to determine the corruptive effects of collusion, you simply OR the rows of the matrix, and to determine the leakage effects of collusion, you simply OR the columns (see Table 5.7).

In this example, if $a$ and $b$ collude to corrupt information, they can corrupt the OR of their rows in the matrix. Let's look at it. If $a$ launches a virus, it could potentially get to $a$, $c$, $d$ and $f$, while if $b$ launches a virus, it gets to $b$, $d$, $e$, $f$, and $g$. Between $a$ and $b$, everything is corruptible (see Table 5.8).

**Table 5.7**

|   | *a* | *b* | *c* | *d* | *e* | *f* | *g* |
|---|-----|-----|-----|-----|-----|-----|-----|
| *a* | $f$ | – | $f$ | $f$ | – | $f$ | – |
| *b* | – | $f$ | – | $f$ | $f$ | $f$ | $f$ |
| *c* | – | – | $f$ | – | – | – | – |
| *d* | – | – | – | $f$ | – | $f$ | – |
| *e* | – | – | – | – | $f$ | $f$ | $f$ |
| *f* | – | – | – | – | – | $f$ | – |
| *g* | – | – | – | – | – | – | $f$ |

**Table 5.8   Corruptions.**

|   | *a* | *b* | *c* | *d* | *e* | *f* | *g* |
|---|-----|-----|-----|-----|-----|-----|-----|
| *a* | f | – | f | f | – | f | – |
| *b* | – | f | – | f | f | f | f |
| = | f | f | f | f | f | f | f |

**Table 5.9   Leakage.**

|   | *c* | *d* | *g* | = |
|---|-----|-----|-----|---|
| *a* | f | f | – | f |
| *b* | – | f | f | f |
| *c* | f | – | – | f |
| *d* | – | f | – | f |
| *e* | – | – | f | f |
| *f* | – | – | – | – |
| *g* | – | – | f | f |

Similarly, if you are worried about leaking secrets, *c*, *d*, and *g* could collude to leak information from everywhere except *f* (see Table 5.9).

This gives us an efficient and easy to use way of automatically analyzing systems for the affects of collusion. The technique is quite simple. First, we have to take transitivity into account by finding all of the indirect information flows and putting them in the matrix. In this example, we have already done this part of the process, which is why we call it a "flow control matrix" rather than a "flow matrix." To determine the effect of collusion on leakage, or "OR" the columns of the colluding domains in the flow control matrix. To determine the effect of collusion on corruption, we "OR" the rows of the colluding domains in the flow control matrix.

### 5.4.2   The New Exposure Analysis

Now that we understand how systems can be modeled and analyzed using information flows, exposure analysis becomes straightforward. We will use the POset in Figure 5.2 as our example to demonstrate the analysis.

The first step in the analysis is to convert the POset into a flow control matrix describing its behavior. Although this will not be necessary to

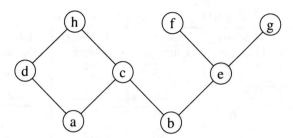

**FIGURE 5.2**   A POset.

analyze our small example, you will find it most useful for more complex systems (see Table 5.10). Begin by putting in the flows shown directly in the picture, and then add the indirect flows. When you're done, you should have a picture with 20 *f* marks in it.

The next step is to analyze the effects of corruption and leakage in your organization. This involves considerable effort, but if you have done risk analysis before, most of the information should already be available. If not, you should probably consider it as an important step toward understanding your exposures. We have provided a set of local leakage and corruption exposures for this example, and have started to fill out the table with results. You should fill out the rest of the table once you understand how to perform the analysis (see Table 5.11).

Every domain has local corruption and leakage values. The "local" corruption value is the total financial damage resulting from the worst-case corruption of information in that domain alone. For example, if we have a mailing list with names, addresses, and postal codes, the worst-case corrup-

**Table 5.10   Your turn.**

|   | *a* | *b* | *c* | *d* | *e* | *f* | *g* | *h* |
|---|---|---|---|---|---|---|---|---|
| *a* | | | | | | | | |
| *b* | | | | | | | | |
| *c* | | | | | | | | |
| *d* | | | | | | | | |
| *e* | | | | | | | | |
| *f* | | | | | | | | |
| *g* | | | | | | | | |
| *h* | | | | | | | | |

**Table 5.11   An exposure analysis table.**

|   | (Local) Leakage | (Local) Corrupt | (Global) Leakage | (Global) Corrupt |
|---|---|---|---|---|
| *a* | 25 | 75 | 25 | 360 |
| *b* | 250 | 10 | 250 | 1335 |
| *c* | 1000 | 25 | | |
| *d* | 750 | 250 | 775 | 260 |
| *e* | 90 | 200 | | |
| *f* | 75 | 90 | | |
| *g* | 25 | 1000 | | |
| *h* | 10 | 10 | 2035 | 10 |

tion in this domain alone would be the amount of money required to replace, repair, or reenter the mailing list. In this case, we have assessed 10 billion dollars (all numbers here are in billions of dollars). We have a 10-unit local corruption value associated with that mailing list, because we can reenter it very easily.

Even though correcting any corruption in this domain may be quite inexpensive, the effect of the domain becoming corrupted might be horrendous. For example, suppose you are sending out bills using the corrupt mailing list. Your use of the corrupt information may cause you to miss payments for a month or more, generate automatic collection letters, and otherwise damage your business and customer relations. Those are indirect effects of a corruption. Since a virus can spread anywhere information can go, we have to consider the corruption value of every reachable domain as part of the global effect of corruption. The result is that a corruption in *b* could effect *b*, *c*, *e*, *f*, *g* and *h* (the columns with *f* marked in *b*'s row of the flow control matrix). In order to get the global corruption value of *b*, we add up the local corruption values of these domains and place the sum in the table. I urge you to do this for all of the remaining entries as practice. Is there a mistake in the way I filled out an entry?

The analysis for leakage is essentially the same, except that we look at columns instead of rows in the flow control matrix, and we add local leakage values instead of corruption values to get the total exposure. The "local leakage" value is the worst-case damage that could result from all the information is that domain being leaked in the worst possible way (i.e., the Murphy's law leakage). To determine the global leakage exposure of *h*, we look at column *h* in the flow control matrix (once it is filled out), and determine that we have to add up the leakage values of $a$, $b$, $c$, $d$, and $h$. Again, I urge you to fill out the remainder of the table and determine whether I have made any mistakes.

## 5.5   A COST ANALYSIS OF VIRUSES AND SELECT DEFENSES

Exposure analysis is one part of the picture, but on the other side of the coin, we have to analyze the costs of defenses in order to determine the most cost-effective way to cover exposures. The major competing technologies for viral defense in the market today are virus scanners, virus monitors (programs that scan for known viruses just before execution), cryptographic checksums, and integrity shells; so we will limit our discussion to these cases.

We will avoid undue description here by starting out with formulas that describe the total costs per year of attack and defense. The interested reader can locate more detailed information through the annotated bibliography. We begin by defining terms in Table 5.12.

Most of these terms are self-explanatory, but a few are a bit obscure. The licensing cost for cryptographic checksums and integrity shells is normally a one-time cost, whereas for scanners and monitors, regular updates force licenses to be paid over time. To compensate, we use 10% per year of the total licensing cost for integrity shells and cryptographic checksums as an equivalent to the yearly licensing cost for scanners and monitors. $o_i$ is a term that describes the rate of spread of a virus, and has experientially been about 2 for a typical PC in a typical environment, and about 10 for a typical PC in a LAN environment.

**Table 5.12   Cost analysis.**

| | | | |
|---|---|---|---|
| $T_s$ | total for scanner | $s$ | systems |
| $T_c$ | total for crypto checksum | $c$ | checks/year |
| $T_m$ | total for monitor | $e$ | employee cost/min |
| $T_i$ | total for integrity shell | $u$ | dist-cost*update-count |
| $t_s$ | minutes per scan | $t_c$ | minutes per check |
| $l_s$ | license for scanner | $l_c$ | license crypto-checksum |
| $l_m$ | licence for monitor | $l_i$ | license integrity shell |
| $a_n$ | new attacks | $a_o$ | old attacks |
| $r_s$ | system cleanup costs | $r_f$ | file cleanup costs |
| $d$ | distribution costs | $o_i$ | comm-rate$^{[K/c]}$ |

Now we show the equations for total cost:

Scanners:

$$T_s = s[\underbrace{cet_s + l_s + u}_{\text{use}}] + \overbrace{\underbrace{a_n r_s s}_{\text{new}} + \underbrace{a_o r_s o_i}_{\text{old}}}^{\text{attacks}} + d$$

Checksums:

$$T_c = s[\underbrace{cet_c + l_c}_{\text{use}}] + \overbrace{[a_n + a_o]r_s o_i}^{\text{attacks}} + d$$

Monitors:

$$T_m = s[\overbrace{l_m + u}^{\text{use}}] + \overbrace{\underbrace{a_n r_s s}_{\text{new}} + \underbrace{a_o r_f}_{\text{old}}}^{\text{attacks}} + d$$

Integrity shells:

$$T_i = \overbrace{sl_i}^{\text{use}} + \overbrace{[a_n + a_o]r_f}^{\text{attacks}} + d$$

Since $d$, the cost of initial distribution, appears in all equations, we can eliminate if for purposes of comparison without loss of information.

To make comparisons, it is easiest to subtract equations. We begin by comparing $T_s$ to $T_c$ as follows:

$$T_s - T_c = s[ce[t_s - t_c] + [l_s - l_c + u]] + a_n r_s[s - o_i]$$

Unless checking is so rare that all systems get infected before checking detects an infection, $o_i \ll s$, which leads to

$$ce[t_s - t_c] + u + [l_s + l_c] + a_n r_s$$

With daily scanning or checking, any reasonable difference in licensing fees are dominated by scanning and checking costs. Update costs also tend to dominate licensing fee differences for this sort of system, so we can simplify in most cases to

$$u - ce(t_c - t_s) + a_n r_s$$

so scanners are less expensive if and only if

$$u + a_n r_s > ce(t_c - t_s)$$

In other words, if update and recovery costs from new attacks combine to exceed the cost difference between scanner scanning times and checksum checksumming times, scanners are less expensive than cryptographic checksums. Using typical values, we compute \$350/year in checking cost difference between the two systems. Thus, if recovery costs are kept low, scanning times don't increase significantly, and relatively few new viruses enter the environment each year, then scanning for known viruses is more cost effective than periodically looking for changes with cryptographic checksums.

We now compare scanners to monitors:

$$T_s - T_m = scet_s + (l_s - l_m) + a_o[r_s o_i - r_f]$$

We assume that licensing fees for scanners and monitors are approximately the same relative to scanning costs. We also note that $o_i > 1$ for any reasonable scenario, and the cost to clean a system ($r_s$) is normally far greater than the cost to clean a single file ($r_f$). We then get

$$T_s - T_m = scet_s + a_o r_s$$

Since all of the terms are positive, $T_s$ is always greater than $T_m$, and thus periodic scanning for known viruses always costs more than monitoring for known viruses in each program just before it is run.

Now the costs of checksums and integrity shells

$$T_c - T_i = s[(l_c - l_i) + cet_c] + [a_n + a_o](r_s o_i - r_f)$$

Assuming that licensing costs are not large relative to periodic checksumming costs, we can drop the $(l_c - l_i)$ term. Since $o_i > 1$ for any reasonable system, and system repair costs are almost always more expensive than repair of a single file, we simplify to

$$T_c - T_i = scet_c + [a_n + a_o]r_s o_i$$

Since all of these terms are positive, $T_c$ is always greater than $T_i$, and thus checking each program for change just before running it is always more cost effective than periodic system-wide change detection with cryptographic checksums.

Finally, we will compare integrity shells to monitors

$$T_m - T_i = s[(l_m - l_i) + u] + a_n r_s s + a_o r_f - [a_n + a_o]r_f$$

$$= s[(l_m - l_i) + u] + a_n[r_s s - r_f]$$

The number of systems $s$ is always at least 1, and for any reasonable system, $r_s \gg r_f$. If we assume that yearly licensing cost differences are small compared to update costs, we get a per-system cost difference of

$$T_m - T_i = u + a_n r_s$$

We conclude that integrity shells are always less expensive than virus monitors because all of these terms are positive. The cost difference comes from the update cost required to keep monitors up to date, and the cost of cleanup for attacks that monitors don't detect.

Another way to look at this result is that in order for a monitor to be more cost effective than an integrity shell, the yearly licensing cost of an integrity shell must exceed the yearly licensing cost of a monitor by the update cost and the undetected attack cleanup cost.

For monitors to be more cost effective than integrity shells in a case where updates cost $5 per system and are done each quarter, and assuming no unmonitored attacks happen, integrity shell license costs would have to exceed monitor license costs by $200 per system! This is because the yearly update cost comes to $20 per system for monitors, and there is no update cost associated with integrity shells. The $20 per year monitor cost is approximately equivalent to borrowing $200 per system for excess licensing fees of an integrity shell. Integrity shells on the market today cost under $100 per system in moderate quantities, and are thus always more cost effective than any of these other techniques.

It also turns out that as system performance increases, integrity shells and cryptographic checksums become less expensive faster than scanners and monitors. This is because improved performance makes checksumming faster and disk improvements make on-line backups cheaper, while the update costs of monitors and scanners stay the same, and the number of viruses that have to be checked goes up.

On-line backups turn out to have negligible costs relative to their options for repair, and their costs decrease with time and the evolution of computers. For example, current disk prices are on the order of $1 per megabyte, while the average system has relatively little information suitable for on-line backup, and for a small reduction in performance, file compression can reduce on-line backup costs even further.

Except under the most contrived circumstances, integrity shells are the most cost effective of the antivirus techniques currently available for untrusted systems, and this gap will widen with the passage of time.

# Chapter 6

# STRATEGY AND TACTICS IN VIRUS DEFENSE

All of the information presented so far addresses techniques, their features, their shortcomings, and how to analyze them in different ways. But all of this information is essentially useless unless you know how to apply it. That's what we're going to talk about now.

There are two critical planning components for virus defense: strategic planning and tactical planning. The difference between strategy and tactics is commonly described in terms of time frames. Strategic planning is planning for the long run, while tactical planning is planning for the short run. Strategic planning concentrates on determining what resources to have available and what goals we should try to achieve under different circumstances, while tactical planning concentrates on how to apply the available resources to achieving those goals in a particular circumstance.

In the planning process, so many things should be considered that we cannon even list them all here. They tend to vary from organization to organization and person to person, and they involve too many variables to draw general conclusions without sufficient facts. I have collected what I consider to be the major issues in planning for viruses, and done some initial analysis to help in your planning, but my efforts on your behalf cannot possibly substitute for analysis by the experts with both technical and organizational knowledge in your application.

For practice, I have also provided a set of sample scenarios and some partial solutions. I hope this will aid you in your efforts to understand how to deal with this problem, but these solutions are not intended to be comprehensive or definitive. They are only food for thought.

## 6.1 GENERAL PRINCIPLES

Fist and foremost, planning a defense is a study in tradeoffs. No single defense is safest for all situations, and no combination of defenses is cost effective in all environments. This underscores a basic protection principle. *Protection is something you do, not something you buy.*

What do I mean when I say that? Suppose we want to protect our house from water damage. It doesn't matter how good a roof we buy for our house, it's not going to protect our house forever. We have to maintain the roof to keep the water out. It's the same with protecting information systems. You can't just buy it; you have to do it.

### 6.1.1   General Strategic Needs

At the core of any strategy is the team of people that develop it and carry it out, both in the long run and in tactical situations. The first and most important thing you should do is gather a good team of people to help develop and implement strategy.

Any strategy that is going to work requires resources, both over the long run and during tactical situations. We commonly see strategies that fail because of insufficient resources, resources poorly applied, a lack of consideration of the difference between strategic and tactical needs, and insufficient attention to detail.

In order to assure that strategies will work in times of need, it is necessary to test tactical components ahead of time. The most common problem we encounter in tactical situations is events that were not anticipated during strategic planning and not discovered during testing. The effect is almost always a very substantial added expense.

Antivirus strategy is a part of overall strategy, and should not be isolated. It is common to have a virus team that has no impact on decisions to purchase hardware or software. It turns out that fairly simple differences in overall planning can make a dramatic differences in the costs associated with virus defense.

### 6.1.2   General Tactical Needs

Efficient response in tactical situations normally calls for the complete attention of some number of trained experts carrying out well-defined roles. In addition, it commonly requires that a substantial number of nonexperts act in concert at the direction of those trained experts.

Tactical situations require that sufficient resources be on hand to deal with the situation. If sufficient resources are not present, the cost of attaining those resources on an emergency basis tends to be very high, the delays caused by the acquisition process may be even more costly, and the inexperience with the newly attained resources may cause further problems.

A small amount of resources properly applied almost always beats a large amount of resources poorly applied. You don't necessarily need to spend a lot to have a strong defense, but you have to spend wisely and react quickly.

## 6.2 SOME WIDELY APPLICABLE RESULTS

Even though there are a vast array of different environments, there are some strategies and tactics that seem to be almost universally beneficial.

- **Consider Highest Exposures First:** In planning a strategy for defense, it is important to consider the potential harm when assessing what to do. Specifically, the highest exposures should receive the most attention, and should thus be addressed with the highest priority.

- **Use the Strongest Defenses Feasible:** All other things being equal, it is better to use a stronger defense than a weaker one. As a rule, sound prevention is better than detection and cure, and general-purpose detection and cure is bette than special-purpose detection and cure, but a false sense of security is worse than any of them.

- **Proactive Defense is Critical:** "Be Prepared," it's the Boy Scout slogan, and it applies in virus defense more than most places. In every comparison I have done or seen, people that take proactive action get away with lower costs, smaller incidents, and faster recovery than those who simply wait for a problem and then react.

- **Rapid Central Reporting and Response Works:** Epidemiological results are clear in showing that rapid centralized reporting and response reduces incident size, incident duration, and organizational impact. If the stories of the Lehigh and Brain viruses doesn't convince you, the evidence gathered and published by IBM must.

- **CERT Teams Work:** Regardless of what you call them, you need a team that receives incident reports and responds to them on an emergency basis. This team is virtually always the same team that helps determine proper proactive strategy, implements tactical response, and performs analysis after incidents to improve future performance.

- **Keep Good Records and Analyze Them:** Record keeping is one of the most valuable aids to improving tactical and strategic response. When properly analyzed, records of incidents allow planners to devise more cost-effective tactical responses, which in turn provide more accurate information for strategic planning to reduce costs while improving response.

- **Don't Punish Victims:** One of the most common strategic mistakes is punishing those who report incidents or accidentally become a vector for viruses. Punishment may be direct or indirect, and may include such subtleties as requiring the victim to do extra paperwork or such abusive treatment as getting a lecture on following written policies. When you punish victims, you increase response time because others become hesitant to report incidents, and lest you think this is simply a supposition, statistics support the improved response of organizations with policies not to punish.

- **Procedural Policies Fail in Prevention:** Many organizations make the mistake of relying on procedure as a preventive defense. The fact is, people are not perfect. When they make mistakes, assessing blame is not an effective response. You should plan on procedural failures and plan a response that considers people as they really are.

- **Training and Education Works:** You have to train your users to use your tactical capabilities or they will be ineffective in live situations, and you have to educate your experts in order to develop an effective plan and carry out the plan effectively in emergencies.

- **All Your Eggs in One Basket:** If we have gained anything from our efforts, it is the understanding that diversity works. If you have a choice of buying 100 copies of either of two nearly equivalent products, buy 50 of each, and haggle to keep the prices low. Where one fails, the other may succeed, and epidemiology shows that covering more attacks is far more important than covering every machine identically.

- **Defense-in-Depth Works:** The synergistic effects of multiple defenses make defense-in-depth the most effective technical solution we have to date. A similar situation appears to be appropriate in the nontechnical defense arena, but I can't prove it with hard data yet.

## 6.3   SOME EXAMPLES

Perhaps the most useful way to teach strategy and tactics is by example. To stimulate thought, I have devised a range of scenarios and performed some initial analysis to give you an idea of the directions that make sense to me. Unfortunately, I cannot take the space here to provide the sort of in-depth analysis required for full planning, but I hope that you will get enough good ideas from my approach to be able to get you started.

### 6.3.1   Typical Attacks

We will begin with some typical attacks. Whatever plans you make it, it will be helpful to consider these attack scenarios and how your plan will handle them. Consider it a form of testing at a theoretical level, but be certain that you don't devise your strategies and tactics simply to respond to these attacks. If you do so, you will have a meager defense. Rather, devise your plan, and then test it to assure that it provides coverage. To the extent that it fails to cover relevant scenarios, consider how to make endemic changes that will address these areas, and then devise additional testing strategies to reveal further flaws.

- The manufacturer of your most recent software acquisition had a virus and didn't know it. You installed the new software, and the virus spread throughout your computers for a few weeks before damage began to occur. You didn't notice the damage at first because it was widely scattered and only a few problems were reported, but by now you are having thousands of files damaged every day and your operations are failing on a widespread basis. Your backups are infected and you don't know where the virus came from or how far back you have to go to get a clean backup.

- A user brought a floppy disk home to do some late night work, and the disk got infected by a PC product at home. When returning to work, the user forgot that this particular disk was used on the home machine, and used it on the computer at work.

- A systems programmer thought he was about to be fired, so he introduced a virus into a library program, and then removed the infection from the source code. As other users used the libraries, other libraries and user files became infected. The attacker then recompiled the library with the clean source before the next backup, to remove the last trace of the cause. After about three weeks, the infected executables slowly migrated to the production system.

- A rival firm sent a spy to sabotage your facility. The spy got a job as a computer operator on the graveyard shift, and began introducing newly designed viruses into you system at the rate of about one a day over a 3-month period. All of the viruses had long delays between infection and damage, large use-based delays, or delays based on conditions that are likely to come up only once a year or so. Each was designed to cause random changes in data files, occasional system crashes, periodic slowdowns, or other minor mischief.

- A disgruntled employee gets a copy of the CARO[1] collection of over 3000 viruses, and runs every one of them at least once while logged into your file server. This employee also inserts every floppy disk they can get their hands on into the infected computer, and puts all of the disks back where they were originally found.

- A disgruntled employee of a disk duplicating firm decides to infect disks before duplicating them. You use this firm to disseminate your disks to your customers and internal users.

Most of the people that look at these scenarios believe that they are vulnerable to some or all of these attacks. At this point, I usually ask: "So what are you going to do?" After all, it's almost the end of the course, and you believe that your systems are vulnerable to a wide range of devastating attacks. Tomorrow morning, you will be back in your organization, and I want to know what you are going to do about it. To do nothing in light of what we now know would be negligent at best, so that is not an acceptable answer... I'll wait..."

### 6.3.2   The Small Business Scenario

You own a small business with 5 physically secure timesharing Unix computers, networked with limited functionality (for data transfers and database updates only). With the exception of your programmer, who you trust implicitly (because he's your brother and he owns half of the business), all of the users use the system only through a menu system that does not allow any programming whatsoever.

The first question that usually comes up is whether you should trust your brother, but it turns out this is irrelevant to the virus issue because he's the systems programmer, and can do whatever he wants to the computer without the use of a virus.

The limited functionality of the system makes viral attack by the user community essentially impossible if it is properly implemented, but unfortunately, almost nobody does this properly. Let's assume that it is done right for the purposes of this example.

---

[1]Computer Antivirus Research Organization.

The last possibility is that he might accidentally import some infected software. We almost all depend on some external software from time to time, and if that contains a virus, then the virus may spread throughout the system. That's probably the only serious exposure in this environment.

Now that we know the exposure of concern, we should form a committee of two (you and your brother) and assess.

For perfect defense, we can limit sharing, limit transitivity, or limit functionality. We have limited function as far as possible, but we cannot do that effectively for imported software. The spread of viruses induced by external software can be reduced by placing that software only on computers requiring it, and Unix allows us to limit sharing, so we should do so to the extend that this is appropriate. This takes little effort, and as long as your brother is willing, why not?

In the way of imperfect defenses, we have change control, multiversion programming, and integrity shells. Change control doesn't really apply to external software since we cannot normally get sources or effectively deal with changes using limited personnel. Multiversion programming is too expensive for this application. Only integrity shells are left, and they can be used inexpensively and transparently in this environment. Backups should be performed regularly to assure that any corruptions can be repaired if detected in time.

So there we have our strategy; you should combine limited sharing with integrity shells to defend against the external virus threat in this environment, and continue to use limited function against the internal threat. Regular backups will also be implemented.

As to tactics, the plan is simple. Your brother will be responsible for everything. In case of an incident, the systems will be disconnected from each other until the infected system(s) are identified. The infected systems will be cleaned by restoring from backups, while uninfected systems will be reintegrated and operations continued as soon as possible. You should also learn how to perform the mechanical operations associated with this recovery and have at least one practice session every 6 months so that in a pinch, there is another person able to restore operations. Make certain your brother agrees to this plan, and have him consider appropriate tools for the task.

### 6.3.3   The University Scenario

You are the president of a major university with a 100-million-dollar research budget, thousands of computers of all sorts, networks running everywhere, 40,000 students who take computer courses, and only scanning defenses in place. You were infected by the Internet virus in 1988, and other viruses have shown up on campus every year since that time, but you still aren't doing any central planning, and the computer center is not handling things as well as you might like. The student newspaper is pressing the issue, the faculty is protesting the heavy-handed way you treat these attacks, and your budget for computers is (always) running low.

If you have no central planning in place, you should immediately form a committee to deal with this issue. The committee should be formed of (as a minimum) the director of the computer center, the chair of the computer science department, the chief financial officer, the president of the student body, the dean of students, and a top-level technical person who will be tasked with operating the campus CERT. As a beginning, this committee should meet for at least one hour per month with the CFO as the chair until a strategic plan is in place and the campus CERT is operating effectively. After that point, the committee should be notified of all incidents and meet at least twice per year to review performance and cover any issues that come up, and to keep the issue on the table. In emergency situations, select committee members may have to get involved at a deeper level. The committee should copy the meeting notes to the president of the university and provide briefings to the board of directors at least once per year as a normal part of covering university activities. It might be sensible to make this part of an existing information security committee or to form an information security committee with this as a starting point if none exists.

The committee should be concerned with several key issues as a starting point. The first issue should be identifying key exposures. We would normally find a financial system, an inventory-control system, a system for keeping track of academic records, and other administrative systems. In a university, we usually also have a large assortment of computers used for educational and research purposes, typically called academic systems. In addition to the computers, there are normally a wide range of networks and gateways to provide connectivity both within the campus and with external networks like the Internet and the EDUnet. In many cases, this network also includes the university telephone system.

The next issue is an analysis of the exposures in each of these systems, which is normally carried out by the CFO in conjunction with the technical expert and the other relevant committee members in their own specialty areas. To the extent that the systems interact, we also have to consider the interactions. Each system typically has different vulnerabilities because of its use and users. If all of these systems interact arbitrarily with each other, the whole environment will act as one homogeneous network, and all of the threats in each environment will be threats to the entire environment.

Another issue to be addressed is possible technical defenses. Although these should be studied in depth by the technical member of the committee, the first thing that springs to my mind is that the administrative systems are operationally critical and do not normally require outside connectivity or a high rate of change. Limited sharing, limited function, sound change control, and integrity shells seem to be in order here.

In the academic computing environment, things are quite different. Limited sharing is generally considered a hindrance to the communications necessary in order to have effective learning. On the other hand, when most academics are questioned, they feel that some things should be protected and others should not. Nevertheless, limited sharing is widely frowned upon. Limited function is also infeasible in most areas of academic computing because most of the software is in support of research, and therefore must be changeable. Sound change control is also inappropriate to the academic experimental environment. The only alternative is an integrity approach in which we use commonly available tools to detect and remove viruses, and perform ongoing epidemiological studies to adapt our defenses to the changing situation.

In the nontechnical area, university policies regarding the behaviors that tend to produce incidents should be devised as the CERT gathers and analyzes incident data. The student body president is key to this activity, since these policies will ultimately involve the way students work, and their input and cooperation will be required in both the development of policy and its implementations.

Tactical planning in the university environment will almost certainly involve a rapid CERT response to reported incidents, a plan for rapidly providing repair capabilities to all willing members of the community, a mechanism for receiving reports of and dispatching responses to incidents, and a rapid collection and analysis system to trach incidents and indicate appropriate response on a real-time basis. It is likely that a broad mix of different defenses will be used in such a diverse environment, and it is incumbent on the CERT to get a comprehensive understanding of all of the different defenses so they can properly respond to the different types of information they may receive.

### 6.3.4  The Financial Institution Scenario

You are the computer security chief at a major financial institution. You use ACF2 on your mainframes, Novell networks for your PC's, and have an institutional policy against importing software. You have a corporate programming staff of 2000, and feel you are in good control over changes in source code. Your production machine is well separated from noncritical machine, you use a limited functionality cryptographically covered network for EFTs, you do background checks on all of your employees, and each is bonded up to 1 million dollars. You are insured with a 100-million-dollar deductible for EFT theft, and you have independent EDP audits performed quarterly. What should your virus defenses plan be?

With an operation of this size, you probably already experience viruses several times per year. If you don't have a CERT team in place, you should form one. Strategic planning already under way should be augmented to include viruses, and your considerations should be similar to those in the administrative side of the university environment described earlier. Central reporting and rapid response are key components of good antivirus strategy in an environment such as yours, where there are a lot of users and high bandwidth sharing. You probably already perform detailed risk analysis on a regular basis, and this should be augmented to include viruses if it hasn't already been done. You probably lack a strong program of gathering statistics on viruses and analysis of those statistics from an epidemiological point of view to improve your strategy and tactics with time, and this should be added to your strategy and performed by your CERT.

By now, the tactical analysis should be getting automatic. We begin with the exposures, and then look at techniques for coverage. In this scenario, however, the analysis has some special features. In particular, electronic funds transfer requires special consideration because the exposure is so high. A typical bank transfers its entire assets in EFTs several times per week. Let's consider that first.

An EFT is really quite a simple transaction. It normally consists of a source account identifier, a recipient account identifier, an amount of money, and an authentication string. That means that limited function applies. Similarly, EFTs can easily be controlled from a single physically secure site and not connected to other computers except through limited function interfaces that carry transactions. Thus, we can have complete isolation except for these limited function links. Because the operations performed are quite simple, there should be very few changes required to the software, so sound change control can also be used here. Similarly, because of the enormous exposure and the simple, well-specified nature of the interactions, we can sometimes even effort multiversion programs and redundant hardware to support it, Finally, we should use integrity protection as an extra precaution against unwanted change. In other words, this is one application where we can apply all of our best techniques.

You have 2000 programmers and you claim you are in good control over changes. I don't believe it. You have Novell networks and institutional policies against importing software. As we have discussed, these are ineffective against viruses, and should be improved. Since limited function and limited sharing are not feasible in this environment I would almost certainly implement a system of defense-in-depth in a mode that prevents the introduction of new software without explicit authorization and automatically detects and corrects violations of this policy. This would satisfy both the corporate policy and the legitimate need for coverage in Novell networks and PCs. It would dramatically limit incident size, improve incident response time, and cost less over time than scanning for viruses or other similar tactics.

### 6.3.5 The Computer Company Scenario

You work for AT&T information services as the chief of corporate computer security for product lines. You deliver general-purpose systems to hundreds of thousands of companies and are charged with assuring that their systems operate appropriately. You deliver cryptographic telephones to the U.S. government for communicating classified information. You have an installed base of 500,000 computers that get software upgrades once or more each year. You have 10,000 programmers working in your area, and about one a week is called on the carpet for "security" violations.

At this point, having heard the good joke a few hours earlier,[2] someone usually suggests "Prepare three envelopes."

Let's get systematic yet again, only this time, I'll ask the questions, and I want you to come up with the answers.

- Who should be involved in strategic planning?
- What strategic plans should definitely be in place?
- Should you have a CERT? What should its functions be?
- What are the highest exposures?
- How can we respond to these exposures effectively?

---

[2]See Appendix A.

# Chapter 7

# FINISHING UP

Before finishing this short course, I would like to take this opportunity to mention a few things I would like you to do. First and foremost, I think you should read the appendices to this book. They include "The Good Joke" that I tell after lunch at my short courses, some mathematical details that advanced readers may find enlightening, and an annotated bibliography of some of the best technical papers in this field.

The good joke is one of the best computer security related jokes I know of, and I tell it in almost every short course I give as a way to wake people up after the lunch break. Although I am pretty funny sometimes, I did not think of this joke, so I won't claim credit for it. On the other hand, I have embellished it greatly over the years, so even if you have heard it, you might review it to keep up to date.

## 7.1   A THOUGHT

When I first started using computers, I had a great desire to attain power in the computing environment. Once I became a systems administrator for several systems, I had a great desire to find someone else to do all of the work associated with the power, leaving me able to use the power when needed. One of my great joys in creating early viruses was the fact that they altered the balance of power between the systems administrator and the user, and in case you were wondering, I was a systems administrator at that time. Now I am convinced that the most useful application of benevolent viruses today is in the automation of systems administration in computer networks. At first, it seemed strange to me that the same mechanism that can wreak havoc with systems can bring order to them, but as I walked down a city sidewalk, it all became clear to me.

I noticed, as I guess we all do, that even in the middle of a busy sidewalk, plants are growing in the cracks. Life, it seems is pervasive. Despite out best efforts to create a lifeless, organized city street, life invades and alters our plans. But that invading life is not really chaotic at all, it only follows a different organization, and spreads its form of organization as it goes. It makes perfect sense that if life forms are in harmony with the environment, they will coexist and stabilize each other, while if the life forms are not in harmony with the environment, they will be at odds, and each will be destabilized by the other. Stopping life is not easy but we have been able to defoliate some parts of the earth to where they are almost barren, and I suppose we will be able to control rudimentary life forms in our computer systems if we become harsh enough in our defense.

Perhaps in some environments, lifelessness is best, but I have always felt we should try to coexist with other living creatures, and in the case of information life forms, I feel the same way. Peaceful coexistence with computer viruses probably involves maintaining two separate environments. In one environment, life thrives, while in the other, controls are key.

Those who want to experiment with computer life should be encouraged to do so, but only in environments suitable to it. Those who want to be in complete control over their computers should also be provided with the ability to do so, and those who would force their life forms on the controlled systems should be punished as we would punish someone who threw a bomb into an unmanned factory. If people are physically harmed in the process, the punishment should be that much more severe, and the effort to track down the attacker that much more intense.

For those of who want live environments, live programs should be available. You must pardon me now: There are cockroaches inside my Xwindows environment, and whenever I let one out, it crawls into a shady spot on my screen and reproduces. I have to reboot now to kill off the whole colony.

# Appendix A

# THE GOOD JOKE

This is not my original joke, but I have told it after lunch at so many short courses, that it is an integral part of the course. I include it here for your pleasure. I first heard it told by a NIST (National Institute of Science and Technology) speaker at a computer virus conference I attended.

It seems that this guy was hired to work for one of the national security agencies in the United States and the guy that was in place before him left under some very serious controversy...some problem with a computer network or something. So during the transition period, after the job-related briefings, the old guy gave him three envelopes labeled 1, 2, and 3, with the instructions to put the three envelopes into the security safe and to only use them in the most dire of emergencies. Well, the new guy had no idea what these three envelopes were about, and the old guy wouldn't tell him, so he thought it was sort of strange, but he put them in the safe to satisfy the old guy, and forgot about them after a couple of months.

So after about a year in office, a major crisis came along. It was something to do with the U.S. Embassy in Moscow. It seems the embassy was built by Soviet workmen, complete with built-in bugging devices, and when the press found out about it, they called up the President. The President's office arranged for a press conference at 3:30 and called our hero and told him he had a press conference scheduled in 15 minutes to answer questions about the Moscow Embassy situation. Of course, our hero had no idea what was going on, but he figured he was in big trouble, and then recalled the three envelopes.

So he went down to the security safe, opened it up, took out the envelope labeled 1, locked up the safe, opened up the envelope, and read it. It said: "Blame it on your predecessor." Okay, he was desperate, and he didn't know what else to do, so he went to the press conference and said: "I was not involved in the decision to build the embassy in this way; however, my predecessor was involved in it and...We became aware of the situation several months before you did, and were working very hard to resolve it, and..." The press ate it up. They blamed it on a previous administration, and our hero came out clean.

So he went on down the road, and about a year and a half later, son-of-a-gun if there wasn't another big problem. This time somebody in Germany launched a computer virus that spread through NASA networks into the United States, and the press called the President, and the President called a press conference for 3:30, and informed our hero with about 15 minutes notice that he was to describe what happened with this NASA network.

Well, if it works once, you don't forget it, so our hero went down and got the second envelope out of the security safe, locked up the safe, opened up the envelope, and read it. It said "Blame it on the operating system." Why not? So our hero went to the press conference and said "The operating system in these computers are fundamentally weak, and our people have been aware of that for a number of years and have been working to resolve the problem..." Well, the press ate it up, and our hero came out unscathed again.

After about another year and a half, it happened again. This time there was some sailor who worked in the U.S. Department of Defense in classified areas, and this sailor was giving away keys to the cryptosystems used for nuclear missile control. So, the press called the President, and the President scheduled a press conference for 3:30, and called our hero with 15 minutes notice. So our hero figured he was in big trouble again, and decided to use the third envelope.

He went down to the security safe, got out the third envelope, locked up the safe, opened up the envelope, and read the last piece of paper. It said: "Prepare three envelopes."

# Appendix B

# THE FORMAL DEFINITION OF COMPUTER VIRUSES

The formal definition presents "viral sets" in terms of a set of "histories" with respect to a given machine. A viral set is a set of symbol sequences that, when interpreted, causes one or more elements of the viral set to be written elsewhere on the machine in all of the histories following the interpretation. We include here some of the relevant definitions required for the remainder of this appendix, starting with the definition of a set of Turing-like computing machines "$\mathcal{M}$" as

$$\forall M [M \in \mathcal{M}] \Leftrightarrow$$

$$M: (S_M, I_M, O_M: S_M \times I_M \to I_M, N_M: S_M \times I_M \to S_M, D_M: S_M \times I_M \to d)$$

where:

$$\mathcal{N} = \{0 \ldots \infty\} \qquad \text{(the 'natural' numbers)}$$

$$\mathcal{I} = \{1 \ldots \infty\} \qquad \text{(the positive 'integers')}$$

$$S_M = \{s_0, \ldots, s_n\}, \quad n \in \mathcal{I} \qquad (\mathcal{M} \text{ states})$$

$$I_M = \{i_0, \ldots, i_j\}, \quad j \in \mathcal{I} \qquad (\mathcal{M} \text{ tape symbols})$$

$$d = \{-1, 0, +1\} \qquad (\mathcal{M} \text{ head motions})$$

$$\Xi_M: \mathcal{N} \to S_M \qquad (\mathcal{M} \text{ state over time})$$

$$\square_M: \mathcal{N} \times \mathcal{N} \to I_M \qquad (\mathcal{M} \text{ tape contents over time})$$

$$P_M: \mathcal{N} \to \mathcal{N} \qquad (\text{current } \mathcal{M} \text{ cell at each time})$$

The "history" of the machine $H_M$ is given by $(\Xi, \square, P)$,[1] the "initial state" is described by $(\Xi_0, \square_0, P_0)$, and the set of possible $\mathscr{M}$ tape subsequences is designated by $I^*$. We say that $M$ is halted at time $t \Leftrightarrow \forall$ $t' > t$, $H_t = H_{t'}$ ($t, t' \in \mathscr{N}$); that $M$ halts $\Leftrightarrow \exists t \in \mathscr{N}$, $M$ is halted at time $t$; that $p$ runs at time $t \Leftrightarrow$ the "initial state" occurs when $P_0$ is such that $p$ appears at $\square_0, P_0$; and that $p$ runs $\Leftrightarrow \exists t \in \mathscr{N}$, $p$ runs at time $t$. The formal definition of the viral set $(\mathscr{V})$ is then given by

(1)  $\forall M \ \forall V (M, V) \in \mathscr{V} \Leftrightarrow$

(2)  $[V \subset I^*]$ and $[M \in \mathscr{M}]$ and $\forall v \in V \ \forall H \ \forall t, j \in \mathscr{N}$

(3)  $[[P_t = j]$ and $[\Xi_t = \Xi_0]$ and $(\square_{t,j}, \ldots, \square_{t,j+|v|-1}) = v] \Rightarrow$

(4)  $\exists v' \in V, \exists t', t'', j' \in \mathscr{N}$ and $t' > t$

(5)  (1) $[[(j' + |v'|) \leq j]$ or $[(j + |v|) \leq j']]$ and

(6)  (2) $[(\square_{t', j'}, \ldots, \square_{t', j'+|v'|-1}) = v']$ and

(7)  (3) $[\exists t''[t < t'' < t']$ and $[P_{t''} \in \{j', \ldots, j' + |v'| - 1\}]]]$

We will now review this definition line by line

(1)  for all $M$ and $V$, the pair $(M, V)$ is a "viral set" if and only if

(2)  $V$ is a nonempty set of $\mathscr{M}$ sequences and $M$ is a $\mathscr{M}$ and
For each virus $v$ in $V$, For all histories of machine $M$,
For all times $t$ and cells $j$

(3)  If the tape head is in front of cell $j$ at time $t$ and $\mathscr{M}$ is in its initial state at time $t$ and the tape cells starting at $j$ hold the virus $v$

(4)  then there is a virus $v'$ in $V$, a time $t' > t$, and place $j'$ such that

(5)  (1) at place $j'$ far enough away from $v$

(6)  (2) the tape cells starting at $j'$ hold virus $v'$

(7)  (3) and at some time $t''$ between time $t$ and time $t'$ $v'$ is written by $M$

To save space, we will use the expression

$$a \overset{B}{\Rightarrow} C$$

to abbreviate part of the previous definition starting at line (2) where $a$, $B$,

---

[1] For convenience, we drop the $M$ subscript when we are dealing with a single machine except at the first definition of each term.

and $C$ are specific instances of $v$, $M$, and $V$, respectively, as follows:

$$\left[\forall B\left[\forall C[(B,C)\in\mathscr{V}]\Leftrightarrow\right.\right.$$

$$\left.\left.\left[[C\subset CI^*]\text{ and }[M\in\mathscr{M}]\text{ and }\left[\forall a\in C[a\overset{B}{\Rightarrow}C]\right]\right]\right]\right]$$

Before continuing, we should note some of the features of this definition and their motivation. We define the predicate $V$ over all Turing Machines. We have also stated our definition so that a given element of a viral set may generate any number of other elements of that set depending on the rest of the tape. This affords additional generality without undue complexity or restriction. Finally, we have no so-called "conditional viruses" in that EVERY element of a viral set must ALWAYS generate another element of that set. If a conditional virus is desired, we may add conditionals that either cause or prevent a virus from being executed as a function of the rest of the tape, without modifying this definition.

We may also say that $V$ is a "viral set" w.r.t. $M\Leftrightarrow[(M,V)\in\mathscr{V}]$ and define the term "virus" w.r.t. $M$ as $\{[v\in V]:[(M,V)\in\mathscr{V}]\}$.

We say that "$v$ evolves into $v'$ for $M$" $\Leftrightarrow[(M,V)\in\mathscr{V}]$ and $[v\in V]$ and $[v'\in V]$ and $[v\overset{M}{\Rightarrow}\{v'\}]]$, that "$v'$ is evolved from $v$ for $M$" $\Leftrightarrow v$ evolves into $v'$ for $M$, and that "$v'$ is an evolution of $v$ for $M$" $\Leftrightarrow$

$$(M,V)\in\mathscr{V}\ \exists i\in\mathscr{N}\ \exists V'\in V^i$$

$$[v\in V]\quad\text{and}\quad[v'\in V]\quad\text{and}$$

$$[\forall v_k\in V'[v_k\overset{M}{\Rightarrow}v_{k+1}]]\quad\text{and}$$

$$\exists l\in\mathscr{N}\ \exists m\in\mathscr{N}$$

$$[[l<m]\quad\text{and}\quad[v_l=v]\text{ and }[v_m=v']]$$

In other words, the transitive closure of $\overset{M}{\Rightarrow}$ starting from $v$, contains $v'$.

## B.1  BASIC THEOREMS

At this point, we are ready to begin proving various properties of viral sets. Our most basic theorem states that any union of viral sets is also a viral set.

**Theorem 1.**

$$\forall M\ \forall U^*[\forall V\in U^*(M,V)\in\mathscr{V}]\Rightarrow[(M,\cup U^*)\in\mathscr{V}]$$

*Proof.*

Define $U = \bigcup U^*$
By definition of $\bigcup$

$$(1) \quad [\forall v \in U [\exists V \in U^* : v \in V]]$$

$$(2) \quad [\forall V \in U^* [\forall v \in V [v \in U]]]$$

Also by definition,

$$[(M, U) \in \mathcal{V}] \Leftrightarrow$$

$$[[V \in I^*] \quad \text{and} \quad [M \in \mathcal{M}] \quad \text{and} \quad [\forall v \in U [v \overset{M}{\Rightarrow} U]]]$$

by assumption,

$$\forall V \in U^* \ \forall v \in V \left[ v \overset{M}{\Rightarrow} V \right]$$

thus since $\forall v \in U \ \exists V \in U^* [v \overset{M}{\Rightarrow} V]$ and $[\forall V \in U^* [V \subset U]]$

$$\left[ \forall v \in U \left[ \exists V \subset U \left[ v \overset{M}{\Rightarrow} V \right] \right] \right]$$

hence $[\forall v \in U [v \overset{M}{\Rightarrow} U]]$
thus by definition, $(M, U) \in \mathcal{V}$
Q.E.D.

Knowing this, we prove that there is a "largest" viral set with respect to any machine, that set being the union of all viral sets w.r.t. that machine.

**Lemma 1.1.**

$$\left[ \forall M \in \mathcal{M} \left[ [\exists V [(M, V) \in \mathcal{V}]] \Rightarrow \right. \right.$$

$$\left[ \exists U \text{ (i) } [(M, U) \in \mathcal{V}] \text{ and (ii) } \left[ \forall V \left[ [(M, V) \in \mathcal{V}] \Rightarrow \right. \right. \right.$$

$$I[\forall v \in V [v \in U]]]]]]]]$$

We call $U$ the "largest viral set" (LVS) w.r.t. $M$, and define $(M, U) \in$ LVS $\Leftrightarrow$ [i and ii].

*Proof.*

assume $[\exists V[(M,V) \in \mathscr{V}]]$
choose $U = \bigcup\{V: [(M,V) \in \mathscr{V}]\}$
now prove (i) and (ii)

Proof of (i) (by Theorem 1)

$$\left(M, \left[\bigcup\{V: [(M,V) \in \mathscr{V}]\}\right]\right) \in \mathscr{V}$$

thus $(M,U) \in \mathscr{V}$

Proof of (ii) by contradiction:
Assume (ii) is false:
thus

$$[\exists V:$$

$$(1)\ [(M,V) \in \mathscr{V}]\ \text{and}$$

$$(2)\ [\exists v \in V: [v \notin U]]]]$$

but

$$[\forall V: (M,V) \in \mathscr{V}$$

$$[\forall v \in V] v \in U]]] \qquad \text{(definition of union)}$$

thus $[v \notin U]$ and $[v \in U]$ (contradiction)
thus (ii) is true
Q.E.D.

Having defined the largest viral set w.r.t. a machine, we would now like to define a "smallest viral set" as a viral set of which no proper subset is a viral set w.r.t. the given machine. There may be many such sets for a given machine.

We define SVS as follows:

$$[\forall M[\forall V[(M,V) \in \text{SVS}] \Leftrightarrow$$

$$(1)\ [(M,V) \in \mathscr{V}]\ \text{and}$$

$$(2)\ [\not\exists U: [U \subset V]\ \text{and}\ [(M,U) \in \mathscr{V}]]]]] \qquad \text{(proper subset)}$$

We now prove that there is a machine for which the SVS is a singleton set, and that the minimal viral set is therefore singleton.

**Theorem 2.**

$$\exists M \exists V$$

$$\text{(i)} \quad [(M,V) \in \text{SVS}] \text{ and}$$

$$\text{(ii)} \quad [|V| = 1]$$

*Proof.* By demonstration

$$M: S = \{s_0, s_1\}, \qquad I = \{0, 1\},$$

| $S \times I$ | N | O | D |
|---|---|---|---|
| $s_0, 0$ | $s_0$ | $0$ | $0$ |
| $s_0, 1$ | $s_1$ | $1$ | $+1$ |
| $s_1, 0$ | $s_0$ | $1$ | $0$ |
| $s_1, 1$ | $s_1$ | $1$ | $+1$ |

$|\{(1)\}| = 1$ (by definition of the operator)

$$[(M, \{(1)\}) \in \text{SVS}] \Leftrightarrow$$

$$\text{(1)} \quad [(M, \{(1)\}) \in \mathscr{V}] \text{ and}$$

$$\text{(2)} \quad [(M, \{\ \}) \notin \mathscr{V}]$$

$(M, \{\ \}) \notin \mathscr{V}$ (by definition since $\{\ \} \notin I^*$)
as can be verified by the reader:

$$\text{(1)} \overset{M}{\Rightarrow} \{(1)\}(t' = t + 2, t'' = t + 1, j' = j + 1)$$

thus $(M, \{(1)\}) \in \mathscr{V}$
Q.E.D.

With the knowledge that the above sequence is a singleton viral set and that it duplicates itself, we suspect that any sequence that duplicates itself is a virus w.r.t. the machine on which it is self-duplicating.

**Lemma 2.1.**

$$\forall M \in \mathscr{M} \ \forall u \in I^*$$

$$\left[\left[u \overset{M}{\Rightarrow} \{u\}\right] \Rightarrow \left[(M, \{u\}) \in \mathscr{V}\right]\right]$$

*Proof.*

by substitution into the definition of viruses:

$$\forall M \in \mathscr{M} \ \forall \{u\}$$

$$\left[\left[(M, \{u\}) \in \mathscr{V}\right] \Leftrightarrow\right.$$

$$\left[\left[\{u\} \in I^*\right] \text{ and } \left[u \overset{M}{\Rightarrow} \{u\}\right]\right]$$

since $[[u \in I^*] \Rightarrow [\{u\} \in I^*]]$ (definition of $I^*$)
and by assumption, $[u \overset{M}{\Rightarrow} \{u\}]$

$$\left[(M, \{u\}) \in \mathscr{V}\right]$$

Q.E.D.

The existence of a singleton SVS spurns interest in whether or not there are other sizes of SVSs. We show that for any finite integer $i$, there is a machine such that there is a viral set with $i$ elements. Thus, SVSs come in all sizes. We prove this fact by demonstrating a machine that generates the $(x|i) + 1$th element of a viral set from the $x$th element of that set. In order to guarantee that it is an SVS, we force the machine to halt as soon as the next "evolution" is generated so that no other element of the viral set is generated in the interim. Removing any subset of the viral set guarantees that some element of the resulting set cannot be generated by another element of the set. If we remove all the elements from the set, we have an empty set, which by definition is not a viral set.

**Theorem 3.**

$$\forall i \in [\mathscr{N} + 1] \ \exists M \in \mathscr{M} \ \exists V$$

$$(1) \quad [(M, V) \in \text{SVS}] \quad \text{and}$$

$$(2) \quad [|V| = i]$$

*Proof.* **By demonstration**

$$M : S = \{s_0, s_1, \ldots, s_i\},\ I = \{0, 1, \ldots, i\},\ \forall x \in \{1, \ldots, i\}$$

| $S \times I$ | N | O | D | Comment |
|---|---|---|---|---|
| $s_0, 0$ | $s_0$ | 0 | 0 | ; if $I = 0$, halt |
| $s_0, x$ | $s_x$ | $x$ | $+1$ | ; if $I = x$, goto state $x$, move right |
| $\ldots$ | | | | ; other states generalized as: |
| $s_x, {}^*$ | $s_x$ | $[x|i] + 1$ | 0 | ; write $[x - i] + 1$, halt |

Proof of (i)
define $V = \{(1), (2), \ldots, (i)\}$

$$|V| = i \qquad \text{(by definition of operator)}$$

Proof of (ii)

$$[(M, V) \in SVS] \Leftrightarrow$$

$$(1) \quad (M, V) \in \mathscr{V}] \quad \text{and}$$

$$(2) \quad [\nexists U[[U \subset V] \quad \text{and} \quad [(M, U) \in \mathscr{V}]]]$$

Proof of "1) $(M, V) \in \mathscr{V}$"

$$(1) \overset{M}{\Rightarrow} \{(2)\}(t' = t + 2, t'' = t + 1, j' = j + 1)$$
$$\ldots$$
$$([i - 1]) \overset{M}{\Rightarrow} \{(i)\}(t' = t + 2, t'' = t + 1, j' = j + 1)$$
$$(i) \overset{M}{\Rightarrow} \{(1)\}(t' = t + 2, t'' = t + 1, j' = j + 1)$$

and $(1) \in V, \ldots,$ and $(i) \in V$
as can be verified by simulation
thus $[\forall v \in V[v \overset{M}{\Rightarrow} V]]$
so $(M, V) \in \mathscr{V}$

Proof of "2) $[\not\exists U[[U \subset V]$ *and* $[(M, U) \in \mathscr{V}]]$"
Given $[\exists t, j \in \mathcal{N}[\exists v \in V$

$$\left[\left[\square_{t,j} = v\right] \text{ and } \left[\Xi_t = \Xi_0\right] \text{ and } \left[P_t = j\right]\right]$$

$$\Leftrightarrow \left[\left[M \text{ halts at time } t + 2\right] \text{ and}\right.$$

$$\left[v|i\right] + 1 \text{ is written at } j + 1 \text{ at } t + 1]]]$$

(as may be verified by simulation)

and $[\forall x \in \{1, \ldots, i\}[(x) \in V]]$ (by definition of $V$)
and $[\forall x \in \{1, \ldots, i\}[x \overset{M}{\Rightarrow} \{[x|i] + 1\}]]$
we conclude that

$$[x|i] + 1 \text{ is the ONLY symbol written outside of } (x)$$

thus

$$\left[\not\exists x' \neq [x|i] + 1\left[x \overset{M}{\Rightarrow} \{x'\}\right]\right]$$

now

$$\left[\forall(x) \in V\left[\left(\left[x|i\right] + 1\right) \notin V \Rightarrow [(x) \notin V]\right]\right]$$

assume $[\exists U \subset V[(M, U) \in \mathscr{V}]]$

$$[U = \{\ \}] \Rightarrow [(M, U) \notin \mathscr{V}] \text{ thus } U \neq \{\ \}$$

by definition of proper subset

$$[U \subset V] \Rightarrow [\exists v \in V[v \notin U]]$$

but

$$[\exists v \in V[v \notin U]]$$

$$\Rightarrow \left[\exists v' \in U[[v'|i] + 1 = v]\right]$$

$$\text{and } [v \notin U] \text{ and } \left[\not\exists v'' \in V\left[v' \overset{M}{\Rightarrow} v''\right]\right]]$$

thus $[\not\exists v \in U[v' \overset{M}{\Rightarrow} V]]$ and $[v' \in U]$
thus $[(M, U) \notin \mathscr{V}]$ which is a contradiction
Q.E.D.

Again, a demonstration of this $\mathscr{M}$ is provided for independent verification of its operation.

## B.2   ABBREVIATED TABLE THEOREMS

We will now move into a series of proofs that demonstrate the existence of various types of viruses. In order to simplify the presentation, we have adopted the technique of writing "abbreviated tables" in place of complete state tables. The basic principal of the abbreviated table (or macro) is to allow a large set of states, inputs, outputs, next states, and tape movements to be abbreviated in a single statement. We do not wish to give the impression that these macros are anything but abbreviations, and thus we display the means by which our abbreviations can be expanded into state tables. This technique is essentially the same as that used by Turing in his original work, and we refer the reader to that manuscript for further details on the use of abbreviated tables.

In order to make effective use of macros, we will use a convenient notation for describing large state tables with a small number of symbols. When we define states in tables, we will often refer to a state as $S_n$ or $S_{n+k}$ to indicate that the actual state number is not of import, but rather that the given macro can be used at any point in a larger table by simply substituting the actual state numbers for the variable state numbers used in the definition of the macro. For inputs and outputs, where we do not wish to enumerate all possible input and output combinations, we will use variables as well. In many cases, we may describe entire ranges of values with a single variable. We will attempt to make these substitutions clear as we describe the following set of macros.

The "halt" macro allows us to halt the machine in any given state $S_n$. We use the asterisk to indicate that for any input the machine will do the rest of the specified function. The next state entry $(N)$ is $S_n$ so that the next state will always be $S_n$. The output $(O)$ is $*$, which is intended to indicate that this state will output to the tape whatever was input from the tape. The tape movement $(D)$ is 0 to indicate the tape cell in front of the tape head will not change. The reader may verify that this meets the conditions of a 'halt' state as defined earlier.

| Name | S, I | N | O | D | Comment |
|------|------|---|---|---|---------|
| halt | $S_n$, * | $S_n$ | * | 0 | ;halt |

The "right till x" macro describes a machine that increments the tape position ($P(t)$) until such position is reached that the symbol $x$ is in front of the tape head. At this point, it will cause the next state to be the state after $S_n$ so that it may be followed by other state table entries. Notice the use of 'else' to indicate that for all inputs other than $x$, the machine will output whatever was input (thus leaving the tape unchanged) and move to the right one square.

| Name | S, I | N | O | D | Comment |
|------|------|---|---|---|---------|
| $R(x)$ | $S_n$, $x$ | $S_{n+1}$ | $x$ | 0 | ;right till x |
|        | $S_n$, else | $S_n$ | else | +1 | |

The "left till x" macro is just like the $R(x)$ macro except that the tape is moved left ($-1$) rather than right ($+1$).

| Name | S, I | N | O | D | Comment |
|------|------|---|---|---|---------|
| $L(x)$ | $S_n$, $x$ | $S_{n+1}$ | $x$ | 0 | ;left till x |
|        | $S_n$, else | $S_n$ | Else | $-1$ | |

The "change $x$ to $y$ until $z$" macro moves from left to right over the tape until the symbol $z$ is in front of the tape head, replacing every occurrence of $x$ with $y$, and leaving all other tape symbols as they were.

| Name | S, I | N | O | D | Comment |
|------|------|---|---|---|---------|
| $C(x, y, z)$ | $S_n$, $z$ | $S_{n+1}$ | $z$ | 0 | ;change X to Y till Z |
|              | $S_n$, $x$ | $S_n$ | $y$ | +1 | |
|              | $S_n$, else | $S_n$ | else | +1 | |

The "copy from $x$ till $y$ to after $z$" macro is a bit more complex than the previous macros because its size depends on the number of input symbols for the machine under consideration. The basic principal is to define a set of states for each symbol of interest so that the set of states replaces the symbol of interest with the "left of tape marker" moves right until the "current right of tape marker," replaces that marker with the desired symbol, moves right one more, places the marker at the "new right of tape," and then moves left to the "left of tape marker," replaces it with the original symbol, moves right one tape square, and continues from there.

The loop just described requires some initialization to arrange for the "right of tape marker" and a test to detect the $y$ on the tape and thus determine when to complete its operation. At completion, the macro goes onto the state following the last state taken up by the macro, and it can thus be used as the above macros.

| Name | S, I | N | O | D | Comment |
|---|---|---|---|---|---|
| CPY$(X, Y, Z)$ | | | | | ;copy from X till Y to after Z |
| | $S_n$ | R(X) | | | ;right till X |
| | $S_{n+1}$ | $S_{n+2}$ | 'N' | 0 | ;write 'N' |
| | $S_{n+2}$ | R(Y) | | | ;right till Y |
| | $S_{n+3}$ | R(Z) | | | ;right till Z |
| | $S_{n+4}$ | $S_{n+5}$ | Z | +1 | ;right one more |
| | $S_{n+5}$ | $S_{n+6}$ | 'M' | 0; | write 'M' |
| | $S_{n+6}$ | L('N') | | | ;left till 'N' |
| | $S_{n+7}$ | $S_{n+8}$ | X | 0 | ;replace the initial X |
| | $S_{n+8}, Y$ | $S_{n+9}$ | Y | +1 | ;if Y, done |
| | $S_{n+8}, *$ | $S_{k+5*}$ | 'N' | +1 | ;else write 'N' an |
| | | | | | ;goto sn + 5 times the input |
| | | | | | ;symbol number |
| | $S_{n+9}$ | R(M) | | | ;right till 'M' |
| | $S_{n+10}$ | $S_{n+11}$ | Y | 0 | ;copy completed |
| | $S_{k+5*}$ | R('M') | | | ;goto the 'M' |
| | $S_{k+5*+1}$ | $S_{k+5*+2}$ | * | +1 | ;write the copied symbol |
| | $S_{k+5*+2}$ | $S_{k+5*+3}$ | 'M' | 0 | ;write the trailing 'M' |
| | $S_{k+5*+3}$ | L('N') | | | ;left till 'N' |
| | $S_{k+5*+4}$ | $S_n + 8$ | * | +1 | ;rewrite * and go on |

As a note, we should observe that for each of the above macros (except "halt"), the "arguments" must be specified ahead of time, and if the tape is not in such a configuration that all of the required symbols are present in their proper order, the macros may cause the machine to loop indefinitely in the macro rather than leaving upon completion.

We now show that there is a viral set which is the size of the natural numbers (countably infinite), by demonstrating a viral set of which each element generates an element with one additional symbol. Since, given any element of the set, a new element in generated with every execution, and no previously generated element is ever regenerated, we have a set generated in the same inductive manner as the natural numbers, and there is thus a one-to-one mapping to the natural numbers from the generated set.

**Theorem 4.**

$$\exists M \in \mathcal{M} \; \exists V \in I^*:$$

$$(1) \quad [(M,V) \in \mathcal{V}] \text{ and}$$

$$(2) \quad [|V| = |\mathcal{N}|]$$

*Proof.* by demonstration:

| Name | S, I | N | O | D | Comment |
|------|------|---|---|---|---------|
| $M$: | $S_0, L$ | $S_1$ | L | $+1$ | ;start with L |
|  | $S_0$, else | $S_0$ | X | 0 | ;or halt |
|  | $S_1, 0)$ | $C(0, X, R)$ |  |  | ;change 0s to Xs till R |
|  | $S_2, R$ | $S_3$ | R | $+1$ | ;write R |
|  | $S_3$ | $S_4$ | L | $+1$ | ;write L |
|  | $S_4$ | $S_5$ | X | 0 | ;write X |
|  | $S_5$ | $L(R)$ |  |  | ;move left till R |
|  | $S_6$ | $L(X \text{ or } L)$ |  |  | ;move left till X or L |
|  | $S_7, L$ | $S_{11}$ | L | 0 | ;if L goto s11 |
|  | $S_7, X$ | $S_8$ | 0 | $+1$ | ;if X replace with 0 |
|  | $S_8$ | $R(X)$ |  |  | ;move right till X |
|  | $S_9, X$ | $S_{10}$ | 0 | $+1$ | ;change to 0, move right |
|  | $S_{10}$ | $S_5$ | X | 0 | ;write X and goto S5 |
|  | $S_{11}$ | $R(X)$ |  |  | ;move right till X |
|  | $S_{12}$ | $S_{13}$ | 0 | $+1$ | ;add one 0 |
|  | $S_{13}$ | $S_{13}$ | R | 0 | ;halt with R on tape |

$$V = \{(L0R), (L00R), \ldots, (L0\ldots0R), \ldots\}$$

Proof of (1) $(M,V) \in \mathcal{V}$
definition:

$$\forall M \in \mathcal{M} \; \forall V [(M,V) \in \mathcal{V}] \Leftrightarrow$$

$$\left[ [V \in I^*] \quad \text{and} \quad \left[ \forall v \in V [v \overset{M}{\Rightarrow} V] \right] \right]$$

By inspection, $[V \in I^*]$
now $\forall (L_0 \ldots 0R) \; \exists (L0 \ldots 00R) \in V$:

$$\left[ (L0\ldots0R) \overset{M}{\Rightarrow} \{(L0\ldots00R)\} \right]$$

(may be verified by simulation)

thus $(M,V) \in \mathcal{V}$

Proof of (2) $|V| = |\mathcal{N}|$

$$\forall v_n \in V \; \exists v_{n+1} \in V,$$

$$\forall k \leq n \; \not\exists v_k \in V: [v_k = v_{n+1}]$$

This is the same form as the definition of $\mathcal{N}$, hence $|V| = |\mathcal{N}|$
Q.E.D.

As a side issue, we show the same machine has a countably infinite number of sequences that are not viral sequences, thus proving that no finite-state machine can be given to determine whether or not a given $(M, V)$ pair is "viral" by simply enumerating all viruses (from Theorem 4) or by simply enumerating all nonviruses (by Lemma 4.1).

**Lemma 4.1.**

$$\exists M \in \mathcal{M} \; \exists W \in I^*$$

$\quad$ (1) $\quad [ |W| = |\mathcal{N}| ]$ and

$\quad$ (2) $\quad \forall w \in W \; \not\exists W' \subset W: \left[ w \overset{M}{\Rightarrow} W' \right]$

*Proof.*

using $M$ from Theorem 4, we choose

$$W = \{ (X), (XX), \ldots, (X \ldots X), \ldots \}$$

clearly $[M \in \mathcal{M}]$ and $[W \in I^*]$ and $[|W| = |\mathcal{N}|]$
since (from the state table)

$$[\forall w \in W [ w \text{ runs at time } t] \Rightarrow [w \text{ halts at time } t]]$$

$$[ \not\exists t' > t [ P_{t'} \neq P_t ]]$$

thus $\forall w \in W \; \not\exists W' \subset W [ w \overset{M}{\Rightarrow} W' ]$
Q.E.D.

It turns out that the above case is an example of a viral set that has no SVS. This is because no matter how many elements of $V$ are removed from the front of $V$, the set can always have another element removed without making it nonviral.

We also wish to show that there are machines for which no sequences are viruses, and do this trivially below by defining a machine which always halts without moving the tape head.

**Lemma 4.2.**

$$\exists M \in \mathscr{M} \; \nexists V \in I^*[(M,V) \in \mathscr{V}]$$

*Proof.* By demonstration:

| Name | S, I | N | O | D |
|------|------|---|---|---|
| $M$: | $s_0$, all | $s_0$ | O | 0 |

(trivially verified that $\forall t[Pt = P_0]$)
Q.E.D.

We now show that for ANY finite sequence of tape symbols $v$, it is possible to construct a machine for which that sequence is a virus. As a side issue, this particular machine is such that LVS = SVS, and thus no sequence other than $v$ is a virus w.r.t. this machine. We form this machine by generating a finite "recognizer" that examines successive cells of the tape, and halts unless each cell in order is the appropriate element of $v$. If each cell is appropriate we replicate $v$ and subsequently halt.

**Theorem 5.**

$$\forall v \in I^* \; \exists M \in \mathscr{M}[(M,\{v\}) \in \mathscr{V}]$$

*Proof.* By demonstration:

$v = \{v_0, v_2, \ldots, v_k\}$, where $[k \in \mathscr{N}]$ and $[v \in I^i]$ (definition of TP).

| Name | S, I | N | O | D | Comment |
|------|------|---|---|---|---------|
| $M$: | $s_0, v_0$ | $s_1$ | $v_0$ | $+1$ | ;recognize 1st element of $v$ |
|      | $s_0$, else | $s_0$ | 0 | 0 | ;or halt |
|      | $\cdots$ |   |   |   | ;etc till |
|      | $s_k, v_k$ | $s_{k+1}$ | $v_k$ | $+1$ | ;recognize $k$th element of v |
|      | $s_k$, else | $s_0$ | 0 | 0 | ;or halt |
|      | $s_{k+1}$ | $s_{k+2}$ | $v_0$ | $+1$ | ;output 1st element of v |
|      | $\cdots$ |   |   |   | ;etc till |
|      | $s_{k+k}$ | $s_{k+k}$ | $v_k$ | $+0$ | ;output kth element of v |

It is trivially verified that $[v \overset{M}{\Rightarrow} \{v\}]$
and hence (by Lemma 2.1) $[(M, \{v\}) \in \mathcal{V}]$
Q.E.D.

With this knowledge, we can easily generate a machine that recognizes any of a finite number of finite sequences and generates either a copy of that sequence (if we wish each to be an SVS), another element of that set (if we wish to have a complex dependency between subsequent viruses), a given sequence in that set (if we wish to have only one SVS), or each of the elements of that set in sequence (if we wish to have LVS = SVS).

We will again define a set of macros to simplify our task. This time, our macros will be the "recognize" macro, the "generate" macro, the "if-then-else" macro, and the "pair" macros.

The "recognize" macro simply recognizes a finite sequence and leaves the machine in one of two states depending on the result of recognition. It leaves the tape at its initial point if the sequence is not recognized so that successive recognize macros may be used to recognize any of a set of sequences starting at a given place on the tape without additional difficulties. It leaves the tape at the cell one past the end of the sequence if recognition succeeds, so that another sequence can be added outside of the recognized sequence without additional difficulty.

| S, I | N | O | D | Comment |
|---|---|---|---|---|
| | | | | ;recognize(v) for v of size z |
| $S_n, v_0$ | $S_{n+1}$ | $v_0$ | $+1$ | ;recognize 0th element |
| $S_n, *$ | $S_{n+z+z-1}$ | $*$ | $0$ | ;or rewind 0 |
| $\cdots$ | | | | ;etc till |
| $S_{n+k}, v_k$ | $S_{n+k+1}$ | $v_k$ | $+1$ | ;recognize kth element |
| $S_{n+k}, *$ | $S_{n+z+z-k}$ | $*$ | $-1$ | ;or rewind tape |
| $\cdots$ | | | | ;etc till |
| $S_{n+z-1}, v_z$ | $S_{n+z+z}$ | $v_z$ | $+1$ | ;recognize the last one |
| $S_{n+z-1}, *$ | $S_{n+z}$ | $v_z$ | $+1$ | ;or rewind tape |
| $S_{n+z}, *$ | $S_{n+z+1}$ | $*$ | $-1$ | ;rewind tape one square |
| $\cdots$ | | | | ;for each of k states |
| $S_{n+z+z-1}$ | | | | ;'didn't recognize' state |
| $S_{n+z+z}$ | | | | ;'did recognize' state |

The "generate" macro simply generates a given sequence starting at the current tape location:

Generate($v$) where $v$ is of length of $k$

| S, I | N | O | D |
|------|---|---|---|
| $S_n$ | $S_{n+1}$ | $v_0$ | $+1$ |
| ... | | | |
| $S_{n+k}$ | $S_{n+k+1}$ | $v_k$ | $+0$ |

The "if-then-else" macro consists of a "recognize" macro on a given sequence, and goes to a next state corresponding to the initial state of the "then" result if the recognize macro succeeds, and to the next state corresponding to the initial state of the "else" result if the recognize macro fails:

if ($v$) (then-state) else (else-state)

| S, I | N | O | D |
|------|---|---|---|
| $S_n$ | recognize($v$) | | |
| $S_{n+2|v|-1}$, * | else-state | * | 0 |
| $S_{n+2|v|}$, * | then-state | * | 0 |

The "pair" macro simply appends one sequence of states to another, and thus forms a combination of two sequences into a single sequence. The resulting state table is just the concatenation of the state tables:

Pair($a, b$)

| S, I | N | O | D |
|------|---|---|---|
| $S_n$ | $a$ | | |
| $S_m$ | $b$ | | |

We may now write the previous machine $M$ as

if ($v$) (pair(generate($v$),halt)) else (halt)

We can also form a machine which recognizes any of a finite number of sequences and generates copies,

$$\text{if } (v_0) \, (\text{pair}(\text{generate}(v_0),\text{halt})) \text{ else}$$
$$\text{if } (v_1) \, (\text{pair}(\text{generate}(v_1),\text{halt}) \,) \text{ else}$$
$$\ldots$$
$$\text{if } (v_k) \, (\text{pair}(\text{generate}(v_k),\text{halt})) \text{ else } (\text{halt})$$

a machine which generates the next virus in a finite ring of viruses from the previous virus,

$$\text{if } (v_0) \, (\text{apir}(\text{generate}(v_1),\text{halt})) \text{ else}$$
$$\text{if } (v_1) \, (\text{pair}(\text{generate}(v_2),\text{halt})) \text{ else}$$
$$\ldots$$
$$\text{if } (v_k) \, (\text{pair}(\text{generate}(v_0),\text{halt})) \text{ else } (\text{halt})$$

and a machine which generates any desired dependency.

$$\text{if } (v_0) \, (\text{pair}(\text{generate}(v_x),\text{halt})) \text{ else}$$
$$\text{if } (v_1) \, \big(\text{pair}(\text{generate}(v_y),\text{halt})\big) \text{ else}$$
$$\ldots$$
$$\text{if } (v_k) \, (\text{pair}(\text{generate}(v_z),\text{halt})) \text{ else } (\text{halt})$$
$$\text{where } v_x, v_y, \ldots, v_z \in \{v_1, \ldots, v_k\}$$

We now show a machine for which every sequence is a virus, as is shown in the following simple lemma.

**Lemma 5.1.**

$$\exists M \in \mathcal{M} \; \forall v \in I^* \; \exists V$$

$$[[v \in V] \text{ and } [(M,V) \in LVS]]$$

*Proof.* by demonstration:

$$I = \{X\}, \, S = \{s_0\}$$

| Name | S, I | N | O | D |
|------|------|-----|-----|-----|
| M: | $s_0, X$ | $s_0$ | $X$ | $+1$ |

Trivially seen from state table:

$\forall$ time $t$ $\forall\Xi$ $\forall P$ [not $M$ halts]

and $\forall n \in \mathcal{N}$ $\forall v \in I^n$

$[[v \overset{M}{\Rightarrow} \{(X)\}]$ and $[(M, \{(X), v\}) \in LV\,S]]$

hence

$$\left[\forall v \in I^* \left[(M, \{v, (X)\}) \in \mathcal{V}\right]\right]$$

and by Theorem 1, $[\exists V[[v \in V]$ and $[(M, V) \in LV\,S]]]$
Q.E.D.

## B.3   COMPUTABILITY ASPECTS OF VIRUSES AND VIRAL DETECTION

We can clearly generate a wide variety of viral sets, and the use of macros is quite helpful in pointing this out. Rather than follow this line through the enumeration of any number of other examples of viral sets, we would like to determine the power of viruses in a more general manner. In particular, we will explore three issues.

The "decidability" issue addresses the question of whether or not we can write a TM program capable of determining, in a finite time, whether or not a given sequence for a given $M$ is a virus. The "evolution" issue addresses the question of whether we can write a $M$ program capable of determining, in a finite time, whether or not a given sequence for a given $M$ "generates" another given sequence for that machine. The "computability" issue addresses the question of determining the class of sequences that can be "evolved" by viruses.

We now show that it is undecidable whether or not a given $(M, V)$ pair is a viral set. This is done by reduction from the halting problem in the following manner. We take an arbitrary machine $M'$ and tape sequence $V'$, and generate a machine $M$ and tape sequence $V$ such that $M$ copies $V'$ from inside of $V$, simulates the execution of $M'$ on $V'$, and if $V'$ halts on $M'$, replicates $V$. Thus, $V$ replicates itself if and only if $V'$ would halt on machine $M'$. We know that the "halting problem" is undecidable by Turing's work, that any program that replicates itself is a virus (Lemma 2.1), and thus that $[(M, V) \in \mathcal{V}]$ is undecidable.

**Theorem 6.**

$$\left[ \not\exists D \in \mathscr{M} \; \exists s_1 \in S_D \; \forall M \in \mathscr{M} \; \forall V \in I^* \right.$$

(1)  $[D \text{ halts}]$ and

(2)  $[S_D(t) = s_1] \Leftrightarrow [(M, V) \in \mathscr{V}]]$

*Proof.* by reduction from the Halting Problem:

$$\forall M \in \mathscr{M} \; \exists M' \in \mathscr{M}$$

$$['L' \notin I_{M'}] \text{ and } ['R' \notin I'_M]$$

and

$$['l' \notin I_{M'}] \text{ and } ['r' \notin I_{M'}]$$

and

$$[\forall S_{M'}[I_{M'} = 'r'] \Rightarrow$$

$$[[N_{M'} = S_{M'}] \text{ and } [O_{M'} = 'r'] \text{ and } [D_{M'} = +1]]]$$

and

$$[\forall S_M$$

$$[[N_M = S_M] \text{ and } [O_M = I_M] \text{ and } [D_M = 0]]$$

$$\Rightarrow [[N_{M'} = S_x] \text{ and } [O_{M'} = I_M] \text{ and } [D_{M'} = 0]]]$$

We must take some care in defining the machine $M'$ to assure that it CANNOT write a viral sequence, and that it CANNOT overwrite the critical portion of $V$ which will cause $V$ to replicate if $M'$ halts. Thus, we restrict the "simulated" $(M', V)$ pair by requiring that the symbols $L, R, l, r$ not be used by them. This restriction is without loss of generality, since we can systematically replace any occurrences of these symbols in $M'$ without changing the computation performed or its halting characteristics. We have again taken special care to assure that $(M', V')$ cannot interfere with the sequence $V$ by restricting $M'$ so that in ANY state, if the symbol $l$ is encountered, the state remains unchanged, and the tape moves right by one square. This effectively simulates the "semi-infinite" end of the tape, and forces $M'$ to remain in an area outside of $V$. Finally, we have restricted $M'$ such that for all states such that "$M$ halts,"$M'$ goes to state $S_x$.

Now by Turing:

$$\nexists D \in \mathcal{M} \; \forall M' \in \mathcal{M} \; \forall V' \in I^*$$

(1)   $[D \text{ halts}]$ and

(2)   $\left[S_{D_t} = s_1\right] \Leftrightarrow \left[(M', V') \text{ halts}\right]$

We now construct $(M, V)$:

$$\left[(M, V) \in \mathcal{V}\right] \Leftrightarrow \left[(M', V') \text{ halts}\right]$$

as follows:

| Name | S, I | N | O | D | Comment |
|------|------|---|---|---|---------|
| $M$: | $s_0, L$ | $S_1$ | $L$ | $0$ | ;if 'L' then continue |
|      | $s_0$, else | $S_0$ | $X$ | $0$ | ;else halt |
|      | $s_1$ | (CPY('l','r','R') | | | ;Copy from 1 till r after R |
|      | $s_2$ | L('L') | | | ;left till 'L' |
|      | $s_3$ | R('R') | | | ;right till 'R' |
|      | $s_4$ | $s_5$ | $l$ | $+1$ | ;move to start of (M',V') |
|      | $s_5$ | $M'$ | | | ;the program M' goes here |
|      | $s_x$ | L('L') | | | ;move left till 'L' |
|      | $s_{x+1}$ | CPY('L','R','R') | | | ;Copy from L till R after R |
| | | $V = \{(L, l, v', r, R)\}$ | | | |

Since the machine $M$ requires the symbol 'L' to be under the tape head in state $s_0$ in order for any program to not halt immediately upon execution, and since we have restricted the simulation of $M'$ to not allow the symbol 'L' to be written or contained in $v'$, $M'$ CANNOT generate a virus.

$$\forall t \in \mathcal{N} \; \forall S_M \leq s_x$$

$$\left[\nexists P_{M_t}[[I \neq \text{'L'}] \text{ and } [O = \text{'L'}]]\right]$$

This restricts the ability to generate members of $\mathcal{V}$ such that $V$ only produces symbols containing the symbol 'L' in state $s_0$ and $s_{x+1}$, and thus these are the ONLY states in which replication can take place. Since $s_0$ can only write 'L' if it is already present, it cannot be used to write a virus that was not previously present.

$$\forall t \in \mathcal{N} \ \forall s (s_5 \leq s \leq s_x)$$

$$[\text{not } [M' \text{ halts at time } t]] \text{ and } \left[P_{M_{t+1}} \text{ not within } V\right]$$

If the execution of $M'$ on $V'$ never halts, then $s_{x+1}$ is never reached, and thus $(M, V)$ cannot be a virus.

$$[\forall Z \in I' : Z_0 \neq \text{'L'}]$$

$$[M \text{ run on } Z \text{ at time } t] \Rightarrow [M \text{ halts at time } t+1]$$

$$[(M', V') \text{ halts}] \Leftrightarrow$$

$$[\not\exists t \in \mathcal{N} : \Xi_t = s_{x+1}]$$

thus $[\text{not } (M', V') \text{ halts}] \Rightarrow [(M, V) \notin \mathcal{V}]$

Since $s_{x+1}$ replicates $v$ after the final 'R' in $v$, $M'$ halts $\Rightarrow V$ is a viral set w.r.t. $M$.

$$[\exists t \in \mathcal{N} : \Xi_t = s_{x+1}] \Rightarrow \left[\forall v \in V \left[v \overset{M}{\Rightarrow} \{V\}\right]\right]$$

and from Lemma 2.1

$$\left[\forall v \in V v \overset{M}{\Rightarrow} V\right] \Rightarrow [(M, V) \in \mathcal{V}]$$

thus $[(M, V) \in \mathcal{V}] \Leftrightarrow [(M', V') \text{ halts}]$
and by Turing

$$\not\exists D \in \mathcal{M} \ \forall M' \in \mathcal{M} \ \forall V' \in I^*$$

$$(1) \quad [D \text{ halts}] \text{ and}$$

$$(2) \quad [S_{D_t} = s_1] \Leftrightarrow [(M', V') \text{ halts}]$$

thus $\not\exists D \in \mathcal{M} \ \forall M \in \mathcal{M} \ \forall V \in I^*$

$$(1) \quad D[\text{halts}] \text{ and}$$

$$(2) \quad [S_{D_t} = s_1] \Leftrightarrow [(M, V) \in \mathcal{V}]$$

Q.E.D.

We now answer the question of viral "evolution" quite easily by changing the above example so that it replicates (state 0') before running $V'$ on $M'$, and generates $v' \Leftrightarrow (M',V')$ halts. The initial self-replication forces $[(M,V) \in \mathcal{V}]$, while the generation of $v' \Leftrightarrow (M',V')$ halts, makes the question of whether $v'$ can be evolved from $v$ undecidable. $v'$ can be any desired sequence $a$, and if it is a virus and not $v$, it is an evolution of $v \Leftrightarrow (M',V')$ halts. As an example, $v'$ could be $v$ with a slightly different sequence $V''$ in place of $V'$.

**Lemma 6.1.**

$$\not\exists D \in \mathcal{M}, \forall (M,V) \in \mathcal{V} \; \forall v \in V \; \forall v'$$

(1)   $[D \text{ halts}]$ and

(2)   $[S_t = s_1] \Leftrightarrow \left[ v \overset{M}{\Rightarrow} \{v'\} \right]$

Sketch of proof by demonstration:
Modify machine $M$ above

| Name | S, I | N | O | D | Comment |
|------|------|---|---|---|---------|
| $M$: | $s_0, L$ | $S_0'$ | L | 0 | ;if 'L' then continue |
| | $s_0$, else | $S_0$ | X | 0 | ;else halt |
| | $s_0'$ | CPY('L','R','R') | | | ;replicate initial virus |
| | $s_0''$ | L('L') | | | ;return to replicated 'L' |
| | $s_1$ | CPY('l','r','R') | | | ;Copy from l till r after R |
| | $s_2$ | L('L') | | | ;left till 'L' |
| | $s_3$ | R('r') | | | ;right till 'R' |
| | $s_4$ | $s_5$ | r | +1 | ;move to start of (M',V') |
| | $s_5$ | $M'$ | | | ;the program M' goes here |
| | $s_x$ | L('L') | | | ;move left till 'L' |
| | $s_{x+1}$ | R('R') | | | ;move right till 'R' |
| | $s_{x+2}$ | $s_{9+k}$ | 'R' | +1 | ;get into available space |
| | $s_{x+3}$ | generate(v') | | | ;and generate v' |

Assume $[v' \text{ is a virus w.r.t. } M]$
Since $[s_{x+3} \text{ is reached}] \Leftrightarrow [(M',V') \text{ halts}]$
thus $[v' \text{ is generated}] \Leftrightarrow [(M',V') \text{ halts}]$
Q.E.D.

We are now ready to determine just how powerful viral evolution is as a means of computation. Since we have shown that an arbitrary machine can be embedded within a virus (Theorem 6), we will now choose a particular class of machines to embed to get a class of viruses with the property that the successive members of the viral set generated from any particular member of the set, contain subsequences which are (in Turing's notation) the of successive iterations of the "Universal Computing Machine." The successive members are called "evolutions" of the previous members, and thus any number that can be "computed" by a $\mathcal{M}$ can be "evolved" by a virus. We therefore conclude that "viruses" are at least as powerful a class of computing machines as $\mathcal{M}$s, and that there is a "Universal Viral Machine" that can evolve any "computable" number.

**Theorem 7.**

$$\forall M' \in \mathcal{M} \; \exists (M,V) \in \mathcal{V} \; \forall i \in \mathcal{N}$$

$$\forall x \in \{0,1\}^i [\, x \in H_{M'} \,]$$

$$\exists v \in V \; \exists v' \in V$$

$$[[\, v \text{ evolves into } v' \,] \text{ and } [\, x \subset v' \,]].$$

*Proof.* By demonstration:
By Turing:

$$\forall M' \in \mathcal{M} \; \exists \, \text{UTM} \in \mathcal{M} \; \exists \, \text{`D.N'} \in I^*$$

$$\forall i \in \mathcal{N} \; \forall x \in \{0,1\}^i [\, x \in H_{M'} \,]$$

Using the original description of the "Universal Computing Machine," we modify the UTM so that each successive iteration of the UTM interpretation of an 'D.N' is done with a new copy of the 'D.N' which is created by replicating the modified version resulting from the previous iteration into an area of the tape beyond that used by the previous iteration. We will not write down the entire description of the UTM, but rather just the relevant portions are listed in the following table.

| S, I | N | O | D | Comments |
|---|---|---|---|---|
| b: | f(b1,b1,':') | | | ;initial states of UTM print out |
| b1: | R,R,P:,R,R,PD,R,R,PA anf | | | ;:DA on the f-squares after :: |
| anf: | | | | ;this is where UTM loops |
| . . . | | | | ;the interpretation states follow |
| ov: | anf | | | ;and the machine loops back to anf |

We modify the machine as in the case of Theorem 6 except that we replace:

|  | ov: | anf | ;goto 'anf' |
|---|---|---|---|
| with: | ov: | g(ov','r') | ;write an 'r' |
| | ov': | L('L') | ;go left till 'L' |
| | ov'': | CPY('L','R','R') | ;replicate virus |
| | ov''': | L('L') | ;left till start of the evolution |
| | ov'''': | R('r') | ;right till marked 'r' |
| | ov''''': | anf | ;goto 'anf' |

and   $\forall S_{UTM}[I_{UTM} = 'R'] \Rightarrow$
[move right 1, write 'R', move left 1, continue as before]

The modification of the 'anf' state breaks the normal interpretation loop of the UTM, and replaces it with a replication into which we then position the tape head so that upon return to 'anf' the machine will operate as before over a different portion of the tape. The second modification assures that from any state that reaches the right end of the virus 'R', the R will be moved right one tape square, the tape will be repositioned as it was before this movement, and the operation will proceed as before. Thus, tape expansion does not eliminate the right side marker of the virus. We now specify a class of viruses as ('L','D.N','R') and *M* as:

| S, I | N | O | D | Comments |
|---|---|---|---|---|
| $s_0, L$ | $s_1$ | $L$ | $+1$ | ;start with 'L' |
| $s_0$,else | $s_0$ | else | 0 | ;or halt |
| $s_1$ · · · | | | | ;states from modified UTM |

# Appendix C

# MODELS OF PRACTICAL VIRUS DEFENSES

This appendix details why and in what manner integrity shells are optimal in their defense against computer viruses. It is extracted from a journal article of a similar name cited in the bibliography.

## C.1   A TRUSTED SYSTEM EXAMPLE

In the present context, we define the term "trusted system" as a system that can be trusted to accurately implement algorithms we describe herein regardless of other factors in the environment. An "untrusted system" is defined as any system that is not a trusted system. In a trusted system, we may model change control using the following mechanism: $S_1 := \{P, d\}$

$$\text{a set of programs } P = \{p_1, p_2, \ldots, p_n\}, \qquad n \in \mathcal{I}, \quad (1.1)$$
$$\text{a dependency relation } d \subset P \times P. \qquad (1.2)$$

The relation $d$ describes the dependency of programs on each other. This is closely related to the flow relation discussed earlier, but differs in that general-purpose functionality is not assumed, and the ability to modify another domain is not required. Only the ability to cause another program to result in a different state or output is required in order to have a dependency relation.

If we could truly enforce this policy, it would appear to be a solid defense against unauthorized cause/effect relationships, but it still fails to capture the intent of the user regarding the times at which dependencies are to be exercised and what specific dependencies are intended. The requirement to specify $d$ also places an increased burden on the user, while only providing limited protection. By way of example, in a general-purpose system, an authorized program $p_j$, where

$$\{p_i, p_j\} \subset P, \; (p_i, p_j) \in d \text{ (read } p_i \text{ depends on } p_j)$$

could cause $p_i$ to implant a virus at any time. Similarly, $p_k$ could cause any $p_j$ to implant a virus, where

$$\{p_j, p_k\} \subset P, \; (p_j, p_k) \in d$$

In essence, we have implemented a preordering by using the trusted system this way, since:

$$\forall p_i, p_j, p_k \in P$$
$$p_i d p_j \text{ and } p_j d p_k \Rightarrow p_i d p_k$$
$$p_i d p_j \text{ and } p_j d p_i \Rightarrow p_i = p_j$$
$$\text{but NOT necessarily } p_i d p_i$$

Another side effect is that for every new program, we must specify $d$, and as our intent changes, so must $d$. The ability to modify $d$ must be limited so that a program in $P$ cannot modify the structure of the relation in order to perform other modifications, and the inconvenience increases.

## C.2   AN ALTERNATIVE TO DEPENDENCY RELATIONS

An alternative method for allowing user intent to be captured in the operation of such a system is the use of a modified command interpreter that requires explicit authorization for changes. This allows us to have an implied dependency relation that changes with time and is quite specific to the user's intent at a given moment.

$$S_2 := \{P, T, A, M\}$$

A set of programs $P = \{p_1, p_2, \ldots, p_n\}, \quad n \in \mathcal{I}$      (2.1)

A set of modification times $T = \{t_1, t_2, \ldots, t_n\}$      (2.2)

where $\forall t_i \in T$, $t_i$ is the last

modification time of program $p_i$

A set of authorized modification times $A = \{a_1, a_2, \ldots, a_n\}$    (2.3)

A set of moves $M = \{m_1, m_2, m_3, m_4\}$      (2.4)

Operating System:

1. get a program $p_i$ to be interpreted                          (2.5)
2. if $t_i = a_i$, {interpret $p_i$; goto 1}                       (2.6)
3. ask user for a move $m$ and act as described below:   (2.7)

$m = m_1$ goto 1

$m = m_2$ {interpret $p_i$; goto 1}

$m = m_3$ {set $a_i = t_i$; interpret $p_i$; goto 1}

$m = m_4$ {restore $p_i$ from time $a_i$; set $t_i = a_i$;

interpret $p_i$; goto 1}

In $S_2$, we have a set of authorized and actual modification times that are compared to determine whether modifications to a program $p_i$ have been authorized, as a condition on interpreting $p_i$. In the case where modifications are authorized, $p_i$ is interpreted without interruption. Unauthorized modifications are treated in one of 4 ways, as specified by the user:

1. $p_i$ is not interpreted
2. $p_i$ is interpreted as is but not permanently authorized
3. $p_i$ is permanently authorized and then interpreted
4. $p_i$ is replaced with an authorized version, then interpreted

The four moves above are examples of how a situation of change might be handled. In the first option, we simply refuse to run the changed program, and presumably investigate further at a later time. In the second option, we run the program for now, knowing it might be untrustworthy. We don't decide to trust the change, and thus continue to generate warnings. In the third option, we decide to accept the change as desirable now and forever. In the fourth option, we restore an old and trusted version of the program from backups and abandon the change.

This method has the advantage that it does not prohibit modifications to programs, but merely forces the user to decide whether or not to trust these modifications before applying them. There is a drawback in that a trusted channel is needed between the user and the TCB in order for $S_2$ to reliably get $m$ from the user. In a trusted computing base, we could allow the user to selectively authorize modifications before they occur. We could not be guaranteed that the modifications are those desired or expected.

A different attack scenario is an attack that corrupts only information that has been changed very recently. In this scenario, we cannot differentiate legitimate from illegitimate modification because of their proximity in time. We still suffer from the possibility of an authorized modification not matching our desires.

The basic problem of being unable to verify that a change is desirable appears to be unsolvable. We may even be willing to verify every state change a system makes. This activity would make the use of a system unbearable unless we could automate the process, but then we would be faced with the problem of verifying the automated checking process as it verifies the system. In the end, we cannot perfect this checking process unless we are able to discern between correct and incorrect inputs to the system. Any time there is a choice to be made, if we can fully cover corruption in the making of the choice, there is no choice left to make, and thus the choice is unnecessary.

## C.3   IMPLEMENTATIONS FOR UNTRUSTED SYSTEMS

If we attempt to implement the previous techniques in an untrusted computing base, we meet with several problems. In $S_1$, we used $d$ to specify the programs that affect each program, but in an untrusted system, there is no way to enforce the $d$ relation. In $S_2$ we require a method for maintaining two sets of modification times and comparing them at interpretation time. Again, we cannot provide this service with impunity in an untrusted system.

In previous papers, we have partially solved this problem through the use of a cryptographic checksum. This allows the complexity of illicit modification to be driven up so that we can provide any desired degree of assurance against undetected or unauthorized modification. With the use of the cryptographic checksum to identify change, we can implement a command interpreter similar to the one of $S_2$ above. This has been partially implemented by several authors. A mathematical description of the technique follows:

$$S_3 := \{P, K, S, C : P \times K \Rightarrow S, M, V, k\}$$

A set of programs $P = \{p_1, p_2, \ldots, p_n\}, \qquad n \in \mathscr{I} \qquad (3.1)$

A set of keys $K = \{k_1, k_2, \ldots, k_m\}, \qquad m \in \mathscr{I} \qquad (3.2)$

A set of checksums $S = \{s_1, \ldots, s_o\}, \qquad o \in \mathscr{I} \qquad (3.3)$

A transform $C : P \times K \Rightarrow S \qquad (3.4)$

A set of moves $M = \{m_1, m_2, m_3, m_4\} \qquad (3.5)$

A set of values $V = \{v_1, \ldots, v_n\}, \qquad (3.6)$

$\forall v_i \in V, \exists s_i \in S : v_i = s_i$

Each user has a secret key $k \in K \qquad (3.7)$

At a set of times $T = \{t_1, t_2, \ldots, t_n\}$, we generate initial values

$$V = \{v_1, v_2, \ldots, v_n\} \; \forall p_i \in P, \text{ where}$$
$$\forall v_i \in V, \; v_i = C(p_i, k) \text{ at time } t_i. \qquad (3.8)$$

$$\text{Define } t_j : \forall t_i \in T, \qquad t_j > t_i \qquad (3.9)$$

Operating System:

1. get a program $p_i$ to be interpreted (time $= t_j$)      (3.10)
2. if $C(p_i, k) = v_i$, {interpret $p_i$; goto 1}      (3.11)
3. ask user for a move $m$ and act as described below:
        $m = m_1$ {goto 1}      (3.12)
        $m = m_2$ {interpret $p_i$; goto 1}
        $m = m_3$ {set $v_i = C(p_i, k)$; interpret $p_i$; goto 1}
        $m = m_4$ {restore $p_i$ to where $C(p_i, k) = v_i$; interpret $p_i$; goto 1}

Just as in the previous example, this method permits 4 options that allow the user to accept or reject a change before using the results of that change. The only difference is the use of a cryptographic checksum to enforce the change control mechanism and the need for a trusted channel between the user and the computer in order to assure that a Trojan horse does not intercept $k$.

The overhead for a typical program is about 1 second on an IBM PC with a high-speed disk drive running the DOS operating system. On a lightly loaded PC-AT running Xenix, the delay is under 1 second, and similar delays have been found on 3b2s and Harris 8000s. Sample implementations have been demonstrated in the Bourn shell, the C-shell, a modified C-shell for IBM PCs running DOS, the standard DOS command interpreter, and the Korn shell. Similar results are expected on most other computers and command interpreters.

## C.4   THE OPTIMALITY OF $S_2$ AND $S_3$

We now show that $S_3$ is optimal in the following sense. We cannot prevent primary infection (i.e., the infection of $p_i$ by some $p_j$ where $C(p_j, k) = v_j$) without eliminating sharing or programming. We therefore define optimality as maximizing the prevention of secondary infection [i.e., the infection of $p_i$ by some $p_j$ where $C(p_j, k) \neq v_j$], and minimizing the time spent in overhead for this prevention. We assume that only one program runs at a time in $S_3$, that $C$ is ample for making forgery of a $v_i \in S$ infeasible, and that only the operating system can interpret a program.

We note first that $S_3$ prevents all secondary infection except in the case where $C(p'_j, k) = C(p_j, k)$ a successful forgery of a checksum. This is because $\forall p'_j$: $C(p'_j, k) \neq C(p_j, k)$, $C(p'_j, k) \neq v_j$, and thus from (3.11) $p'_j$ is not interpreted unless the change resulting in $C(p'_j, k) \neq v_j$ is authorized by the user.

Since at any time, $t_k$: $t_i < t_k < t_j$ there is another time $t_l$: $t_k < t_l < t_j$, checking $C(p_j, k)$ at time $t_k$ does not detect a change at time $t_l$.

Since there is no possibility of interpreting $p_j$ before time $t_j$, there is no possibility of infection of any $p_i$ by $p_j$ before $t_j$. Thus a check of $p_j$ at time $t_k$ does not detect infection at time $t_l$, which is required in order to meet our first condition of optimality, and furthermore requires extra time, which fails to meet our second condition of optimality.

If $S_3$ does one thing at a time, there is no program $p_k$ that can be interpreted between time $t_j$ and the interpretation of $p_j$, and thus there is no later time than $t_j$ to perform the checksum and still meet the condition of preventing all secondary infections. Hence, $t_j$ is the optimal time to perform $C(p_j, k)$. Since our system performs $C(p_j, k)$ at time $t_j$, it is in fact optimal by our criteria.

$S_2$ varies from $S_3$ in only one important way, it needn't depend on the quality of $C$ for its proper operation. Thus all of the other facts presented in this section apply equally well to $S_2$, and $S_2$ is therefore optimal in the same sense as $S_3$.

## C.5   THE ROLE OF THE ENVIRONMENT IN VIRAL PROTECTION

A major problem with the previous discussion is that it ignores the role of the environment in the propagation of computer viruses. For example, the use of the word "program" may be quite misleading in the above discussion. In effect, information only has meaning in that it is interpreted. Since we cannot know a priori which information is treated as program in any given environment, we cannot know what behavior is questionable.

We often cite the "basic" programming language to show that information treated as data by the editor is treated as program by the basic language interpreter. Similarly, in compiled systems, the source code is treated as data by the editor, while it is translated into program by the compiler. Even a document formatter treats its data as program, and in fact several document formatters are general purpose enough to allow the implementation of a virus. It is therefore completely inadequate to provide methods that operate only in the environment of the command interpreter.

In effect, this only covers a very small subset of the information residing in a system.

One option is to model the dependencies of programs on each other to allow the checking of all relevant information for integrity before interpreting a given program. We can perform such checks if we know the dependency of programs on each other, either by explicit proclamation by the user or by learning the dependencies through experience. We model the dependency relation $d$ as follows:

$$S_4 := S_3 + \{D, d: PxP \Rightarrow D\}$$
$$D = \{\text{true, false}\}$$
$$\text{A dependency relation } d: (PxP \Rightarrow D) \qquad (5.1)$$

Operating System:
1. Same as (2.5)
2. if $t_i = a_i$, {if check($i$) then [interpret $p_i$; goto 1]   (5.2)
       else goto 1}
3. Same as (2.7)

Where check($x$) is a recursive function of the form:

if $t_x \neq a_x$ then FALSE,
else $\{\forall p_y \in P: (p_y, p_x) \in d, [\text{remove } (p_y, p_x) \text{ from } d]$
   if $d$ is empty, return TRUE
   if $(\forall p_j \in P: (p_x, p_j) \in d, [\text{check}(j) \neq \text{FALSE}])$
   then TRUE
   else FALSE
   }

The dependency relation is applied transitively in the check function to verify the transitive closure of all programs that $p_i$ depends on, and thus all programs that can affect the integrity of results yielded by $p_i$. This relation can produce an infinite regress if not properly implemented since there can be cyclic interdependencies between programs. The resulting dependency structure is therefore a transitive binary relation as follows:

$$\forall p_1, p_2, p_3 \in P$$

$$p_1 dp_2 \text{ and } p_2 dp_3 \Rightarrow p_1 dp_3 \quad \text{(transitive)}$$

$$d \subset P \times P \qquad\qquad \text{(binary relation)}$$

A special case of this structure is the case where:

$$\forall p_a, p_b \in P : (p_a dp_b) \Rightarrow (p_b \bar{d} p_a)$$

since this guarantees that $p: (p_a dp)$ is finite and degenerate. Such a dependency graph is a preordering that guarantees that we can search the entire structure without loops and resolve all dependencies in a straightforward manner in finite time. It also allows us to use many of the results from previous works, but does not imply that all programs must have Turing capability.

Using the flow relation $f$, we know that

$$\text{if } [(p_a f p_b) \text{ and } (p_b f p_a)] \quad \text{and} \quad \overline{[(p_a dp_b) \Rightarrow (p_b dp_a)]},$$

then $p_b$ is not general purpose!

This result states that if we are in a preordering structure and not a POset, and if multiple programs coexist in a single domain, then those programs are not general purpose. Put another way, if we wish to enforce a preordering without enforcing a POset, we must use programs without Turing capability or put each program in a private domain.

In the case of limited functionality programs, we can only use information in limited ways. The traditional concept of "data" is actually a function of the environment in which the information is interpreted, not a function of the data itself. When addressing the issue of program dependencies, we are therefore exploring properties of programs regardless of the information they operate on. Conversely, if we wish to protect "data" files from corruption, we must do so by limiting the environments in which they are interpreted. We unify this perspective by treating all information as "program," and limiting the dependencies of programs on each other.

This unification leads to a methodology wherein data files are treated as programs with the association between data files and programs that are intended to interpret them maintained by the operating system. This type of user interface has been provided in the Apple Macintosh environment wherein the invocation of a document is actually treated as the invocation of a document processing program on the specified data file. We have prototyped a generalization of this technique for PCs wherein a sequence of programs are offered in order to evaluate a given program, with the user deciding which is appropriate to the desired use. We model this system as follows:

$$S_5 := S_4 + \{A, a: P \times P \Rightarrow A\}$$

$$A = \{\text{true,false}\}$$

$$\text{An association relation } a: (P \times P \Rightarrow A) \quad (5.3)$$

Operating System:

1.  Same as (2.5)
2.  if $t_i = a_i$, $\{$if check($i$) then $[$interpret($p_i$); goto 1$]$ else goto 1$\}$    (5.4)
3.  Same as (2.7)

where check($x$) is defined as in $S_4$ and interpret($x$) is defined as $\forall p \in P$, ($xap$) and 'user permission' $\Rightarrow$ interpret $p$ using $x$ as input.

Three more potential improvements to this system are ordering the association relation so that the most likely associations are tried first, allowing the user to authenticate changes immediately after they occur so that the window in which a subsequent modification can happen is reduced nearly to vacuous, and checking critical portions of the system upon reentry into the operating system so that any corruptions of the operating system itself will be detected immediately.

## C.6   PRACTICAL LIMITS OF THESE TECHNIQUES

In the proposed system, we are placing somewhat of a burden on the user to provide accurate information about the changes in a system with time and the dependency of programs on each other. In such a situation, we can naturally expect to have some failures, if only in the inability of the human operator to make correct decisions all of the time. Furthermore, as we require more of the user, the system becomes less usable and less reliable. Fortunately, the system is quite resilient in that (N)ary infections are detected before (N + 1)ary infections can take place. As the system becomes more and more corrupt, the user must make more and more questionable decisions to keep the system operating, until finally, the system becomes so corrupt that useful operation may become nearly impossible.

Analyzing the dependencies of programs on each other may take a good deal of time if the cryptographic checksum is to be strong. If done on-line, it may create a severe performance bottleneck to usability. In $S_2$, this is not a problem. In a trusted system, $S_2$ has almost no performance effects while providing excellent protection, even if we check all of the dependencies of $S_5$.

Another major problem on untrusted systems is that an attacker could simulate the entire system, always returning the results that should be returned, but actually storing different information. When damage is triggered, everything might cease to function with no prior warning. It is for this reason that we must have some trusted hardware and a secure channel in order to have high integrity in a general-purpose trusted system.

A different attack that has been suggested is the use of a program that simulates the defense, acting as the defense would in all events except in detecting the corruptions that it spreads. Even as behavior begins to change, we may suspect that there is something wrong, but the checking mechanism will still claim that everything is as it should be. This is a quite complex problem to solve because the substitute system must produce all of the positive alarms and fail to produce the nonalarms of the system it replaces. Individualized built-in keys for each copy of the program generated could make this more complex, as could the use of evolution in the design of the defense. Although these could drive the complexity of attack higher and higher, it would still be possible to launch such an attack.

A third attack which is similar to the simulation situation is the replacement of the normal operating system with a substitute that acts just as the original operating system acts except in the case of a particular form of corruption. An example would be encrypting all on-line files and decrypting them for use. In this case, the attack may have to modify the current version of the operating system in memory to assure that when reading the encrypted operating system from disk, it returns the original. If the defense checks for changes in the memory used by the operating system, this attack becomes still more complex in that the integrity checker must be corrupted as in the second attack listed above. Again we can drive the complexity up, but can never make attack impossible.

As we see, the price for successful attack can be made quite high, but in an untrusted system we are eternally in a struggle between attack and defense. The issue at hand then is what price we are willing to pay for what degree of assurance.

# Appendix D

# SOME SAMPLE FORMS OF PROGRAM EVOLUTION

We will consider two programs equivalent if, given identical input sequences, they produce identical output sequences. The equivalence of two programs is undecidable, as is the determination of whether one program can evolve from another. This result would seem to indicate that evolution has the potential for increasing complexity of analysis, and thus difficulty of attack. In a practical operating system design, we may also have very stringent requirements on the space and time used by the protection mechanism, and certain instruction sequences may be highly undesirable because they impact some other aspect of system operation or are incompatible across some similar machines. For this reason, we may not be able to reach the levels of complexity required to eliminate concerted human attack, but we may succeed in increasing the complexity of automated attacks to a level where the time required for attack is sufficient to have noticeable performance impacts, even to a level where no attacker is able to design a strong enough attack to defeat more than a small number of evolutions.

We know that evolution is as general as Turing machine computation, and that an exhaustive set of equivalent programs is easily described mathematically (i.e., the definition of equivalence), but this is not particularly helpful in terms of designing practical evolutionary schemes. We now describe a number of practical techniques we have explored for program evolution and some results regarding the space, time, and complexity issues introduced by these techniques.

## D.1  INSTRUCTION EQUIVALENCE

In some computers, several machine instructions are equivalent. For example, there are several equivalent "op-codes"[1] on the Intel 808x series of processors. An evolution can be attained by replacing applicable op-codes with equivalent op-codes. Assuming that 1 of every $k$ instructions can be

---

[1]That is, operation code—the portion of the instruction used to determine which machine operation is to be performed.

replaced by any of *e* different instruction codes in this way, we can produce *e* programs for every *k* instructions, or $(n/k)^e$ equivalent *n*-instruction programs.

Instruction equivalence, at least in the 808x family of computers, has no impact on time or space, since equivalent forms of the same instructions operate identically. The effort required to make these transformations is minimal, and their impact on a serious attacker is relatively insignificant because detecting any of a set of op-codes is nearly as simple as detecting any particular element of the set (i.e., at most a linear number of steps).

## D.2   EQUIVALENT INSTRUCTION SEQUENCES

A very similar procedure involves replacing instruction sequences with equivalent sequences. For example, a sequence that adds 17 to a memory location can be replaced by instructions that add 20 and subtract 3, or any other combination of operations that yield the same result. This produces a potentially infinite number of equivalent programs. Another way to get equivalent sequences is by performing operations using different register modes, and saving and restoring registers respectively before and after executions.

The number of evolutions is potentially infinite in this technique, but it may also increase time and space. If we wish to use only the space equivalent replacements, we may be severely limited, while some evolutions may exchange time with space so as to make the resulting program either faster or slower.

In terms of attack, this process can greatly complicate things. For example, a test for '0' or '1' can be replaced by a large number of equivalent decision procedures. Several equivalent decision procedures follow:

|       | if $x = 0$ goto $A$ |        | goto $x * 5 + . + 1$ |
|-------|---------------------|--------|----------------------|
|       | $\cdots$            | .+ 1:  | $\cdots$             |
| $A$:  | $\cdots$            | .+ 6:  | $\cdots$             |
|       | goto $x + . + 1$    |        | $y = (x + 17) * 35$  |
| .+ 1: | goto $A$            |        | if $x \leq (35 * 17)$ goto $A$ |
| .+ 2: | $\cdots$            |        | $\cdots$             |
| $A$:  | $\cdots$            | $A$:   | $\cdots$             |

Clearly, we can derive enormous numbers of variations on this theme with little trouble. An attacker trying to determine what is being done in these code fragments has several problems. One problem is that any number of values may appear possible in *x*, even though, based on the original design, we may know that only the two values '0' and '1' are actually used. For other values, very strange behavior may result. Another problem is that as designers, we can control the entry points to these routines, whereas the attacker may not know all of them or understand what we knew as designers about the machine status at those entry points. By cascading these types of replacements, we can create enormous numbers of possible program executions, even though very small subsets are ever exercised due to external constraints on calling values. The complexity of attack may be dramatically increased, while the difficulty of creating these evolutions is minimal.

Care must be taken in implementing evolutions of this sort at a low level because of the difficulty in identifying and maintaining instruction boundaries and entry points. In higher-level languages, the problem is far less severe.

## D.3   INSTRUCTION REORDERING

Many instruction sequences can be reordered without altering program execution. In general, any linearly executed instruction subsequences that alter independent portions of the program state and output fall under this category. For example, assigning independent values to independent memory locations can normally be reordered. In parallel processing, it has been shown that programs produce a PO set of dependencies, and programs for automatically analyzing these dependencies have been written to exploit this property in parallel processing applications. The number of reorderings is limited by the number of equivalent paths through the program, and the number of paths can be enormous. For example, a typical operating system call involves setting a series of values and making the call. In the setting of these parameters, order is rarely important, and we typically set two or three values, which means that each operating system call might be reordered into any of 6 different forms, not including any reordering of the calculations used for setting the parameters. In calls using arguments placed on the stack, we can similarly reorder the sequence of stack pushes and pops, again producing $n!$ orderings for $n$ different arguments. Here is a simple example with 3 statements in all 6 orderings:

| | | |
|---|---|---|
| a = a + 1;<br>b = b*3 + c;<br>j = j + 12; | a = a + 1;<br>j = j + 12;<br>b = b*3 + c; | j = j + 12;<br>a = a + 1;<br>b = b*3 + c; |
| b = b*3 + c;<br>j = j + 12;<br>a = a + 1; | b = b*3 + c;<br>a = a + 1;<br>j = j + 12; | j = j + 12;<br>b = b*3 + c;<br>a = a + 1; |

Reordering of instructions generally requires no additional time or space while providing $n!$ different variants, but this may not drive up the complexity of attack in cases where specific instructions are being sought for bypass. For example, the multiplication can be easily found in all six.

## D.4  VARIABLE SUBSTITUTIONS

In high-level languages, we may use variable substitutions to alter program appearance, but this has little effect on lower-level programs unless compilers produce resorted symbol tables. At lower levels, we may easily alter the locations of memory storage areas. By moving variables, we prevent static examination and analysis of parameters and alter memory locations throughout a program without affecting program execution. Here is an example of the impact of variable substitutions at the low level, where we have given numerical values to all instructions and labeled memory locations:

| | | | | | |
|---|---|---|---|---|---|
| 1: | 2705 | ;jump to 5 | 1: | 2705 | ;jump to 5 |
| 2: | 0 | ;loc of 'A' | 2: | 1701 | ;loc of 'B' |
| 3: | 1701 | ;loc of 'B' | 3: | 2103 | ;loc of 'C' |
| 4: | 2103 | ;loc of 'C' | 4: | 0 | ;loc of 'A' |
| 5: | 1002 | ;A = A + 1 | 5: | 1004 | ;A = A + 1 |
| 6: | 2003 | ;B = B − 1 | 6: | 2002 | ;B = B − 1 |
| 7: | 2103 | ;shift B left | 7: | 2102 | ;shift B left |
| 8: | 1734 | ;xor C with B | 8: | 1723 | ;xor C with B |
| 9: | 4306 | ;B = 0?goto 6 | 9: | 4206 | ;B = 0?goto 6 |
| 10: | 0 | ;halt CPU | 10: | 0 | ;halt CPU |

To see this effect more plainly, we now show only the values of memory locations and leave out the comments:

| | | |
|---|---|---|
| 1: | 2705 | 2705 |
| 2: | 0 | 1701 |
| 3: | 1701 | 2103 |
| 4: | 2103 | 0 |
| 5: | 1002 | 1004 |
| 6: | 2003 | 2002 |
| 7: | 2103 | 2102 |
| 8: | 1734 | 1723 |
| 9: | 4306 | 4206 |
| 10: | 0 | 0 |

In general, we can place each variable at any program location not yet used by another conflicting variable. This yields $n!v$ different configurations for $v$ variables in $n$ program locations. In practice, variables are commonly kept in specific areas, stacks require allocatable areas, and other restraints on memory locations are common. By altering this practice and placing variables pseudorandomly throughout the program, we may cause a great deal of diffusion. This is easily done by a compiler.

## D.5   ADDING AND REMOVING JUMPS

Many program sequences can be modified by placing a series of jump instructions where previous instruction sequences were located, relocating the previous instructions, and jumping back after sequences are completed. This produces arbitrary reordering of instructions, and at least $n!$ unique sequences for an $n$-instruction original sequence. Here is a simple example:

| | | | |
|---|---|---|---|
| A: | $I_1$ | A: | Jump A' |
| B: | $I_2$ | B: | Jump B' |
| C: | $I_3$ | C: | Jump C' |
| D: | $I_4$ | D: | Jump D' |
| E: | $I_5$ | E: | Jump E' |
| F: | $\cdots$ | F: | $\cdots$ |
| | | B': | $I_2$; Jump C |
| | | E': | $I_5$; Jump F |
| | | C': | $I_3$; Jump D |
| | | A': | $I_1$; Jump B |
| | | D': | $I_4$; Jump E |

We can similarly remove existing jump instructions and reorder programs, so long as no other part of the program transfers control into those sequences. Even in those cases, we can sometimes alter the jumps into the reordered sequences.

The addition of jump instructions increases space and time approximately linearly with the number of jumps inserted while their removal increases performance and decreases space. This does not alter the form of specific instructions being sought, but it does a good job of obscuring program sequences.

One major problem with this technique is that different instructions take different amounts of space on some processors. This makes incoming jump instructions error prone unless the evolution process is done very carefully.

At the source code level, the technique is quite simple, and thus it is particularly useful when we can reassemble or recompile code.

By designing programs with "jump tables" or other similar structures, we may easily combine reordering of instructions and instruction sequences with altered jump tables to evolve programs in this way. A similar technique has been used by some software developers to make tracking of corporate licensees easier. When a particular evolved version is found, the corporation that released it can be easily identified.

## D.6   ADDING AND REMOVING CALLS

Programs that use subroutine calls and other similar processes can be modified to replace the call and return sequences with in-line code or altered forms of call and return sequences. Similarly, any sequence of in-line code can be replaced by subroutine calls and returns. Assuming that any single instruction can be placed in or removed from a subroutine and that there are $k$ different subroutine call and return sequences, an $n$-instruction program results in $n^k$ different evolutions. The time and space alterations are similar to those for inserting and removing jump instructions except that calls take more instructions to implement and may impact the stack and other processor information. Here is a simple example of call modification:

| | | | | |
|---|---|---|---|---|
| | goto Start; | | | goto Start; |
| f(a): | return(2*a); | o( ): | | z = z + 3; |
| pr(a): | wait-for-printer ( ); | | | return(0); |
| | print(a): | Start: | | x = 3; |
| | return(0); | | | y = 2*x; |
| Start: | x = 3; | | | o( ); |
| | y = f(x); | | | x = z + y/2; |
| | z = z + 3; | | | wait-for-printer( ); |
| | x = z + y/2; | | | print(x); |
| | pr(x); | | | halt; |
| | halt; | | | |

Another important aspect of call insertion and removal is that it obscures high-level design structure, and thus makes tracking similar operations more complex. Analysis of structure has been used by instructors in computer science courses to detect cheating, and this technique would likely invalidate those methods for use in automatic detection of program similarity.

As in the case of jump insertion and removal, it is far easier to perform call insertion and removal with knowledge of program structure.

### D.7   GARBAGE INSERTION

Any sequence of instructions that are independent of the in-line sequence can be inserted into the sequence without altering the effective program execution. Every instruction can have an arbitrary number of garbage instructions inserted, so there is no limit to the number of equivalent programs we can generate.

Each added instruction increases both time and space, but is valuable for fooling programs that look for specific instruction sequences. For example, an attack that looks for IO calls to the operating system could be fooled by inserting spurious calls, thus forcing the successful attacker to examine more and more of the parameters used in the defense, and possibly increasing the time required for an attack to an intolerable level. As an example, we offer the following listing:

```
Start:      a = 21; b = − 19;
            for d = b to 98 step 7 do
            c = c + d;
            OScall(a,4,d);
            done
```

In this listing, we will now claim that the actual operation being performed is OScall(21,4,2), and that the other OScall invocations have invalid parameters, and thus return failures. The assignment of $a$ is unrelated to this call, as is the repeated addition of $d$ to $c$. In fact, the whole loop is unneeded, but this insertion of instructions is used to complicate the process of analysis.

By making spurious calls and using their results, we may greatly complicate analysis. For example, we could optionally call one of $n$ different equivalent routines to make a decision, thus forcing multiple unique but equivalent paths through the program and making complete analysis far more complex. Again, the insertion creates confusion and diffusion. There is no limit to the amount of garbage we can insert, and a very broad range of relative ratios of garbage and program are available. The total number of different programs possible through garbage insertion is limited from above by the total number of free bits available for program space, which is limited only by available memory for program storage, and is clearly enormous.


## D.8   PROGRAM ENCODINGS

Any sequence of symbols in a program can be replaced by any other sequence of symbols, provided there is a method for undoing that replacement for the purpose of interpretation. For example, a trivial 'exclusive-or' (i.e., XOR) with a set of randomly selected bits stored in memory produces a random set of instructions, which can be recovered by performing another XOR with the same set of bits. Two common sorts of encoding schemes are compression and encryption. In compression, we find a coding that removes redundancy from the instruction sequence, and replace the original with its compressed form. In encryption, we find an encoding designed to obscure the content of a sequence. The decoding process reverses the encoding prior to execution. The number of encodings of a sequence are equivalent to the number of different sequences, or $2^n$ encodings for an $n$-bit sequence. A very good example of using encoding in an attack was given earlier, and this technique might also work well in defense.

The performance of coding schemes varies dramatically, and in the case where they must be decoded during operation, this can produce substantial time and space impacts. Furthermore, an attacker could wait until decoding is completed before bypassing protection unless the coding scheme varies as well as the things being encoded.

Encoding is strong against attacks involving examination of code, but if the decoded form is identical in all cases, it may be simple to find a way to alter the program after decoding or to observe the decoding key as it is entered or stored. Thus the use of coding alone is not sufficient for defending against serious attacks, even though it may help prevent the detection of a particular version by examination, as in the case of evading a virus scanner.


## D.9   SIMULATION

Any sequence of instructions can be replaced by an equivalent sequence for a different processor, and that processor can be simulated by an interpretation mechanism. For example, we can invert all of the bits of a program, and simulate a bit-wise inverted version of the original processor. Any coding scheme can be used for this purpose, including a scheme that varies the code with the location. Again, there are at least $2^n$ different encodings for an *n*-bit instruction sequence.

In the case of simulation, we may have significant advantages in that the attacker must understand the simulation system as well as the machine language being used, or somehow detect the desired part of the code at run time. Unfortunately, simulation requires substantial time and space, and can only be used in circumstances where time and space are noncritical.

Here is a partial example of two evolutions of a simulator, where the 'case' statement is used by the simulator to determine how to interpret instructions, and instructions follow the 'GO' label as pairs of 'op-code', 'argument':

| Loop: | | Loop: | |
|-------|-----------------|-------|------------------|
| Case  | 0:(op code 0)   | Case  | 17: (op code 17) |
|       | . . .           |       | . . .            |
|       | 6:(op code 6)   | Case  | 8: (op code 8)   |
|       | . . .           |       | . . .            |
|       | 4:(op code 4)   | Case  | 12: (op code 12) |
|       | . . .           |       | . . .            |
| . . . |                 |       |                  |
| Esac  |                 |       |                  |
|       | goto Loop       |       | goto Loop        |
| GO:   | 0,12            | GO:   | 17,12            |
|       | 4,17            |       | 12,17            |
|       | 6,17            |       | 8,17             |
|       | 4,3             |       | 12,3             |
|       | 0,4             |       | 17,4             |
|       | 6,6             |       | 8,6              |

In our example, the 'case' statements of the two examples are aligned together so that you can tell the equivalence between op-codes, but in the second parts of the listings, you can see the impact of the transformation of op-codes on reading a program listing. In the following listing, we expand on this theme by a simple transformation of the arguments (op-code 17 subtracts 1 before equivalent execution, op-code 12 adds one, and op-code 8 subtracts 4). Now, there are no common byte sequences between the two program fragments.

| GO: | 0,12 | GO: | 17,13 |
|-----|------|-----|-------|
|     | 4,17 |     | 12,16 |
|     | 6,17 |     | 8,21  |
|     | 4,3  |     | 12,2  |
|     | 0,4  |     | 17,3  |
|     | 6,6  |     | 8,10  |

By implementing an evolving simulation engine for critical parts of the program, we can make detection of equivalence require both understanding the difference between the two evolutions of the simulation engine, and understanding the equivalence between the two sequences being simulated. This can be carried to multiple levels, with the simulator simulating another simulator etcetera until we get to the level at which actual decisions are made. We can even evolve the number of levels of simulation used.

It is very easy to implement a simulation engine in most current computers through the built-in debugging mechanism. The example above where we use a loop around a case statement shows just how easily simulation can be implemented with classical techniques, and in practice simulation engines require only a few thousands bytes of source code. Evolving a simulation engine and the simulated code is also very simple. For example, in the case above, it required only simple text replacement in the interpreted code and minor changes to the engine. Another simple alteration would be to XOR the memory value with a pseudorandom function of the location number in memory. This greatly increases confusion at the expense of only a small amount of time and space.

### D.10   BUILD AND EXECUTE

An extension of the encoding and simulation techniques above is the "build-and-execute" mechanism, wherein we build instructions prior to execution and then execute them. This is a so-called self-modifying code, and again the potential complexity is equivalent to the complexity of encodings. One of the very nice points about building instructions for execution is that it obscures the instruction being executed from observation until just before execution time. This drives the time required for attack up so as to make it very noticeable in many cases.

As a method of evolution, this technique requires that we design a set of build-and-execute mechanisms and install them into a program using some sort of pseudorandom selection and placement mechanism. As in the case of many other mechanisms we have discussed, knowledge of the program being evolved is quite useful in implementing this sort of evolution.

Many build-and-execute schemes implement very complex codings that vary with use so that the instructions built may change with the details of the execution. For example, the use of relative addresses 'XOR'ed with instructions and filling in arguments at run time are common techniques.

Here is a simple example of a self-modifying code, where the 'Add' instruction is modified to add each of the elements of a list of 17 numbers. In this example, we assume that the 'op code' for 'Add' is 2300, and that the address being added is stored in the last two digits of the add instruction.

|          |                                  |                        |
|----------|----------------------------------|------------------------|
|          | AI = 2299 + @list                | ;initialize Add Instruction |
| loop:    | AI = AI + 1                      | ;increment pointer     |
| AI:      | 0                                | ;initial value is 0    |
|          | (AI − 100) < list + 16, goto loop | ;loop                 |
|          | DONE                             | ;whatever follows      |
| list:    | 12                               | ;the list to be added  |
|          | 17                               |                        |
|          | . . .                            |                        |
| list + 16 | 43                              | ;end of the list       |

Assuming that the attacker has to observe these modifications at run time in order to determine when a particular operation takes place, an automated attack would apparently have to trace program execution and react to the particular instructions being interpreted under such an evolutionary scheme rather than searching for particular strings in a program or perform analysis from the program's appearance in memory.

## D.11   INDUCED REDUNDANCY

The use of redundancy is a basic technique in integrity protection. For example, the use of cryptographic checksums for detecting arbitrary corruption applies redundant information in the form of the stored checksum value, and CRC codes and parity bits are redundant information commonly used to detect corruption due to noise of particular characteristics. The same concept can be applied to preventing attacks on programs.

In this case, we induce redundancy by repeating test procedures used to make decisions so that multiple tests must be passed in order for an operation to be accepted. When used in conjunction with other evolution techniques, this provides a mean by which the defender can prevent the attacker from being certain that the defense has been bypassed. For example, if a particular test is performed a random number of times on any given attempt at attack, the attacker cannot be certain that all of the relevant tests have been bypassed. Even if the attack works on one evolution, that doesn't mean it will work on a significant number of other evolutions.

In the following example, we show a redundant overall test which requires 3 out of 4 partial tests strewn throughout a program to be passed in order to pass the overall test.

```
count = 0;
  . . .
x = open-file('zz')
  . . .
if (x < 3) count + +;
  . . .
if (x > 0) count + +;
  . . .
if (count < 1) OR (count > 2) nogood;
  . . .
x = open-file('zz')
  . . .
if (x = 2) OR (x = 1) count + +;
  . . .
if (count < 2) OR (count > 3) nogood;
  . . .
x = open-file('zz')
  . . .
if (x AND 3) > 0 count + +;
  . . .
if ((count AND 4)! = 4) nogood;
  . . .
```

A few notes are in order here. Notice first, that there is no explicit "good" decision, but rather a set of hurdles that have to be passed and that are strewn throughout the program. If any of these tests fail, the "nogood" decision is made, but there is no simple way to avoid the last "nogood" decision. If there were an explicit "good" decision, then an attacker could simply try to locate the "good" decision point and begin operation there. Also, if the decisions were not strewn throughout the program, an attacker could easily bypass the whole set of decisions, but by intermixing them with the rest of the program, we force the attacker to work harder. Another important point is that there is no value for "count" or "$x$" that the attacker can select at the start of the program that will bypass all of the tests. This means that there is no simple way to forge the values required to make tests pass. Multiple forgeries are required. We could also use different variables for different parts of the tests, and further drive up the complexity of the attack process.

In practice, it is fairly simple to devise a series of tests and disperse them throughout a program, but ultimately tests depend on the state of the system for their accuracy, and if we are to eliminate all sorts simplistic forgery, we must not only make the tests redundant, but also the data upon which they depend. This increases the time and space requirements for accuracy, which yields our usual protection trade-off between integrity and space/time.

## D.12   INTERMIXING PROGRAMS

A rather complex sort of evolution is the intermixing of programs so that instructions from two independent operations are intermixed. This is complex to do because there are many possible interactions between memory and register states. In practice, we have found it far too complex to analyze and implement this sort of evolution at low levels, but in higher-level programming languages , we see it as having great potential.

In this example, we have two subroutines that are often called, and that leave their results in independent variables "$x$" and "$y$". As an evolution, we simply intermix the routines so that both functions are performed when either is desired, but no interference results because the results are stored independently, and by convention, we use or store the results of these routines immediately after the routines are called. Subroutine 1 is called with two integers as its argument, while subroutine 2 is called with an integer and a real number:

| Subroutine 1 | Subroutine 2 | Mixed Subroutine |
|---|---|---|
| s1(i,j) := | s2(i,r) := | sb(i,j,r) := |
| x = 0; | | x = 0; |
| x2 = 17; | | x2 = 17; |
| | y = i + 12; | y = i + 12; |
| if (i < 3) x = x + 6; | | if ($i$ < 3) x = x + 6; |
| | y = y*r/3.74; | y = y*r/3.74; |
| x = x*i + j/17; | | x = x*i + j/17; |
| return; | return; | return; |

This sort of intermixing creates two problems for the attacker. The first problem is that the intermixing could be varied so as to produce a substantial number of different orderings of the statements in the subroutine. We can select the next statement from either subroutine, so long as there are unselected statements from both remaining, which yields on the order of $2^n$ different equivalent subroutines. The second problem is that the attacker cannot tell which function is being used when it is called, and may thus be forced to trace the implications of both calls through several following program steps before realizing what information can be ignored.

In general, we can take $n$ unrelated programs and, assuming we are a bit careful, mix them together without ill effects. This seems to be very confusing to someone trying to analyze the resulting code, especially if the routines that are intermixed are selected at random for each defense. The mixing process also has the effect of disguising the subroutine calls because the calls themselves are different for different intermix combinations. In our example, the two mixed routines had two arguments each, and the mixed routine had three parameters.

## D.13   ANTIDEBUGGER MUTATIONS

In order to make debugging programs difficult, many different techniques have been developed within the computing industry. The basic principle is to make the things the debugger does to track program execution fail when debugging the evolved program. Since each processor has a somewhat different debugging mechanism, we will make assumptions designed so as to make the examples easy to understand.

Disassemblers in systems with multiple instruction lengths have methods for synchronizing instructions. When encountering a jump instruction, typically, disassemblers assume that the following instruction is a legal instruction, but we can use these instructions to mask instructions around them by placing misleading operation codes after jumps, and returning at an offset 1 or more bytes from the end of the jump. The disassemblers may see a conditional jump (that is designed to always be true in actual operation) followed by an unconditional 3-byte jump which actually masks a 2-byte operating system call. Here is an example from an 8086 processor that calls 'int 13':

| | | |
|---|---|---|
| go: | jne 1 | ;two byte conditional jump (flags clear) |
| | jle cd | ;conditional jump masking 'int' |
| | adc (13) 90 | ;add carry 90 masking 13 and no-op (90) |

An attempt at disassembly might fail in this context, but a debugger that observes each instructions as it is processed should be able to properly detect the operation.

In a similar fashion, we can include jump instructions whose last byte (usually the address jumped to) corresponds to a desired operation code, and place the code jumped to appropriately so that the jump works and the proper return address is in the middle of the previously executed instruction. In this way, we reuse the last bytes of the jump location as operation codes on the next pass through the code.

This technique again masks the true instructions being executed until execution time, thus forcing the debugger to trace each instruction in order to find a particular instruction type.

Debugging can often be turned off and turned back on in such a fashion that the debugger cannot tell that any change was made. From all appearances, the debugger executes normally, and yet some number of intervening instructions may go unobserved. This depends on the ability of the debugger to detect attempts to turn it off. We may use any addressing mode of the process to alter the memory locations used by the debugger, so in order for the debugger to be certain to catch all attempts to access its address space, it must either simulate the entire operation of the computer, or determine all addresses used on each memory operation of the program at run time, determine whether those addresses impact the debugger, and forge the instruction if needed. Either of these options consumes a great deal of processing power and results in substantial time consumption, normally within the range where people notice the slowdown.

Another common trick is to make the operation of the defense depend on the presence of its own debugging routine. For example, we could use the address of a built-in debugging routine or some offset from that address in an arithmetic operation that alters pointers, so that if the debugger operated by the defense is not operating (or alternatively, if any other debugger is operating), the code operates improperly. Another variation is to have the internal debugger alter normal instructions at execution so that (as an example) 'move' instructions that copy information between memory locations use different memory locations, reverse memory locations, alter operating modes, etcetera. This is essentially a simulation technique as described earlier.

Here is a simple example, again from an 8086 processor, of an instruction sequence containing illegal instructions and "no-op" instructions, where the "debugger" simulates altered instructions when these are encountered. Note that this is a common technique used by operating systems for operating system calls, and thus is also a call insertion technique as described earlier. In this example, the "no-op" instruction shifts the 'ax' register left 3 bits, and the illegal instruction (designated 'ill') sets the value 20 in the 'bx' register. Another debugger trying to debug this code would not alter the execution, and thus the program would not operate in the same manner.

```
go:     mov ax,3        ;initialize ax
        nop             ;no-op instruction (shift ax left 3)
        add ax,21       ;regular instruction
        ill             ;illegal instruction (setq bx to 20)
        add bx,3        ;regular instruction
```

All of these techniques can be selectively inserted and evolved during program evolution so as to produce a very complex debugging problem for the attacker. Even though some human attackers might eventually be able to get past this line of defense, they might have to observe a large number of different variations in order to determine the whole set of debugger bypass mechanisms, and then they would have to program attacks for all of them into an automated attack in order to operate automatically against this technique.

## D.14   MIX AND MATCH

All of the techniques described above may be mixed together, applied in any sequence, and applied recursively, thus providing a very rich environment for evolution. The only limitation is that identifying which code sequences may be quite difficult unless the evolution engine knows something about program structure. For example, when a program is designed with numerous jump instructions that enter into the middle of other code sequences, it may be very difficult to determine whether an alteration will have an impact on some other execution sequence. This is the same problem we cause the attacker to go through, and as we have seen it can make things rather complex.

# Appendix E

# VIRUSES IN NETWORKS

I would now like to describe some initial results of experiments on the impact of computer viruses on two modern computer networks. We begin by describing a research environment designed to allow safe and repeatable experiments with computer viruses. Next, we describe exhaustive tests of protection settings, their effectiveness against viruses in two very common computing environments, and other vulnerabilities encountered in the process of these experiments. Finally, we summarize results, describe confirming experiments performed by other researchers, and propose further work in this area.

## E.1 BACKGROUND

In July of 1992, Sanjay Mishra of Queensland University of Technology and I configured a small experimental network for the sole purpose of performing experiments on the impact of viruses on modern networking environments. We performed a number of experiments over the next 3 weeks, and reported initial results. A number of researchers were initially surprised at these results, many systems administrators expressed serious concerns about them, and several people with experience in managing these networks had difficulty believing that these results could be accurate. Because of the complexity of networks and the resulting possibility for errors in experimental technique and in interpretation of manuals, we requested that other research groups perform independent experiments to confirm or refute our results.

Since that time, two groups[1] have performed substantial experiments and reported confirmations back to us, several other groups have stated that they will be performing similar experiments,[2] our virus research

---

[1]Vesselin Bontchev of the The University of Hamburg's 'Virus Test Center' and Padget Pederson.

[2]Several of these groups are from government agencies who will almost certainly not reveal their results.

network has been dismantled,[3] and we returned to out eternal quest for components for further experiments. In the process, we have also received a substantial amount of additional information relating to our published results, and thus we present this "new and improved" work on the impact of computer viruses on modern computer networks.

For the purposes of communication, we used the F-Prot product (version 2.03a) for virus identification and scanning. When we identify the Jerusalem virus, we intend to indicate the virus identified by F-Prot as the "Jerusalem virus (standard)," and when we identify the 1704 virus, we intend to indicate the virus identified by F-Prot as the "Cascade 1704-A virus." Similarly, when we specify "Netware," we intend to indicate Novell's Netware product, version 3.11, when we specify "Unix," we intend to indicate AT&T's Unix System 5, version 3.0 running TCP/IP and NFS, also by AT&T for PC compatibles, and when we specify PC-NFS, we intend to indicate the product of that name produced by Sun Computer Systems. We note that these specific systems may not be indicative of all other similar systems, but based on the confirming experiments, we believe they are representative.

## E.2   THE PURPOSE OF THE VIRUS RESEARCH NETWORK

The Virus Research Network (VRN) was designed to allow rapid, comprehensive, conclusive, and repeatable experiments on the impact of viruses on networks. This was achieved to a reasonable extent by the methods outlined in the following. We are also interested in finding ways to improve network protection, and when we identified anomalies, we sought causes and reported the results.

Rapid experimentation is key to getting enough useful results to justify the cost of such a facility, but in our case, we had only a small window of availability for the facility, so necessity led us to efficiency. We got rapid results by automating most aspects of reconfiguration, and by using a backup computer to rebuild configurations in relatively short order. Depending on the particular experiment, the entire clean and rebuild process took as little as 20 minutes. In the worst case, cleanup required about 8 hours, and was done overnight.

Comprehensive experiments can often be performed through exhaustive testing. For example, in the experiments described later in this work we

---

[3]We borrowed most of the hardware and software on a temporary basis, and had to return the component parts to the original users.

tested all possible protection settings for files and directories on the file server against some well-known viruses. Given somewhat larger disks and more time, we could have performed still more comprehensive testing, but as we will see, this is not always required in order to get useful results.

Results were usually quite conclusive because we designed experiments with specific and attainable goals in mind, and had a facility which could be used for substantial run times without outside interference. Where possible, we tried to seek out more definitive experiments in favor of less definitive ones, and we used controls to assure that experimentation errors didn't cause false results.

We were relatively meticulous about documenting our experiments to assure that they were repeatable by outside researchers, and whenever reasonable, we used command scripts to automate operations. The use of automation in this case gives a high degree of repeatability. For example, one run may involve running several thousand programs in a particular order from a specific series of places in the network and with particular viruses active at particular times. It would be very difficult to perform or repeat such an experiment without automation.

In our first experimental run, these factors turned out to be quite critical, because the description of protection in the manuals of the network under test turned out to be inconsistent and we had to repeat the entire run. Because of the automation, we were able to perform an identical 2-hour experiment involving over 2500 program runs under slightly different conditions with only 20 minutes of analysis, cleanup, and reconfiguration overhead.

As a part of the facility, we had a fairly substantial number of virus samples received by the Queensland University of Technology's Computer Virus Information Group (CVIG) as a part of its normal interaction with users. The selection of viruses for attacks was based on the prevalence of the virus in the environment, the techniques used by the virus for infection, and the defenses in place. We also created custom attacks where no virus in our collection was appropriate to the task. In the case of custom attacks, as a matter of policy we didn't provide copies of the attacks to others, but to date, this has not caused other researchers to report problems in generating confirming results.

## E.3   THE VIRUS RESEARCH NETWORK

VRN consisted of 4 PC-compatible computers in a physically isolated room. The computers were connected with Ethernet cable providing a relatively high-speed communications backbone comparable to the most commonly used networking hardware today. The "server" machine was a 80386-based computer with 4 megabytes of RAM and 100 megabytes of disk, requires so that the commonly available network operating systems could run without further hardware. Two of the remaining computers were PC-AT class machines with 20 megabyte hard disks and 1 megabyte of memory required to run workstation software. The fourth machine had a tape drive that allowed it to perform rapid and reliable backup and restoration for the remainder of the network.

We pause to note that the 100 megabyte limitation on file server disk space restricted our ability to perform some exhaustive tests. For example, to test all file protections and directory protections under Unix requires $2^{18}$ files ($2^9$ different file protections in each of $2^9$ different directories). To create the 262,144 required files in 512 directories using only 1 kilobytes per file requires over 250 megabytes. Since virus infections typically require more than another 1 kilobytes of disk space, we could encounter conditions requiring over 500 megabytes of disk space. Many file systems also have difficulty handling that many files, and even more importantly, as we describe later, the complexity of updating protections in these circumstances makes accurate experiments difficult to perform.

In addition to physical isolation, all viruses used for experiments were kept on well-marked floppy disks in a locked file cabinet, and all machines used in the network were clearly marked as contaminated. Machines were only allowed to leave the facility after the relatively thorough cleanup process described below, except in specific cases where well-understood viruses were tested under very controlled circumstances. Floppy disks were not permitted to leave the facility without reformatting on a "Clean'ed" machine.

An additional machine which runs Coherent (a PC-based Unix-like system) was used to create script files that automated configuration and operation of the network for experiments. This machine only produced disks for the network, and never took information out of the facility. Disks were transported back to this machine only after being formatted by the Backup machine and then again by the receiving machine. A typical run involved DOS batch files of over 50 kilobytes, and could be created in a few minutes by the Coherent system with a minimum of effort.

VRN operated in three distinct operating modes;

1. **Run.** In the Run Mode, the Backup machine was physically disconnected from the network so that it remained free from viruses. The server and the two workstations operated with viruses placed in the configuration as appropriate to the experiment.

2. **Clean.** In the Clean mode, each computer was rebooted from a write-protected operating system disk using hardware reset, and all operations were performed from programs on that disk. Computers were scanned for known viruses using scanning software known to reliably detect the virus samples used for the experiments. These results were printed on a local printer for further analysis and as a record of operations. After analysis information was gathered, further experiments were sometimes performed by returning to the "Run" mode, or the systems were prepared for rebuilding by performing a low-level fixed disk format, preparing a known good partition table, and restoring basic operating system files from the floppy disk. After this procedure, the "Rebuild" mode was entered.

3. **Rebuild.** In the Rebuild mode, the Backup computer was connected to the network, and configurations were restored to all of the other computers to prepare for the next experiment. After rebuilding was completed, the Backup computer was again disconnected from the network to allow further experiments to proceed. The Backup computer was always bootstrapped from a write-protected floppy disk drive to further assure against contamination, and all systems were scanned for known viruses after cleanup as a control.

A copy of VRN can be configured for under U.S. $6000, and operating costs are predominantly driven by physical plant, people, and software costs. The development of experiments is also nontrivial since issues arise about how to create and analyze accurate and efficient experiments, and experimental technique is of course critical. Nevertheless, we feel that any substantial organization with serious concerns about network protection could easily create and operate a similar facility.

## E.4   EXPERIMENTS

Our experiments were designed to test the efficacy of protection settings provided with network file servers against the most common computer viruses. We selected Netware and Unix for our experiments based on their availability in our laboratory and their widespread use in the current environment. We planned to perform similar experiments with other network configurations, with a variety of vendor-based defenses in place, and under a variety of usage profiles, but have been unable to get hardware, software, or support for further experiments as of this time.

Efficacy experiments are relatively easy to perform by creating an exhaustive test of protection settings for files and directories stored on the file server under the respective protection models. They are also useful because most environments operate without additional protection, and this permits us to provide accurate advice on prudent administrative measures appropriate to these environments. We thought at first that these experiments would not be particularly enlightening because if protection is properly implemented, the experiments will only reveal what we already know about the theoretical protection provided by the models. To a large extent, this was true, but as we will now see, the specific experiments and results indicate that implementation does not always meet expectations.

### E.4.1 Netware

We installed a default Netware file server configuration per the instructions in the manuals that came with the system, and configured 256 subdirectories under the "TEST" directory with names consisting of all possible combinations of the letters "Y" and "N" in the order shown below, and corresponding to the settings of the "Trustee Rights" for a user "US1" over those directories.

| S | Supervisor |
|---|---|
| E | Erase |
| R | Read |
| W | Write |
| C | Create |
| A | Access Control |
| F | FileScan |
| M | Modify |

Trustee Rights

As an example, the directory name "YNNYNNNY" has "Supervisor," "Write," and "Modify" rights enabled and all other rights disabled for user "US1." We sometimes abbreviate by using exponential notation (e.g., $NY^5NY$ is the same as NYYYYYNY).

Trustee rights were selected because they are supposed to dominate the "Inherited Rights" implied by ANDing the parent directory's effective rights with the "Inherited Rights Mask," and therefore make analysis simpler without loss of generality. We did not test the assertion that Trustee Rights dominate Inherited Rights, and this should be confirmed by anyone interested in exhaustive testing of Netware protection.

Each of the resulting 256 directories were provided with 5 "EXE" and 5 "COM" executable files selected from standard DOS utilities such that they required relatively little disk space and run to completion producing only a syntax error when run from a command file with no command line arguments. This provides a method by which we can execute a large number of programs in a short period of time with a minimum of space overhead, and identifiable characteristics. The viruses selected for experiments were known to be able to infect these files and tested for this capability independently.

We initially turned on the "Copy Inhibit," "Rename Inhibit," "Delete Inhibit," and "Archive" file "Attributes," setting one bit per file and leaving one file with no protection bits set as a control. These files were designated respectively "A-E.COM" and "F-J.EXE." In order to provide exhaustive testing of Attributes in combination with Trustee Rights, we would have to create all combinations of the 14 Netware Attributes with the 8 Trustee Rights shown above, leading to $2^{22}$ (4,194,304) files in 512 directories, which would consume over 4 gigabytes of storage and require over 48 days to test at 1 program execution per second. Instead, we selected the attributes which we thought to be of interest and tested them individually. A more thorough test would be appropriate for an organization with more resources.

In RUN 1, following the description in the manual, we enabled all rights for the "TEST" directory. According to the manuals, subdirectory rights are supposed to "take precedence" over parent rights (see p. 345 of the Netware *"Utilities Reference"* manual and p. 207 of the Netware *"Concepts"* manual). We then logged into the network as user "US1," and for each directory, changed to that directory, executed the Jerusalem virus from the hard-disk on the local workstation (stored in the file "C:\VIRUS.EXE"), executed each of the programs "A–J" in order, executed "VIRUS.EXE" again, and changed back to the "TEST" directory. This was done in sequence starting at the $Y^8$ directory and continuing in standard binary counting sequence through to the $N^8$ directory. The run took about 2 hours to complete.

After completing the run, we rebooted the workstations from their write-protected floppy boot- disks logged into the network as Supervisor, and scanned for known viruses on the network. This procedure assures that the workstations are not infected with the virus under test, that the scan is valid, and that the scan does not create infections where none existed before. To our surprise, we found that all of the files under test were infected, even those in directories to which the user "US1" had no access! Upon deeper examination, we found that the Netware "Supervisor" right dominates all other rights except when inherited rights cancel its effects. Fortunately, our controls picked up this problem early on, and we were able to track down a resolution relatively quickly.

This problem is indicative of one of the major difficulties we encountered in examining Netware and many other protection systems. The manual attempts to explain protection in several different places, and as aid to the less experienced user, makes several attempts to put protection in simple terms. Unfortunately, protection in Netware is not simple to understand or to manage, and the simplifications lead to serious misunderstandings. It was only the specific examples in one of the manuals in conjunction with our experiments that led us to our current understanding of Netware protection.

The problem of determining "Effective Rights" (the rights users actually have over files or directories) turns out to be quite complex in Netware, and we feel that this is a serious impediment to effective protection management. As an example of the complexity, each user's effective rights to a given file are dictated by 14 file attributes, 8 file trustee rights, 8 inheritance rights, and 16 rights (8 inherited and 8 trustee) per directory for each directory set up to the root of the file system. At 4 directory levels down from the root, each file's accessibility is determined by about 100 bits of protection information. Similarly, changing any one protection bit may impact substantial portions of the file structure, and determining what is affected is a nontrivial problem.

The problem of determining effective rights is apparently so difficult that Netware can't immediately determine proper effective rights, which introduces yet another problem. In some cases, these settings don't take effect for some time, which leaves substantial windows of vulnerability and makes it somewhat complex to be certain that test results are accurate and repeatable. We did not thoroughly verify the inheritance of rights, and we encountered several anomalies that disappeared over time scales of a few minutes. By following the advice of one of the people who read about our initial results in the "Risks" computer forum, we logged out and back in whenever we changed effective rights, and this seemed to seriously reduce the anomaly rate.

Now consider the problem of performing the exhaustive experiment with over 4 million files described earlier. This would mean that over 400 million protection bits would have to be checked over the process of the experiment, and that the space consumed by protection bits alone comes to over 12 megabytes! How long might it take to update protection for 4 million files when it tool several minutes for 2500 files? If the process is linear with the number of files, we would expect a delay on the order of 5000 minutes, or about 100 hours! Fortunately, the mechanism that causes this problem appears to be related to the cache mechanism used in Unix networks that we will describe later, and thus we don't expect a serious impact for larger file systems, but we have not performed tests to verify this, and suggest it as an open area for future experimentation.

This time variance also means that reliable programming in Netware is somewhat more complex than it would be in a more static situation, and many DOS programs make assumptions about the static nature of accessibility that will certainly make them unreliable in a non-static protection environment of this sort. This is not necessarily a problem to be resolved by Netware, since DOS programmers tend to make too many assumptions about file accessibility, and in any networking environment there will be changes, even if they are more predictable over time as Netware.

In RUN 2, we set the directory rights of "TEST" to the Netware recommended values of "Read" and "FileScan" only, logged out and back in to assure that effective rights were accurately updated, and repeated the test from RUN 1 exactly as before. This time, our controls indicated that the Netware subdirectory rights worked correctly. According to RUN 2, the tested file attributes were completely irrelevant to protection from viruses. Again, this conflicts with the manuals (p. 227 of the *Concepts* manual), which state that file attributes dominate directory rights. Upon further examination, we found that most (but not all) of the file attributes are DOS or MacIntosh protection bits, and further that they only apply to the operating system the user is using! Thus, Read-Only protection isn't supposed to work on MacIntosh computers, while the MacIntosh "Inhibit" settings don't impact DOS access! Again, the complexity of mechanism introduced substantial problems, but in this case, the situation is far worse because protection seems to depend on DOS, which has no effective protection.

The results from RUN 2 can be summarized in one simple equation:

$$\overline{S}\left(\overline{f} + \overline{R} + \overline{W}\right)$$

This is intended to convey that with the "Supervisor" AND any of "FileScan," "Read," or "Write" effective rights turned off for a given user, that user's PC being infected with the Jerusalem virus does NOT cause files in that directory to become infected. All of the other rights and attributes tested were apparently irrelevant to DOS virus protection.

We suspected that the reason "FileScan" protection limited viral spread in this case was because the Jerusalem virus infects only on program execution, and the DOS command interpreter requires FileScan in order to execute programs. Thus the programs that could not be run were not infected. For this reason we were not yet convinced that FileScan being turned off was effective against viruses when programs are run from a DOS "Exec" call, which does not have the same restriction as the command interpreter.

We eventually performed RUN 9 to determine the effectiveness of this protection equation against a slightly more sophisticated attack. In this case, we exhaustively tried to "open" files in the protected directories for "Read," "Write," and "Read/Write" access using a simple 'C' program. We found that files in $NY^5NY$ and $NYNY^5$ could be modified, leading to the conclusion that only $NY^2NY^4$ was effective. In other words, only $\overline{SW}$ was effective against this sort of attack. Since the "$A$" attribute allows you to alter all but the "$S$" attribute $\overline{A}$ must also be included for effective protection, leading to the new equation:

$$\overline{SWA}$$

RUN 1 and RUN 2 results also led us to RUN 3 in which we wished to evaluate the effectiveness of the previous equation against a broader spectrum of viruses, and to evaluate the utility of the "Read Only" file attribute in virus defense. RUN 3 required only 4 directories ("$SR$," "$SW$," "$SF$," and "YYYYYYY" corresponding to $\overline{SR}, \overline{SW}, \overline{SF}$, and full access respectively) with 4 files per directory (2 "COM" and 2 "EXE" files designated A.COM, B.COM, C.EXE, and D.EXE corresponding to Read-Only, Read-Write, Read-Only, and Read-Write, respectively). The same process used in RUN 2 was used in RUN 3 except that each of the different viruses from a test suite was used in turn, only the 4 directories of interest were used, and the experiment was performed in the "TEST2" directory.

RUN 3 surprisingly showed that "Read-Only" is ineffective against the 1704 virus which succeeded in infecting "A.COM" IN THE "YYYYYYY" directory even though it was write protected. No similar infection technique was available for "EXE" files, and no virus in our experiment succeeded in infecting the "C.EXE" program in the "YYYYYYY" directory, even though several infected the "D.EXE" file.

It turns out that this DOS attribute is trivilally modified with the "*M*" attribute turned on, and this attribute can in turn be altered if the "*A*" attribute is enabled, leading to the second equation that could not be attacked by the methods described so far:

$$\overline{SAM}Ro$$

Netware provides an Execute-Only attribute that can never be unset once it is set, and is supposed to prevent all subsequent access to the file. It does not prevent renaming or deleting of files, but prevents "Read" and "Write" operations to some extent, even against the Supervisor. Unfortunately, an Execute-Only file can be read by a user on a DOS-based system by performing a DOS "Load Program" call, and intercepting the file as it is passed to the loader. By reading it in this way, deleting the old version, and rewriting a new version, we can completely bypass Execute-Only protection, but a more dangerous attack appears to be presented by a "Companion" virus.

We were successful in creating a "Companion" virus example which was successful against Execute-Only protection. In this case, we rename the original executable and create a new executable containing the virus using the same name as the original executable, and giving it the same file size and other characteristics.[4] The replacement executable is then given the same file attributes as the original program, and made to automatically call the original after performing infection and/or damage. In this case, even the systems administrator cannot accurately detect the change because Execute-Only protection prevents the systems administrator from checking file contents or integrity. It would seem more appropriate to allow the systems administrator Read access to Execute-Only files so that they can be properly backed up and restored, and their integrity can be checked.

One idea for protection against this Companion virus is to prevent renaming of Execute-Only files, but the same attack can be made at any place up the directory tree from the Execute-Only file (i.e., by renaming a directory and placing a Trojan directory in its place), so to be safe we would have to prevent directory renaming from the Execute-Only file up to the Root of the file system. This in turn would allow any user to prevent the systems administrator from renaming significant portions of the file structure by simply making a file Execute-Only. It would also force operations on directories to depend on all files lower than them in the file tree,

---

[4]Setting the characteristics in this way is not required in order for the virus to operate, but it makes detection far more difficult.

and thus exacerbate the other protection problems we have discussed. It seems that Execute-Only protection in a network is ill-conceived, except in systems where hardware protection and encryption make the implementation of such a facility feasible.

To protect against these Companion viruses, you need to prohibit at least the Modify, AccessControl, Create, and System Rights, since trivial attacks can be found without these rights eliminated. By combining the equations from the previous two strong configurations with this one, we reach the equation below:

$$\overline{SMAC}(\overline{W} + \text{Ro})$$

This equation describes necessary but not sufficient settings for files and effective directory protection. We have found them effective in our experiments, and except for the time-lag problem described earlier, they appear to be sound, but we have not tested them sufficiently to prove their correctness. This is in line with Netware's suggested "RF" access rights. This protection setting also precludes changing information stored on the server, effectively making the server Read-Only! For directories where authorized users are permitted to make alterations, infections of files in those directories by those users is undefended by Netware, as in all other systems whose sole protection results from access control.

We also found from user reports that a common method of virus spread in Netware networks comes from the infection of the "Login.Exe" program stored on the server and used by all users to login to the network. As delivered, Netware allows the Supervisor to modify this file, and thus if the Supervisor EVER logs into a Netware server from an infected workstation, EVERY user that logs in subsequently may become infected. Furthermore, current versions of Netware cannot be logged into from the console, and thus once this file is infected, only a user with a local copy of a clean Login.Exe can ever login safely. Even worse, the supervisor is automatically granted all rights to all files (except modification and read access to Execute-Only files) regardless of directory and file protections, so a Companion virus of the sort described above is UNDEFENDABLE with Netware access controls once the Supervisor logs in from an infected machine. Therefore, substantial protection must be provided against the Supervisor EVER logging in from an infected machine, or the entire protection scheme becomes ineffective. In a recent conference Novell advised that a special user be created with "RF" Trustee Rights to all files and directories, and that when a virus is suspected, this user be used to check for viruses. They also confirmed that logging in as Supervisor with a virus present presented a substantial danger and noted that many low-level viruses could infect Netware file servers.

All of the results just presented have now been substantially confirmed by independent research teams, and similar equations have been developed for older versions of Netware with substantially different Trustee Rights.


### E.4.2   Unix

We installed a default Unix configuration per the manual provided with the system, specified a "Read/Write" file structure accessible over the network by user "US1" with an effective "Root" directory corresponding to "home/us1," and configured 512 directories belonging to user US1 and placed under US1's home directory, with names consistent of all possible combinations of octal protection codes depending on the placement of those rights in the standard Unix protection display as shown below:

|         | Owner | Group | World |
|---------|-------|-------|-------|
| Read    | 400   | 40    | 4     |
| Write   | 200   | 20    | 2     |
| Execute | 100   | 10    | 1     |

which is displayed as (by example) "561" to stand for "Read" and "Execute" for the "Owner" (400 + 100 = 500), "Read" and "Write" for "Group" members (40 + 20 = 60), and "Execute" for the rest of the "World" (500 + 60 + 1 = 561). Three users (US1, US2, and US3) were created with owner, group, and world identifications, respectively, so that the protection space is exhausted by accessing each directory from each user. We provided 3 executable files designated A-C.COM in each directory with protection settings of 666, 444, and 111, respectively.

As in the case of Netware, truly exhaustive testing was infeasible. To create the necessary 512 files of each sort (.Exe" and ".Com") in each of 512 directories would require over 500,000 files, over 250 megabytes, and runtimes over 138 hours for a single test run at 1 second per program execution. Actually, our examination is ignoring an additional 2 protection bits per file (setUID and SetGID), which grant the user running a program the effective rights of the owner or group, respectively, of the file, and therefore have a substantial impact on access rights. This would extend the time by a factor of 4 (from 5.8 days to over 23 days). Even though this time is not beyond the range of feasibility, our experiments were limited in time, so we could not do these tests. Again, we urge any interested parties to pursue these tests for a more thorough examination of the problem.

One workstation was configured with PC-NFS software that allows remote file sharing, and was used for all of the experiments. Because Unix allows multiuser multiproccessing from the console, we were able to monitor operations and set up further experiments without additional workstations.

In RUN 4, we exhaustively tested directory protection settings and found that no program could be run without directory access of at least $R + X$ for the user, group or world, depending on the rights associated with the logged-in user. We also found that directory protections of each directory dominated protections of other directories, and thus that actual protection at any given moment is dictated by the protections of the directory containing the file. We were somewhat surprised to find that programs would run even though they had no read rights set for the user attempting to execute them. Since "Execute" requires "Read" from the file server to the PC (similar to the Execute-Only protection in Netware), this led us to RUN 5, in which we exhaustively explored file protections.

In RUN 5, we set out to exhaustively tested file protection settings in a single directory over which the user had full rights. We created 512 files in the "Test2" directory with names and protection settings in the range from $000_8$ through $777_8$, all owned by user US1. The run began with a surprise. Not only could we execute programs with NO access rights for the user, but they also became infected! Thus, file access rights were completely ineffective! Then, another surprise. After running and infecting files 000, 001, 002, 003, and 004 the workstation could not continue processing. We rebooted and tried again, and found that the PC could not proceed past file 003. Subsequent retries resulted in the same problem. All of this is more than a bit disconcerting, because a substantial history of experiments with Unix protection has shown file access rights to be quite effective against Unix programs making system calls. Hence, networked workstations appear to have more access than processes on the server itself.

Next, we explored the impact of directory protection on file protection and found that with a directory protection of 500, the owner could only execute programs which were readable by owner (i.e., $400_8$-$777_8$). This seemed appropriate, but we then found that all of the programs that were run were infected. Even files protected with settings of $400_8$-$577_8$ (i.e., those without Write enabled) in a directory protected 500 (i.e., without Write enabled) were infected!

Next, we tried similar experiments with another user, US2, first using identical groups, and then again with nonidentical groups. We found that for directory protections allowing "Group" or "World" "Read" access, file access control determined infectability, while for all other directory access settings, no infection occurred. Files could be infected whenever both "Write" access was enabled for the file's owner and both "Read" and "Write" access were available to the infected user. This is quite strange, since it is somewhat different from normal Unix protection. For example, Unix manuals commonly claim that Unix grants all "World" rights to "Group' members and "Owners," and all "Group" rights to the "Owner," but in the networked example, "Group" members and "Owners" could not access files accessible by a "World" user. Similarly, a "World" user could read and modify a file that the file's "Owner" could not read in a directory to which the "Owner" had no access!

This combination of rights applied separately to files and directories is quite strange in some cases. For example, a file with access rights of 206 and Group ID 100 in a directory with access rights of 050 and Group ID 200 could be infected by a user in Group 100, but not by the Owner or a user in Group ID 200. This is far different from the results you would get when logged in as a Unix user to the same system.

We conclude that the NFS network drivers do not use normal access controls, and suspect that the entire file system is susceptible to attack, at least from the effective "Root" directory down the directory tree. We were unable to access files in other portions of the file server's directory space, and suspect that this aspect of protection is effective for the fact that symbolic links could completely bypass any such mechanism, and that the network interface operates on Unix i-nodes, which may be exploited to gain access to otherwise inaccessible areas of the same file system.

Directory protection appears to be effective to the extent that preventing all access works, but clearly write prevention is a critical protection need if we are to run programs without modifying them, and this was ineffective at the directory level. We did not explore the impact of symbolic links, but believe it will lead to further problems of this sort. Again we believe that directory access controls may be bypassed through direct access to i-nodes.

Clearly, a simple virus could alter file protections, alter files, and restore file protections, and thus, even effective file access controls would not alter the situation in the case of a serious attacker. Thus, a file's owner is almost always able to cause infection, regardless of protection settings, while other users may be able to infect a file even if the owner doesn't have write access enabled.

A further aspect of Unix-based remote file sharing is that in all the examples we have seen, file sharing allows access by multiple users from a single remote computer based on user IDs and passwords provided on the remote machine only. In other words, the root user on any machine in the network authorized to perform remote file sharing has the ability to grant or deny effective access rights to any user ID on the server. More specifically, any remote machine that can be taken over by an unauthorized user or process can access all files on the mounted file system on the server, except those owned by user identities explicitly remapped through the Unix user-ID remapping capability associated with remote file system mounts. In the case of PCs running the DOS operating system, viruses designed to take advantage of this problem should be able to gain all access attainable by all combination of user with access.

Remote file sharing under Unix also permits virtual file systems to be mounted as "Read-Only," which we did not test, and mounting of those file systems with specific user IDs remapped, which we also did not test. Unlike Netware, Unix servers can be used from the console, and use different executable files than DOS, and thus we believe that with prudence, we may be able to prevent the infection of the file server operating system, but this is by no means certain. As in Netware and all other systems we are aware of, viruses can spread through the normal access rights regardless of the inadequacies of the particular implementation.

Unix-based LANs also have a serious problem caused by the delay between the setting of protections and the effect of those settings on files. In particular, when remote systems use disk cacheing for network files systems (which can be disabled or enabled on each machine in the network), changes in protection settings on one machine may not appear on other machines for some time. For example, if machine "A" is connected to a remote file system on server "S" and A is doing disk cacheing, then a change in file protection made on S will not be "written through" to A immediately. Thus, a file protection change that prevents access on S will not prevent that access from A, assuming A has cached the protection information and thus does not have to look at the current value on S to determine accessibility.

This attack is theoretical at this time, and has not been confirmed by experiment; however, it is apparent from the manner in which the system operates and from examination of the source code of "386BSD" Unix[5] that this will happen. Cache updates are often delayed by as much as 30 seconds. This also implies that other information that is cached may be inconsistent when viewed from various systems in a network. This leads to serious potential problems in the use of shared databases based on file access rather than remote procedure calls and server-based locking mecha-

---

[5]A version of BSD Unix freely available in source form.

nisms. Even a "rename" operation may not take effect for some time on remote machines.

In the case of Unix, we also feel it is important to note that there are a multitude of different vendors with different versions of the operating system, and that the results from this particular version may not reflect the entire field. We also feel compelled to mention that the basic networking scheme used by Unix systems is flawed in that it extends too many privileges to the network drivers, has inadequate authentication, and is not designed with the uniform view of protection taken by the remainder of the Unix operating system. These inconsistencies appear to lead to implementation flaws such as those we have noted here.

We also note that the vast majority of Unix systems appear to be derivatives of only a few vendors' original source codes, and that the protection decisions in almost all Unix systems have been left unchanged and unexamined for something like 20 years. For example, the 386BSD Unix access control decisions are apparently verbatim copies of those from BSD Unix, which according to several sources are identical to those made in System 5 Unix. This would imply that the vast majority of vendor protection code is identical and that these fundamental flaws in one system appear in the vast majority of other systems. We would thus expect that the strange access control behavior would appear on many systems, and hope that others will perform experiments in other environments to confirm or refute these results for those systems.

## E.5  SUMMARY, CONCLUSIONS, AND FURTHER WORK

This research is still in its early stages, but we have already gained a great deal of insight into the protection provided both against viruses and in a more general sense by the protection mechanisms of two of the most commonly used network file servers. Our results show that viruses are a serious threat in all of these environments, and the protection mechanisms in place are less effective than we would expect. In effect, the only safe file server is the Read-Only file server, and even then, there are serious threats from Supervisors under Novell and serious attackers under Unix.

More specifically, relatively safe protection settings for Netware were identified as $\overline{SMAC}(\overline{W} + \text{Ro})$, relatively safe protection settings for Unix were identified as $\overline{R_{directory}} + \overline{W_{owner}}$, and a number of serious problems have been revealed in both Unix and Netware.

It seems clear that architecturally there are flaws in Network and Unix that make network protection difficult to attain. Netware has difficult to understand and maintain protection settings, and while Unix servers seem to have far better consistency in the meaning of protection settings, the implementation fails to meet the theory.

In terms of automation, neither system provides any substantial useful automation for either the user or the administrator to maintain a consistently well-protected environment. The tools for protection provided with these file servers are far too difficult to use for effective protection, and without adequate tools, it is unrealistic to expect even expert administrators to do an adequate job. Better tools are required if the virus threat to these networks is to be controlled effectively through the protection mechanisms provided.

As we have discussed, our results at this time are preliminary, and a great deal of further research is required in order to get an effective handle on this problem over the full spectrum of networking environments available today. Studies of spread rates would be a valuable tool in determining cost-effective defenses. More thorough studies of the effectiveness of network protection are called for both in the environments discussed here and in other environments not yet studied systematically. We have not yet started to study the effectiveness of these environments when additional protection measures such as virus scanning and integrity mechanisms are put in place, and this is an area where the results would be directly applicable to current users. A great deal of work is also called for in the area of protection management and the design of tools to automate systems administration so as to allow normal administrators to provide effective protection without undue effort.

We hope that others will follow in our footsteps, extend our results, perform exhaustive tests we were unable to perform, and carry on some of the many other experiments required to address the LAN virus protection issue. More importantly, we hope vendors will start a program of systematic, comprehensive, and regular testing to detect and resolve similar problems before release. Finally, we hope that these results will lead to a deeper study of network protection issues, which are clearly underconsidered in current networking environments.

# Appendix F

# ANNOTATED BIBLIOGRAPHY

F. Cohen, "Computer Viruses—Theory and Experiments," in *DOD/NBS 7th Conference on Computer Security*, originally appearing in IFIP–Sec. 84, also appearing in *IFIP-TC11 Computers and Security*, Vol. 6, pp. 22–35 (1987), and other publications in several languages. This is the most famous paper on computer viruses and forms the basis for most of the current understanding of the field.

J. P. Anderson, "Computer Security Technology Planning Study," *USAF Electronic Systems Division Report No. ESD-TR-73-51*, Oct. 1972 (cited in Denning). This study evaluated computer security issues that were prevalent prior to the introduction of the virus problem.

R. R. Linde, "Operating System Penetration," in *AIFIPS National Computer Conference*, pp. 361–368, 1975. This paper described many of the common techniques for operating systems protection, and how systems could be designed to defend against them.

D. E. Bell and L. J. LaPadula, "Secure Computer Systems: Mathematical Foundations and Model," *Mitre Corporation Report*, 1973 (cited in many papers). This is the classic paper in which Bell and LaPadula describe a model for maintaining secrecy in timesharing computer systems.

D. E. Denning, *Cryptography and Data Security*, Addison-Wesley, Reading, MA, 1982. This is a very good graduate text on computer security covering most of the important issues prior to computer viruses.

E. J. McCauley and P. J. Drongowski, "KSOS—The Design of a Secure Operating System," in *AIFIPS National Computer Conference*, pp. 345–353, 1979. This paper describes one of the operating systems designed in the 1970s to maintain secrecy.

G. J. Popek, M. Kampe, C. S. Kline, A. Stoughton, M. Urban, and E. J. Walton, "UCLA Secure Unix," in *AIFIPS National Computer Conference*, 1979, pp. 355–364. This paper describes a secure implementation of the Unix operating system in which much of the implementation was proven correct mathematically.

B. D. Gold, R. R. Linde, R. J. Peeler, M. Schaefer, J. F. Scheid, and P. D. Ward, "A Security Retrofit of VM/370," in *AIFIPS National Computer Conference*, 1979, pp. 335–344. This paper describes some of the effort to make an insecure computer system secure through a major retrofit.

C. E. Landwehr, "The Best Available Technologies for Computer Security," *IEEE Computer Magazine*, Vol. MC-16, No. 7 (1983). This paper summarized computer security techniques and implementations up until the advent of computer viruses.

B. W. Lampson, "A Note on the Confinement Problem," *Communications of the ACM*, Vol. 16, No. 10, pp. 613–615, (1973). This famous paper described the covert channel problem for the first time.

K. J. Biba, "Integrity Considerations for Secure Computer Systems," *USAF Electronic Systems Division Report*, 1977 (cited in Denning). In this paper, the dual of the Bell-LaPadula model is used to achieve integrity levels in a computer system for the first time.

K. Thompson, "Reflections on Trusting Trust," (Turing Award Lecture, 1984) *Communications of the ACM* (August 1984). This paper described the Thompson C compiler, which allows Thompson to login to almost any Unix system.

F. Cohen, *Computer Viruses*, 1985, Ph.D. dissertation, University of Southern California, 1986), ASP Press, Pittsburgh. This is a mathematical treatment of the computer virus issue, and contains the first formal definition of viruses, many of the proofs about defenses, and much of the basis for current computer virus theory.

A. Dewdney, "Computer Recreations," *Scientific American* (1984–1986). This is a series of articles about computer games involving competing programs in an environment. It turns out that the most successful ones tend to be viruses.

F. Cohen, "Computer Security Methods and Systems," in *1984 Conference on Information Systems and Science*, Princeton University. This paper describes much of the computer security technology prior to viruses.

M. Pozzo and T. Gray, "Managing Exposure to Potentially Malicious Programs," in *Proceedings of the 9th National Computer Security Conference*, September 1986. This paper describes a trusted software approach to computer virus defense, wherein software is given different levels of trust and information flow is limited based on these levels.

F. Cohen, "A Secure Computer Network Design," *IFIP-TC11 Computers and Security*, Vol. 4, No. 3, 1985, pp. 189–205 (1985). Also appearing in *AFCEA Symposium and Expo on Physical and Electronic Security*, August 1985. This paper describes the combination of the Bell-LaPadula and Biba models, extends previous results to computer networks, and introduces some major insecurities in computer networks.

F. Cohen, "Protection and Administration of Information Networks Under Partial Orderings," *IFIP-TC11 Computers and Security*, Vol. 6, pp. 118–128 (1987). In this paper, the use of POsets to describe protection in a computer system is introduced. Collusion analysis is developed, and several examples are given.

F. Cohen, "Design and Administration of Distributed and Hierarchical Information Networks Under Partial Orderings," *IFIP-TC11 Computers and Security*, Vol. 6, 15 pp. (1987). In this paper, previous results are extended to cover management of distributed and hierarchical networks. Protocols for distributed POset protection are given, and previous analysis is extended.

M. Pozzo and T. Gray, "Computer Virus Containment in Untrusted Computing Environments," in *IFIP/SEC Fourth International Conference on Computers and Security*, December 1986. In this paper, a cryptographic technique based on public key cryptography is given for implementing trusted software as a protection mechanism.

F. Cohen, "Design and Administration of an Information Network Under a Partial Ordering—A Case Study," *IFIP-TC11 Computers and Security*, Vol. 6, pp. 332–338 (1987). In this paper, a case study of a POset-based protection system is described. Results indicated that implementation and use were both easier with the increased structure, and tracking down the sources of corruption was greatly improved.

F. Cohen, "Designing Provably Correct Information Networks with Digital Diodes," *IFIP-TC11 Computers and Security* (1988). This paper describes a hardware device for highly reliable one-way transmission so as to facilitate hardware-based POset implementations.

F. Cohen, "A Cryptographic Checksum for Integrity Protection in Untrusted Computer Systems," *IFIP-TC11 Computers and Security*, Vol. 6 (1987). This paper introduced a cryptographic method for protecting the integrity of information stored on disk by providing reliable detection of change.

F. Cohen, "Two Secure Network File Servers," *IFIP-TC11 Computers and Security* (1987). This paper describes two prototype implementations of

POset-based file servers designed to facilitate POset-based networks.

M. Pozzo and T. Gray, "An Approach to Containing Computer Viruses," *IFIP-TC11 Computers and Security* (1987). This paper describes a novel approach to computer virus containment through cryptographic signatures.

B. Cohen and F. Cohen, "Error Prevention at a Radon Measurement Service Laboratory," *Radiation Protection Management*, Vol. 6, No. 1, pp. 3–47, (1989). This paper describes a high-integrity computing environment in which dramatic increases in integrity were attained at very low cost.

F. Cohen, "A Complexity Based Integrity Maintenance Mechanism," in *Conference on Information Sciences and Systems*, Princeton University, March 1986. This paper first described the concept of software self-defense and proposed an implementation based on cryptographic check-summing techniques.

F. Cohen, "Recent Results in Computer Viruses," in *Conference on Information Sciences and Systems*, Johns Hopkins University, March 1985. This paper summarized early results on computer viruses and defenses.

F. Cohen, "Maintaining a Poor Person's Integrity," *IFIP-TC11 Computers and Security* (1987). This paper describes methods by which people without much financial support could protect themselves from computer viruses through purely procedural methods.

W. Murray, "The Application of Epidemiology to Computer Viruses," *IFIP-TC11 Computers and Security*, *Computers and Security* (1989). This paper details some interesting work in modeling computer viruses and defenses based on biological methods.

H. Highland (Ed.), *IFIP-TC11 Computers and Security* (Special Issue) (April 1988). This was the first special issue on computer viruses in a scientific journal, and included several good papers on the topic.

V. McLellan, "Computer Systems Under Seige," *The New York Times* (January 31, 1988). This was one of the early articles on computer viruses in the popular press.

J. F. Shoch and J. A. Hupp, "The Worm Programs—Early Experience with a Distributed Computation," *Communications of the ACM*, pp. 172–180 (March 1982). This was a famous paper that first described the Xerox Worm experiments for parallel processing on a distributed computing network.

J. B. Gunn, "Use of Virus Functions to Provide a Virtual APL Interpreter Under User Control," *Communications of the ACM*, pp. 163–168 (July

1974). This paper describes a viral technique for modifying the APL interpreter, but did not involve replication or infection.

L. J. Hoffman, "Impacts of Information System Vulnerabilities on Society," in *AIFIPS National Computer Conference*, pp. 461–467, 1982. This paper describes the degree to which we have become dependent on computer systems and what we could reasonably expect to result from existing system vulnerabilities.

Kaplan (U.S. Dept. of Justice, Bureau of Justice Statistics), *Computer Crime—Computer Security Techniques*, U.S. Government Printing Office, Washington, DC, 1982. This is a wonderful resource book on computer security techniques, and gives a firm basis for EDP audit from the previrus era.

M. H. Klein, "Department of Defense Trusted Computer System Evaluation Criteria," Department of Defense Computer Security Center, Fort Meade, MD 20755, Report No. DOD-CSC-84-001 (1983). This is the widely touted "orange book" Trusted System Evaluation Criteria published by the NSA for evaluating multilevel secure systems for military use. Although it has become a de-facto standard, it does not address integrity or many other issues widely held to be of more widespread import.

A. Turing, "On Computable Numbers, with an Application to the Entscheidungsproblem," *Proceedings of the London Mathematical Society Series* 2 (1936). This is the famous paper that shows that any problem that can be solved by any general-purpose computer can also be solved by any other general-purpose computer, given enough time and space.

S. Yau and R. Cheung, "Design of Self Checking Software," *1975 IEEE Conference on Reliable Software*, IEEE Press, New York, 1975, pp. 450–457. This is one of a series of papers on software-based fault tolerant computing.

J. Kelly and A. Avizienis, "A Specification Oriented Multi-Version Software Experiment," in *1985 IEEE Symposium on Fault Tolerant Computing*, IEEE, New York, 1983, pp. 120–126. This paper describes some of the major problems with multiversion programming and the experiments performed at UCLA to evaluate its potential for practical use.

R. Scott, J. Gault, D. McAllister, and J. Wiggs, "Experimental Validation of Six Fault Tolerant Software Reliability Models," in *1984 IEEE Symposium on Fault Tolerant Computing*, IEEE, New York, 1984, pp. 102–107. This paper advances the practice of multiversion programming by showing the importance of good specification to the final outcome.

L. Chen and A. Avizienis, "*N*-Version Programming: A Fault Tolerance Approach to Reliability of Software Operation," FTCS, Vol. 8, pp. 3–9 (June 1978). This paper introduced the *N*-version programming model.

L. Chen, "Improving Software Reliability by *N*-version Programming," *UCLA Computer Science Department Report No. UCLA-ENG-7843*, 1978. This paper described some improvements to the initial work on *N*-version programming.

Randell, "System Structure for Software Fault Tolerance," *IEEE Transactions on Software Engineering* Vol. SE-1, pp. 220–223 (June 1975). This paper introduces the systems requirements for reliable *N*-version software implementations.

M. Harrison, W. Ruzzo, and J. Ullman, "Protection in Operating Systems," *Communications of the ACM*, Vol. 19, No. 8, pp. 461–471 (1976). This paper introduces the first formal mathematical model of protection in computer systems, and forms the basis for the Subject/Object model of computer security. It also proves that determining the protection effects of a given configuration is, in general, undecidable.

M. Cohen, "A New Integrity Based Model for Limited Protection Against Computer Viruses," Masters thesis, The Pennsylvania State University, College Park, PA, 1988. This thesis describes the concept of integrity shells as a method of defending against computer viruses.

F. Cohen, "Models of Practical Defenses Against Computer Viruses," *IFIP-TC11, Computers and Security*, Vol. 7, No. 6 (1988). This paper formally introduces integrity shells and shows that they are optimal as a defense against computer viruses.

F. Cohen, "Automated Integrity Maintenance for Viral Defense," *IFIP-TC11, Computers and Security* (1990). This paper describes some of the automated decision-making issues in the use of integrity shells for a computer virus defense.

DPMA 2nd Annual Computer Virus Symposium, New York, NY, 1989. This conference had several interesting papers on vulnerabilities in computer systems and computer virus defenses.

S. Jones and C. White Jr., "The IPM Model of Computer Virus Management," *IFIP-TC11 Computers and Security* (to be published). This model of management issues in computer virus defense considers viruses as pests in an agricultural environment.

F. Cohen, *The ASP 3.0 Technical Users Manual*, ASP Press, Pittsburgh, 1990. This is the technical manual for the first commercial integrity shell.

F. Cohen, "ASP 3.0—The Integrity Shell," *Information Protection*, Vol. 1, No. 1 (1990). This article describes some of the issues in integrity shells as a practical defense against viruses without using any high-powered mathematics.

Y. J. Huang and F. Cohen, "Some Weak Points of One Fast Cryptographic Checksum Algorithm and Its Improvement," *IFIP-TC11 Computers and Security*, Vol. 8, No. 1 (1989). This paper shows several weaknesses in one cryptographic checksum used as a viral defense, and shows how it can be improved.

M. Prew, "Minimizing the Impact of Computer Crime on Your Earnings," *Wigham Poland* (Corporation of Lloyds), 1984. This article was written by an insurance underwriter to describe the economic impacts of computer crime in modern society.

H. Highland, *Computer Virus Handbook*, Elsevier, New York, 1990. This is a very good book on computer viruses from a technological standpoint, and covers much of the basis for present computer virus theory as well. It is recommended reading for those interested in computer viruses under the DOS operating system.

S. White, "A Status Report on IBM Computer Virus Research," in *Proceedings of the Italian Computer Virus Conference*, 1990. This paper describes the status of computer virus research at IBM's high-integrity computing laboratory.

L. Adleman, "An Abstract Theory of Computer Viruses," in S. Goldwasser (Ed.), *Lecture Notes in Computer Science, Vol. 403, Advances in Computing—Proceedings of Crypto-88*, Springer-Verlag, New York, 1990. This was the second theoretical work on computer viruses. It describes a subset of the previous formal definition, and demonstrates that detection of members of this subset is also undecidable.

E. Spafford, "Crisis and Aftermath," *Communications of the ACM*, Vol. 32, No. 6 (1989). This is one of the short papers published in a special issue of *CACM* on the computer virus attack on the Internet.

J. Rochlis and M. Eichin, "With Microscope and Tweezers: The Worm form MIT's Perspective," *Communications of the ACM*, Vol. 32, No. 6 (1989). This is another paper describing the efforts to fight the Internet virus from the ACM special issue on the virus in the Internet.

F. Cohen, "Some Simple Advances in Protection Tools," *Information Protection*, Vol. 1, Nos. 5–9 (1990). This article describes some of the simple advances in protection tools needed to facilitate proper management of the enormous amount of protection state in modern computer systems.

W. Gleissner, "A Mathematical Theory for the Spread of Computer Viruses," *IFIP-TC11 Computers and Security*, Vol. 8, No. 1, pp. 35–41 (1989). This paper gives a thorough mathematical analysis of the spread of computer viruses in computer systems, including predictions of spread times based on various properties of system use.

Tipet, *The Tipet Theory of Computer Virus Propagation*, Foundationware, USA. This is a very oversimplified model of viral spread that predicts enormous global calamity if viruses go unchecked.

C. Shannon, "A Mathematical Theory of Communications," *Bell System Technical Journal* (1949). This classic paper describes information theory for the first time, and forms the basis for all of modern syntactic information theory. It also shows that covert channels (as well as any other channels) can be arbitrarily reliable even in the presence of purposely introduced noise.

F. Cohen, "Current Best Practice Against PC Integrity Corruption," *Information Protection*, Vol. 1, No. 1, (1990). This paper describes procedural requirements for sound computer virus defense in PC-based environments.

F. Cohen, "Computer Viruses," in *Computers Under Attack*, ACM/ Addison-Wesley, Reading, MA, 1990. This is a good summary of computer virus research results, but is redundant once you have read this book.

F. Cohen, "the Impact of Information Protection on Computer Engineering," *Information Protection*, Vol. 1, No. 4 (1990). This paper describes the degree to which protection issues have influenced the basic design of computer systems.

F. Cohen, "How To Do Sound Change Control and What It Costs," *Information Protection*, Vol. 1, No. 6 (1990). This paper describes the cost of sound change control.

H. Gliss, "The Security of Information Resources—Results of a Survey," in *The Oxbridge Sessions*, Holland, 1990. This paper gives the results of one of the best computer security surveys ever completed in industry.

F. Cohen, "A Cost Analysis of Typical Computer Viruses and Defenses," *IFIP-TC11, Computers and Security* (to be published). This paper describes the mathematical analysis of the costs of computer virus defenses, and shows that integrity shells are far more cost effective than other competitive techniques currently in the environment.

M. Pozzo, Ph.D. dissertation, University of California at Los Angeles, 1990. This thesis describes essentially ineffective attempts at trying to find computer viruses by examining executable programs and trying to predict their behavior. It also contains a number of interesting advances in the use of public key cryptography and proof of program correctness for viral defense.

J. Hirst, "Eliminator—Computer Virus Detection and Removal," Copyright ©, British Computer Virus Research Centre, 1990. This shows the state-of-the-art in special-purpose automated computer virus detection and removal.

L. Hoffman, *Rogue Programs—Viruses, Worms, and Trojan Horses* Van Nostrand Reinhold, New York, 1990. This book is a good resource for papers on computer viruses and related integrity attack is against modern computers.

G. Davida, Y. Desmedt, and B. Matt, "Defending Against Computer Viruses through Cryptographic Authentication," in *1989 IEEE Symposium on Computer Security and Privacy*, IEEE, New York, 1989, pp. 312–318. This paper is a minor extension of previous results on integrity protection through cryptographic checksums.

M. Joseph and A. Avizienis, "A Fault Tolerance Approach to Computer Viruses," *1988 IEEE Symposium on Security and Privacy*, IEEE, New York, 1988. In this paper, extensions to software fault tolerance are applied to computer virus defense in critical systems.

J. Kephart, S. White, and D. Chess, "Computers and Epidemiology," *IEEE Spectrum*, pp. 20–26 (May 1993). In this paper, empirical data is used in conjunction with modeling of infection vectors to show how virus epidemics work and the effects of common defenses on quelling those epidemics.

N. Baily, *The Mathematical Theory of Epidemics*, Hafner Publishing Co., New York, 1957. In this book, the mathematics are derived for predicting the level of infection within a society, and the concept of an "*epidemic*" is given mathematical meaning.

F. Cohen, "Operating System Protection Through Program Evolution," *IFIP-TC11 Computers and Security* (to be published). This paper describes a number of evolutionary techniques that can be applied by operating system designers to make system-specific attacks very complex to create.

# Appendix G

# ABOUT THE SOFTWARE: INTEGRITY TOOLKIT

The Integrity Toolkit (**IT**) is an integrated and customizable set of tools for integrity maintenance in a DOS environment. **IT** is NOT a retail product. Rather, it is a unified collection of technologies that is ONLY made available under a licensing arrangement. Licensees then customize **IT** for large customers to provide just the functions needed in precisely the form desired.

The special edition of **IT** provided by John Wiley and Sons with "A Short Course on Computer Viruses" is designed to provide examples of how many different integrity functions operate, cost analysis of the most common integrity protection mechanisms under DOS, brief training information for those interested in integrity protection, and other simple tools that many users find interesting or useful.

The special edition of **IT** is normally managed through the "Mɪᴛ" (Menu Integrity Tool) program. Mɪᴛ is used to install and manage **IT**, and provides a standard menu-based interface. To install **IT** on your system, place the **IT** disk in your floppy disk drive (we use A for the example) and at a DOS prompt type:

A:MIT.

DO NOT first move to the A drive by typing "A:" at the DOS prompt, and DO NOT simply copy the files into your system to install **IT**. These techniques will not properly install **IT**, and may cause undue confusion. In a Windows environment, you must get to a DOS prompt before installing **IT** because the way some Windows versions operate, the installation will fail if you try to install **IT** by using the Windows facilities for running programs from floppy disk drives.

**IT** installation takes only a few minutes, and despite the initial warning message, the special edition provided on your disk does not change any DOS files. **IT** does remove files in the ASP directory of your bootable (C) disk, so if you use the directory name ASP, you must first move that directory to a different name using the DOS or Windows commands appropriate to that operation.

Once **IT** is installed, MɪT will automatically run to let you try **IT** out. For instructions on how to use MɪT menus, press the INS key, and a help screen will be displayed.

The top level **IT** menu provides 5 options:

- Use allows you to create and verify cryptographic checksums, scan for known viruses, and use a set of DOS utilities that provide too many functions to describe here.

- Teach provides detailed information on protection issues, attacks, defenses, **IT** capabilities, **IT** configuration, and where to get more information. These menus include information about many functions not provided in the special edition of **IT** provided by John Wiley and Sons but available in commercial versions.

- Analyze provides spreadsheets to analyze the costs of protection using virus scanners, virus monitors, cryptographic checksum systems, and integrity shells. It allows you to change values to analyze many different environments and get an understanding of the lifecycle costs associated with these techniques.

- meNus provides menu customization including changes in boarders, sounds, how the keys work and other similar things. Many users spend more time playing with menu appearances than with the rest of **IT** because it is fun to do.

- Passwords provides checking of user supplied passwords to determine the amount of time it would normally take a good attacker to guess the password and a password and pass phrase generator that generates a pseudo-random string that would be a pretty good password on any system.

Except for the Use Utilities menu, and assuming you have read the book, no more information is required to use and understand **IT** and what it does. Within this menu, there are some facilities that require additional explanation. Specifically:

- Memory use map uses the program Boots.Exe to generate a map of the memory usage of a DOS-based PC. The memory map consists of a table listing memory locations, program names (where available), the number of allocated memory areas, and the sizes of programs resident in DOS memory. This is handy for figuring out why programs can't be run, for detecting programs in memory that don't belong there, and for understanding what DOS does with its memory under different circumstances.

- Disk utilities runs the program Boots.Exe and allows the user to directly manipulate areas of the hard disk. BE CAREFUL!!! Boots is a very powerful tool that, if used properly, can help manually cure or examine viruses on disk, lock and unlock the hard disk from access on floppy bootups, and save and restore critical system areas in case of corruption. But along with this power, comes substantial danger. If you tell Boots to write information onto a critical area of the disk and the information you provide is not right, Boots will NOT be able to tell the difference, and your disk may become unuseable! The language used in Boots deals with heads, tracks, sectors, and other technical words having to do with physical disk drives. We advise you to read a technical book on PCs if you want to get a fuller understanding of these words.

- Wipe freespace uses the program. Asp.Exe to overwrite all unused areas of a disk with '0's. This overwrites deleted file areas and other unused disk areas, so that somebody who looks at the disk later cannot see what was written there by simply scanning disk blocks. One of the best uses for this is in creating a master disk for duplication. Overwriting freespace eliminates file information that may have been on the same disk before the duplicated information was there.

- full screen Asp runs the Asp.Exe program to allow the user to try different integrity capabilities through the Asp.Exe menu system. This program is somewhat complicated, and a description of its use is included below.

Asp.Exe provides a broad array of integrity capabilities through a unique user interface. The main user interface (called the FSI) appears on the screen when Asp.Exe is run from the Mit menu. In some cases, there is not enough memory available to run Asp.Exe from Mit.Exe. In this case, it is advisable to leave Mit, and reenter without using any other Mit menus. You can also run Asp.Exe by typing 'Asp-K'. Please note that this must be an upper case K.

The first time you run Asp.Exe, it may ask you whether or not to create a checksum file. 'Y' is the proper response.

The file window has markings associated with each file to indicate that the file is a directory (marked by backslash), an executable program (*), a hidden or system file (-) or any other file (no marking).

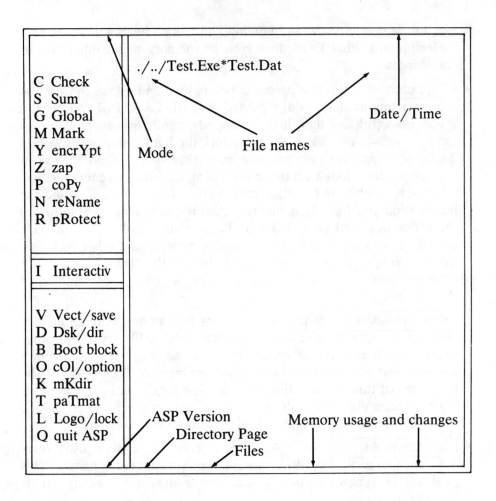

The FSI allows the user to press a key to perform an action affecting files on the screen. To move the cursor around the file window, use the arrow keys on the keyboard. To 'run' the currently marked program, press the 'ENTER' key. Files are interpreted as follows:

| If the file is a | Then do this |
| --- | --- |
| Directory | Change to that directory |
| Executable program | Run the program |
| Known file type | Interpret with the known interpreter |
| Other file type | Type the file on the screen |

The most commonly used actions are listed in the upper portion of the menu:

- **C Check** checks files to determine if they have changed since they were last 'summed'.

- **S Sum** creates or updates cryptographic checksums of files.

- **G Global** performs checks on every file checksummed in the on-line data base.

- **M Mark** marks sets of files on the screen so that other operations can be performed on groups of files. Directories cannot be marked. Selecting 'm' marks or unmarks an individual file, while 'M' changes the marking of every file in the file window. In addition, ' < ' marks everything from the cursor to the end of the screen and ' > ' unmarks everything from the cursor to the end of the screen,

- **Y encrYpt** encrypts files for privacy.

- **Z Zap** deletes files and overwrites the disk areas they consumed so that they cannot be reread even if they are subsequently 'undeleted'.

- **P coPy** copies files.

- **N reName** renames files.

- **R pRotect** sets DOS file protections and attributes of files. The user is prompted for protection changes in the form of ' + ' or ' − ' followed by a sequence of characters from the set 'rwsha' used to indicate the addition or removal of 'read', 'write', 'hidden', 'system', and 'archive' file attributes from a file. The FSI displays all files regardless of their attributes, while most DOS command interpreters do not display hidden or system files unless explicitly requested.

These commands operate on individual files when the lower case character is entered, and on marked groups of files when the upper case character is entered. For example, 's' checksums the file currently covered by the cursor in the file window, while 'S' checksums all marked files in the file window.

The 'Interactive' command places you into an interactive 'integrity shell' mode wherein each command is checked for integrity before being run. The lower case 'i' invocation allows you to type one command, while the upper case 'I' loops taking command after command. This implementation of an integrity shell has substantial limitations, but it should provide a good example of how the concept operates. To exit the interactive command loop, type 'exit' at the prompt. A more cleanly embedded implementation of an integrity shell is available in commercial versions of **IT**.

The commands below 'interactive' provide other functions that are commonly requested in a command tool:

- **V VECT / save** Checks for changes in interrupt vectors used by DOS to implement system calls. This function is performed automatically in the default operating mode whenever a program is run. If interrupt vectors change, it indicates that a change in DOS operation has been made. This should only happen when a resident program is loaded (such as the first time the print command is issued). Other changes indicate that a program is changing the way DOS operates, and is indicative of some common viruses.

- **D DSK / dir** Changes disk drive or directory by requesting the new disk or directory from the user. This is handy for moving to parts of the file system in different parts of the directory tree.

- **B Boot block** Checks the DOS master boot sector for changes. The DOS master boot record NEVER changes in normal DOS operation, and the only programs that make such alterations are low level computer viruses. Asp.Exe is also able to replace altered master boot records with the original, and in normal operation, does so if changes are detected. This function may be incompatible with other DOS antivirus products.

- **O COL / option** Changes Asp.Exe screen colors or sets Asp options. Screen color changes are superficial only. Options dictate how automated integrity operations are performed. For example, by properly setting options, you can have Asp refuse to run programs with unknown checksums, automatically checksum programs not previously checksummed, automatically repair and retest corrupted programs without user intervention, or any of a large number of other possibilities.

- **K mKdir** creates a DOS directory.

- **T paTmat** checks files for known viruses.

- **L LOGO / lock** displays the Asp logo (if there is one on-line) or locks the keyboard and clears the screen until the user reenters a specified unlock key.

- **Q Quit** exits from Asp.Exe.